Ruling England, 1042–1217

Ruling England, 1042–1217

Richard Huscroft

PEARSON
Longman

Harlow, England • London • New York • Boston • San Francisco • Toronto
Sydney • Tokyo • Singapore • Hong Kong • Seoul • Taipei • New Delhi
Cape Town • Madrid • Mexico City • Amsterdam • Munich • Paris • Milan

PEARSON EDUCATION LIMITED

Edinburgh Gate
Harlow CM20 2JE
United Kingdom
Tel: +44 (0)1279 623623
Fax: +44 (0)1279 431059
Website: www.pearsoned.co.uk

———————————————

First edition published in Great Britain in 2005

© Pearson Education Limited 2005
The right of Richard Huscroft to be identified as author of this work has been
asserted by him in accordance with the Copyright, Designs and Patents Act 1988.

ISBN 978-0-582-84882-5

British Library Cataloguing-in-Publication Data
A CIP catalogue record for this book can be obtained from the British Library

Library of Congress Cataloging-in-Publication Data
Huscroft, Richard.
  Ruling England, 1042–1217 / Richard Huscroft. — 1st ed.
    p. cm.
  Includes bibliographical references (p.) and index.
  ISBN 0–582–84882–2 (pbk. : alk.paper)
    1. Great Britain—History—Norman period, 1066–1154.   2. Great
  Britain—History—Angevin period, 1154–1216.   3. Great Britain—History—Edward, the
  Confessor, 1042–1066.   4. Power (Social sciences)—Great Britain—History—To 1500.   5.
  Great Britain—Politics and government—1066–1485.   6. Great Britain—Politics and
  government—449–1066.   I. Title.
  DA195.H96 2005
  942.02—dc22

                                                                    2004044558

10   9   8   7   6   5   4
10   9

Set by 35 in 9.5/12.5pt Stone Serif
Printed in Malaysia (CTP-PJB)

The Publishers' policy is to use paper manufactured from sustainable forests.

Contents

Acknowledgements

We are grateful to the following for permission to reproduce copyright material:

Maps 1 and 6 after maps in *Feudal Britain: The Completion of the Medieval Kingdom, 1066–1314*, pub. Edward Arnold, reprinted by permission of the author (Barrow, G.W.S. 1956, reprinted 1971); Map 2 after map in *The Penguin History of Britain: The Struggle for Mastery: Britain 1066–1284*, pub. Penguin Press, reproduced by permission of Penguin Books Ltd. (Carpenter, D. 2003); Map 3 after map in *A Companion to the Anglo-Norman World*, published and reprinted by permission of Boydell Press (van Houts, E. and Harper-Bill, C., eds 2003); Map 4 after map in *The Angevin Empire, 2nd Edition*, pub. Hodder Arnold, reprinted by permission of the author (Gillingham, J. 2002); Map 5 adapted from map in *The Atlas of Anglo-Saxon England*, published and reprinted by permission of Blackwell Publishing and University of Toronto Press (Hill, D. 1981).

In some instances we have been unable to trace the owners of copyright material, and we would appreciate any information that would enable us to do so.

Introduction

This book is about the exercise of political power in England from the beginning of the reign of Edward the Confessor to the beginning of the reign of Henry III. Consequently it deals overwhelmingly with the affairs of the kings of England, how they tried (some more successfully than others) to rule their kingdom, and the relationships they had with their political élites. Although it addresses wider developments in culture, society and the economy, and by no means ignores those social groups below the level of the governing classes, these are not areas with which I have been mainly concerned. This emphasis on high politics and government has been deliberate, in part because of limited space, but more because I believe strongly that there is merit in such an approach. Of course it is possible to study the history of a period from any number of perspectives, but, in my opinion, social, economic and cultural developments are more readily comprehensible if they are based on a solid understanding of mainstream politics. I am also aware that the prominence I have given to England fails to do justice to the efforts made by historians over the past thirty years or so to construct the wider history of the British Isles and those parts of the continent ruled by the English kings during this period. Again, the available space meant that a longer and broader discussion was impossible. However, I also think that specifically *English* history is still a valid area of study, especially at a time when England's future within the United Kingdom is as uncertain as the United Kingdom's future within Europe. Therefore, my intention has been to provide a basic yet still challenging introduction to the main political events and developments of this hugely important period. I hope it will be useful to A-level students and new undergraduates taking relevant courses, and to enthusiastic amateur historians who have heard of the Battle of Hastings and Magna Carta, but are otherwise largely unfamiliar with England during these years. I also hope it will be stimulating enough to be of interest to students and professionals who already have a working knowledge of the areas I have covered.

The book is divided into three parts: Late Anglo-Saxon England (1042–66), Anglo-Norman England (1066–1154) and Angevin England (1154–1217), and each part is subdivided into four chapters. The first chapter in each part contains an outline reign-by-reign narrative of the principal political events. I have attempted to make these chapters as neutral as possible in order to give readers a basic, uncontroversial idea of what happened and when. The other three chapters in each part are more thematic, and they deal in turn with developments in central and local government, the law and in the king's relationship with the English Church during the periods in question. From time to time, I have also included discrete, short discussions of relevant areas of historiographical controversy. These are not intended to be comprehensive syntheses of all the available views on a particular subject; but they are supposed to be helpful and provocative, and to introduce students to some of the ways in which historical debates might be discussed. A chronology has also been provided at the start of the book, as well as a brief account of the main narrative sources and some suggestions for further reading at the end.

It will soon become apparent to readers that this book owes its principal debt to the scholars who have undertaken the original research on which its discussions and conclusions are based. However, individuals have been enormously kind, too. I must thank David Carpenter in particular for all his help, criticism and advice. He is an inspirational teacher and a generous friend. Ken Lawson and Huw Ridgeway have both reassured me when necessary that this project was worthwhile; and my Head of Department at Westminster School, Giles Brown, has always been supportive and encouraging. My father's careful reading of an early draft of the book also pointed up many errors and inconsistencies. My A-level students have played a significant part in the making of this book, too. It began life as a series of handouts for them as they set off sometimes warily but usually willingly down the unfamiliar road of medieval history, and it has developed as they have continued to ask the sort of sensible yet searching questions which professional historians tend to overlook. Their insight and their readiness to suspect what others take for granted make every lesson a challenging one, and I thank them warmly for this. However, two people have inspired me beyond measure. Jo and Matilda have made the months during which I worked on this book very special indeed, and it is as a small token of my love and thanks that I dedicate it to them, my queen and my princess.

Chronology of Main Events, 978–1217

978–1016	**Aethelred II king of England**
996–1031	Robert II king of France
1002	Aethelred marries Emma, daughter of Duke Richard I of Normandy
1013–14	**Sweyn king of England**
	Aethelred II and family flee to Normandy
1014	Death of Sweyn (February)
	Return of Aethelred II
1016	Death of Aethelred II (23 April)
1016	**Edmund Ironside, son of Aethelred II, king of England**
1016	Edmund Ironside and Cnut, son of Sweyn, divide England between them
	Death of Edmund Ironside (30 November)
1016–35	**Cnut king of England**
1017	Cnut marries Emma, widow of King Aethelred and mother of Edward the Confessor
1019–35	Cnut king of Denmark
c.1023	Godwin earl of Wessex
1023/32	Leofric earl of Mercia
1031–60	Henry I king of France
1033	Siward earl of Northumbria
1034–40	Duncan king of Scotland
1035–87	William duke of Normandy
1035–47	Magnus king of Norway
1035–42	Harthacnut, son of Cnut, king of Denmark
1035	Death of Cnut (12 November)
1035–40	**Harold I 'Harefoot', son of King Cnut, king of England**
1040	Death of Harold I (17 March)
1040–2	**Harthacnut king of England**
1040–57	Macbeth king of Scotland
1041	Edward, son of King Aethelred, recalled to England from Normandy by Harthacnut
1042	Death of Harthacnut (8 June)

1042–66	**Edward the Confessor, son of Aethelred II, king of England**
1043	Sweyn Godwinson made an earl
	Stigand bishop of East Anglia
1044–50	Robert of Jumièges bishop of London
1045	Edward the Confessor marries Edith, daughter of Earl Godwin
	Harold Godwinson earl of East Anglia
1047–66	Harald Hardrada king of Norway
1047–76	Sweyn Estrithson king of Denmark
1047	Stigand bishop of Winchester
?1050–51	Duke William of Normandy marries Matilda, daughter of Baldwin V, count of Flanders
1050–2	Robert of Jumièges archbishop of Canterbury
1050	Ralph, nephew of Edward the Confessor, made an earl
1051	Edward the Confessor expels Earl Godwin and his family
	Duke William of Normandy visits England (?)
1052	Return from exile of Earl Godwin and his family
1052–70	Stigand archbishop of Canterbury
1053	Death of Earl Godwin (15 April)
1053–66	Harold Godwinson earl of Wessex
1054	Earl Siward of Northumbria campaigns successfully in Scotland; Macbeth king of Scotland deposed
1055	Death of Earl Siward of Northumbria
	Gruffudd ap Llywelyn sacks Hereford
1055–65	Tostig Godwinson earl of Northumbria
1057	Deaths of Ralph, earl of Hereford, and Leofric, earl of Mercia (31 August)
1057–?62	Aelfgar, son of Earl Leofric, earl of Mercia
1058–93	Malcolm III king of Scotland
1060–1108	Philip I king of France
1060–9	Ealdred archbishop of York
1061	Malcolm, king of Scotland, invades northern England
1062–95	Wulfstan bishop of Worcester
?1062–70	Edwin, son of Earl Aelfgar, earl of Mercia
?1063–66	Earl Harold marries Alditha, sister of Earls Edwin and Morcar
1063	Earls Harold and Tostig campaign successfully in Wales; death of Gruffudd ap Llywelyn (August)

1065	Northumbrian revolt; Earl Tostig exiled
	Morcar, son of Earl Aelfgar and brother of Earl
	Edwin, earl of Northumbria
1066	Death of Edward the Confessor (5 January)
1066	**Harold II Godwinson king of England**
1066	Harold II consecrated at Westminster (6 January)
	Battle of Gate Fulford (20 September)
	Battle of Stamford Bridge (25 September)
	Battle of Hastings; death of Harold II (14 October)
1066–87	**William I king of England**
1066	William I consecrated at Westminster
	(25 December)
1068	Revolt of Earls Edwin and Morcar
	Northern rising; William subdues midland
	England and York
1069	Further northern revolt
	Danish invasion of England led by sons of
	Sweyn Estrithson
1069–70	The Harrying of the North
1070	Stigand, archbishop of Canterbury, and other
	English bishops deposed
	Rising in East Anglia led by Hereward; death of
	Earl Edwin, imprisonment of Morcar
1070–89	Lanfranc archbishop of Canterbury
1071	Malcolm, king of Scotland, marries Margaret,
	sister of Edgar *aetheling*
1072	Peace of Abernethy between William I and
	King Malcolm
1075	Revolt of three earls against William I
1076	Execution of Waltheof, earl of Northumbria
	(May)
1078–80	Revolt against William I by his eldest son,
	Robert Curthose
1080–6	Cnut IV king of Denmark
1080	Robert, son of William I, campaigns in
	Scotland against King Malcolm; establishes
	Newcastle
	Robert de Mowbray earl of Northumbria
1083	Fall of Odo, bishop of Bayeux, William I's
	half-brother
1084	William I quarrels with Robert Curthose again
1085–6	Threatened invasion of England by King Cnut
	VI of Denmark
1085	William I orders Domesday survey (Christmas)

1086	Oath of loyalty to William I sworn at Salisbury by all important English landholders (1 August)
1087	Death of William I (9 September)
1087–1100	**William II king of England**
1087–1106	Robert Curthose duke of Normandy
1087	William II consecrated at Westminster (26 September)
1087–8	Domesday Book compiled
1088	Unsuccessful rebellion led by Odo of Bayeux against William II (spring–summer)
1091	Agreement on succession between William II and Robert Curthose
1092	William II campaigns in Cumbria; constructs castle at Carlisle
1093–1109	Anselm archbishop of Canterbury
1093	Malcolm, king of Scotland, ambushed and killed by Earl Robert de Mowbray (13 November)
1093–7	Donald Ban king of Scotland
1094	William II invades Normandy
1095	Unsuccessful revolt of Earl Robert de Mowbray against William II
1096	Robert Curthose pawns Normandy to William II
1097	Edgar *aetheling* campaigns in Scotland (October); expels Donald Ban
	Anselm leaves England (November)
1097–1107	Edgar king of Scotland
1099–1128	Ranulf Flambard bishop of Durham
1100	Death of William II (2 August)
1100–35	**Henry I king of England**
1100	Henry I consecrated at Westminster (5 August); issues 'Coronation Charter'
	Anselm returns to England (September)
	Henry I marries Edith-Matilda, daughter of Malcolm III, king of Scotland and Queen Margaret (11 November)
1101	Robert Curthose invades England; Treaty of Alton (August)
1102	Robert de Bellême forced out of England by Henry I
1106	Henry I defeats Robert Curthose at battle of Tinchebrai (28 September)
1106–35	Henry I duke of Normandy
1107–39	Roger bishop of Salisbury
1107–24	Alexander I king of Scotland

1107	Investiture dispute settled in England
1108–37	Louis VI king of France
1110	Matilda, daughter of Henry I, betrothed to the Emperor Henry V
1114	Matilda marries Henry V (January)
1118	Death of Queen Edith-Matilda, wife of Henry I (1 May)
	Henry I defeated by Count Fulk of Anjou at Alençon
1119	Henry I defeats Louis VI at Brémule (20 August)
1120	William, son of Henry I, drowned in the wreck of the White Ship (25 November)
1121	Henry I marries Adeliza of Louvain
1124	Henry I defeats Norman rebels at Bourgthéroulde (26 March)
1124–53	David I king of Scotland
1125	Stephen of Blois marries Matilda, daughter of Eustace III count of Boulogne
1127	Empress Matilda recognised as Henry I's heir to England and Normandy (1 January)
1128	Empress Matilda marries Count Geoffrey of Anjou (17 June)
1129–71	Henry of Blois, brother of Stephen, bishop of Winchester
1130	First surviving pipe roll
1135	Death of Henry I (1 December)
1135–54	**Stephen king of England**
1135–44	Stephen duke of Normandy
1135	Stephen consecrated at Westminster (22 December)
1137–80	Louis VII king of France
1138	Scots defeated at the Battle of the Standard (22 August)
1139	Stephen arrests the bishops of Salisbury and Lincoln (24 June)
	Empress Matilda and Earl Robert of Gloucester land in England (30 September)
1141	Stephen defeated and captured at the battle of Lincoln (2 February)
	Matilda's forces defeated and Robert of Gloucester captured at Winchester (14 September)
1142–4	Geoffrey of Anjou conquers Normandy
1144	Geoffrey of Anjou captures Rouen (23 April)

1144–9	Geoffrey of Anjou duke of Normandy
1147	Death of Robert of Gloucester (31 October)
1148	Empress Matilda leaves England
1149–89	Henry of Anjou, son of Empress Matilda and Geoffrey of Anjou, duke of Normandy
1151	Death of Geoffrey of Anjou (September)
1151–89	Henry of Anjou count of Anjou
1152	Henry of Anjou marries Eleanor of Aquitaine (18 May)
1152–89	Henry of Anjou duke of Aquitaine
1153–65	Malcolm IV king of Scotland
1153	Henry of Anjou invades England (January–August)
	Death of Eustace, son of Stephen (17 August)
	Treaty of Winchester; Henry of Anjou acknowledged as Stephen's heir (6 November)
1154	Death of Stephen (25 October)
1154–89	**Henry II king of England**
1154	Henry II consecrated at Westminster (19 December)
?1154–68	Robert, earl of Leicester, and Richard de Lucy justiciars
1154–62	Thomas Becket chancellor
1156	Pipe rolls resume in largely unbroken sequence
1162–70	Thomas Becket archbishop of Canterbury
1164	Constitutions of Clarendon (29 January)
1165–1214	William the Lion king of Scotland
1166	Royal survey of landholding in England – the *Cartae Baronum*
	Assize of Clarendon
1168–78	Richard de Lucy justiciar
1169	Henry II makes his eldest son Henry heir to England, Normandy and Anjou
1169–70	Anglo-Norman conquest and colonisation of Ireland begins
1169–89	Richard, son of Henry II, count of Poitou
1170	Inquest of Sheriffs
	Murder of Thomas Becket (29 December)
1172	Compromise of Avranches (27 September)
March 1173–July 1174	Great Rebellion against Henry II
1176	Assize of Northampton
1177	Henry II designates his son John king of Ireland
*c.*1177–9	*The Dialogue of the Exchequer* written by Richard FitzNigel

?1179–89	Ranulf Glanvill chief justiciar
1180–1223	Philip II king of France
1183	Death of Henry the Young King (11 June)
1185	John's expedition to Ireland
1186	Death of Count Geoffrey of Brittany (August)
1189	Death of Henry II (6 July)
1189–99	**Richard I king of England, duke of Normandy, count of Anjou and duke of Aquitaine**
1189	Richard I consecrated at Westminster (13 September)
	John made count of Mortain; marries Isabelle of Gloucester (29 August); given control over seven English counties
	William de Mandeville, earl of Essex, and Hugh de Puiset, bishop of Durham, co-justiciars
	Death of earl of Essex (November); Hugh, bishop of Durham, sole justiciar
	Richard I leaves England on crusade (11 December)
1190–1	William Longchamp, bishop of Ely, justiciar
1191	Richard I marries Berengaria of Navarre (12 May)
	Richard I reaches Acre (8 June)
	Acre surrenders to the crusaders (12 July)
	Philip II of France returns from Third Crusade (by December)
1191–4	Rebellion by John
1191–3	Walter of Coutances, archbishop of Rouen, justiciar
1192	Richard I sets sail for England (9 October)
	Richard I captured by Leopold, duke of Austria (20 December); placed in custody of Emperor Henry VI
1193–1205	Hubert Walter archbishop of Canterbury
1193–8	Hubert Walter chief justiciar (December)
1194	Richard I released from captivity in Germany (February)
	Richard I lands in England (13 March)
	Richard I leaves England (12 May)
	First surviving 'articles of the eyre'
1195	First tripartite final concord (or 'foot of fine') issued on the instructions of Hubert Walter
1198–1213	Geoffrey FitzPeter, earl of Essex, chief justiciar
1199	Death of Richard I (6 April)

1199–1216	**John king of England, duke of Normandy and Aquitaine and count of Anjou**
1199	John invested duke of Normandy at Rouen (25 April)
	John consecrated at Westminster (27 May)
	First surviving charter roll
1199–1205	Hubert Walter, archbishop of Canterbury, chancellor
1200	Treaty of Le Goulet (22 May)
	John marries Isabella of Angoulême (24 August)
	First surviving close roll
1201	First surviving patent roll
1202	Philip II announces confiscation of John's continental lands (Spring)
	John captures Arthur of Brittany at the Battle of Mirebeau (1 August)
1203	Arthur of Brittany murdered (April)
1204	Philip II captures Rouen (24 June)
1205	Death of Hubert Walter, archbishop of Canterbury (13 July)
1206–28	Stephen Langton archbishop of Canterbury
1208	Papal interdict imposed on England (24 March)
1213–15	Peter des Roches, bishop of Winchester, chief justiciar
1213	John makes England a papal fief (15 May)
1214	John lands in France (February)
	Interdict lifted (2 July)
	John's allies defeated by Philip II at Battle of Bouvines (27 July)
	John returns to England (October)
1214–49	Alexander II king of Scotland
1215	Magna Carta issued (15 June)
	Magna Carta annulled by Pope Innocent III (24 August)
1215–32	Hubert de Burgh chief justiciar
1216	Louis of France lands in Kent (21 May)
	Death of John (15–16 October)
1216–72	**Henry III king of England, lord of Ireland, duke of Normandy and Aquitaine and count of Anjou**
1216	Henry III consecrated at Gloucester (28 October)
	Magna Carta reissued for first time (12 November)

1217	Royalist victory at Lincoln (20 May) Royalist naval victory off Sandwich (24 August) Peace of Kingston between Henry III and Louis of France (12 September) Magna Carta reissued for second time (by November)

A Note on Money

During the period covered by this book, there was only one coin in circulation in England, the silver penny. There were twelve pence in a shilling, 240 pence (twenty shillings) in a pound and 160 pence in a mark. However, shillings, pounds and marks were terms used for accounting purposes only; there were no coins with those values. Throughout the book, and for the sake of simplicity and ready comparability, I have given large sums in pounds.

References and Abbreviations

I have attempted to keep references to a minimum by giving a citation only when a source or secondary work has been quoted or referred to expressly. I have also tried to give references to the most accessible versions of the sources used. If a source (like the *Anglo-Saxon Chronicle*, for example) is included in a readily available volume of collected sources, I have referred in the notes to the collection rather than the source. Full details of most of the works referred to here can be found in 'Suggestions for Further Reading'.

I have used the following abbreviations in the notes:

Eadmer   *Eadmer's History of Recent Events in England*, trans. Bosanquet
EHD II   *English Historical Documents II 1042–1189*, ed. Douglas and Greenaway
EHD III   *English Historical Documents III 1189–1327*, ed. Rothwell
JW   *The Chronicle of John of Worcester*, ed. Darlington and McGurk
NC   *The Norman Conquest of England*, ed. Brown
OV   *The Ecclesiastical History of Orderic Vitalis*, ed. Chibnall
V.Ed.   *The Life of King Edward*, ed. Barlow
WMB   William of Malmesbury, *The Deeds of the Bishops of England*, trans. Preest
WMHN   William of Malmesbury, *Historia Novella*, ed. King and Potter
WMK   William of Malmesbury, *The History of the English Kings*, ed. Mynors, Thomson and Winterbottom

List of Debates

Map 1   The shires and political divisions of England in 1066

Source: After Barrow, G.W.S. (1956, reprinted 1971) *Feudal Britain: The Completion of the Medieval Kingdom, 1066–1314*, pub. Edward Arnold, p. 12. Reprinted by permission of Professor G.W.S. Barrow.

Map 2   The shires of England in 1217

Source: After map 'The countries of England' from Carpenter, D. (2003) *The Penguin History of Britain: The Struggle for Mastery: Britain 1066–1284*, pub. Penguin Press, Copyright © David Carpenter, p. xiii. Reprinted by permission of Penguin Books Ltd.

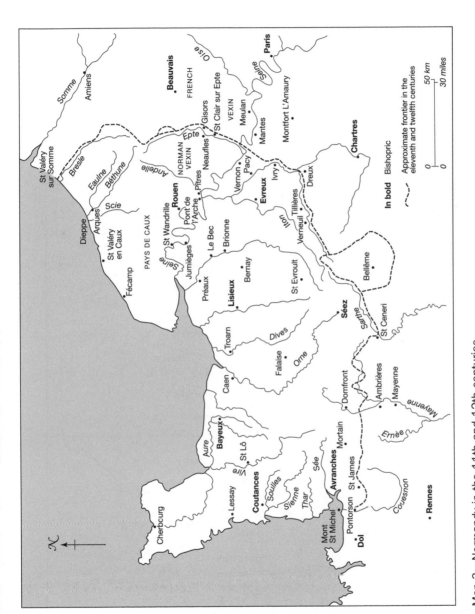

Map 3   Normandy in the 11th and 12th centuries

Source: After van Houts, E. and Harper-Bill, C. (eds) (2003) *A Companion to the Anglo-Norman World*, pub. Boydell Press, p. xiii. Reprinted by permission of Boydell Press.

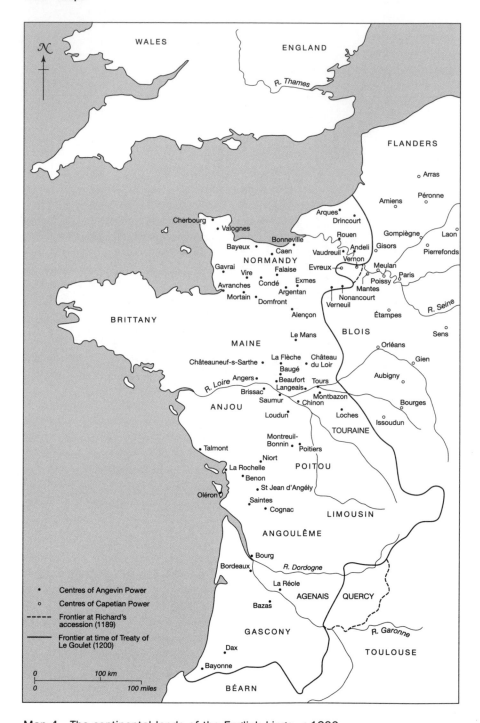

Map 4   The continental lands of the English kings, *c.*1200

Source: After Gillingham, J. (2002) *The Angevin Empire, 2nd Edition*, pub. Hodder Arnold, p. 32. Reprinted by permission of Professor John Gillingham.

Map 5   The dioceses of England in 1066

Source: Adapted from Hill, D. (1981) *The Atlas of Anglo-Saxon England*, pub. Blackwell and University of Toronto Press, p. 148. Reprinted with permission of Blackwell Publishing and University of Toronto Press.

Map 6   The dioceses of England in 1217

Source: After Barrow, G.W.S. (1956, reprinted 1971) *Feudal Britain: The Completion of the Medieval Kingdom, 1066–1314*, pub. Edward Arnold, p. 313. Reprinted by permission of Professor G.W.S. Barrow.

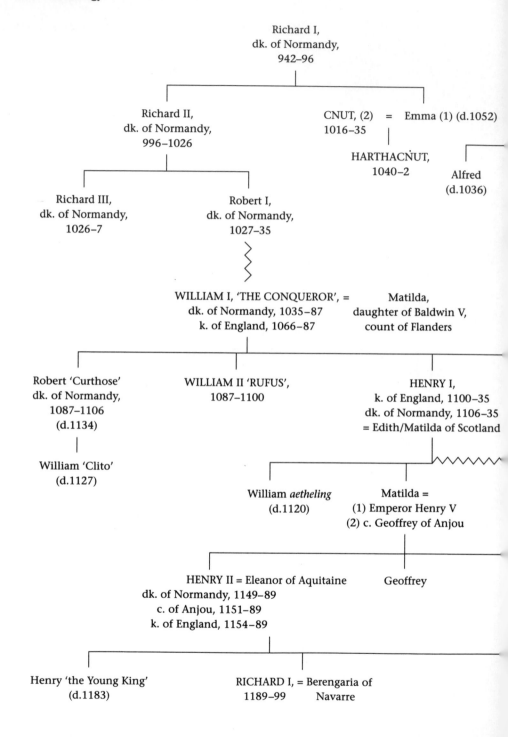

The Kings of England, 979–1272. A Selective Genealogy

This is not exhaustive and only mentions individuals referred to in the text. Kings of England are given in capital letters. The following abbreviations are used:

c. count
css. countess
d. died
dk. duke
e. earl
k. king
www = illegitimate

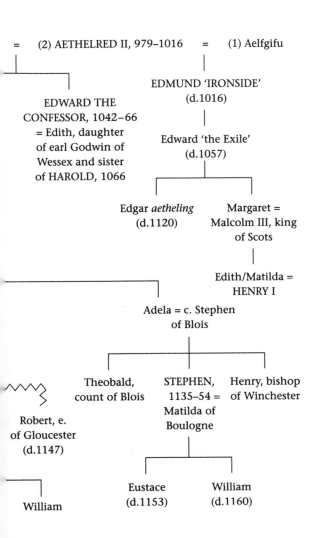

= (2) AETHELRED II, 979–1016   =   (1) Aelfgifu

EDMUND 'IRONSIDE' (d.1016)

EDWARD THE CONFESSOR, 1042–66 = Edith, daughter of earl Godwin of Wessex and sister of HAROLD, 1066

Edward 'the Exile' (d.1057)

Edgar *aetheling* (d.1120)

Margaret = Malcolm III, king of Scots

Edith/Matilda = HENRY I

Adela = c. Stephen of Blois

Theobald, count of Blois

STEPHEN, 1135–54 = Matilda of Boulogne

Henry, bishop of Winchester

Robert, e. of Gloucester (d.1147)

William

Eustace (d.1153)

William (d.1160)

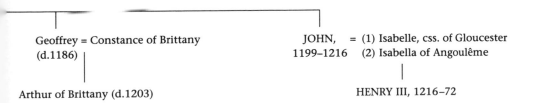

Geoffrey = Constance of Brittany (d.1186)

Arthur of Brittany (d.1203)

JOHN,   = (1) Isabelle, css. of Gloucester
1199–1216   (2) Isabella of Angoulême

HENRY III, 1216–72

The Kings of England, 970–1272: A Simplified Genealogy

Part I

Late Anglo-Saxon England,
1042–1066

1

The Reigns, 1042–1066

Edward the Confessor, 1042–1066

1042–1050

Edward the Confessor was the surviving son of King Aethelred II (978–1016) and Emma of Normandy, and the half-brother of King Harthacnut (1040–2). However, despite his lineage he was an unlikely king. He had fled England after the invasion of King Sweyn of Denmark in 1013 and, although he had returned for a short period in 1014 and again, perhaps, in 1036, he had spent his formative years in Normandy at the duke's court and out of the mainstream of English politics. His chances of becoming king must have appeared slim when his father died in 1016 (there were several potential claimants at that stage) and even slimmer in 1035 on the death of King Cnut (1016–35), who left two sons to continue the Danish line. Edward's prospects had improved since being summoned back to England in 1041, to rule either alongside or as a deputy for the second of Cnut's sons, Harthacnut; but the latter's death in 1042 was probably unexpected and, after only a year back in England, the traditions, structures and systems of his new kingdom must still have been unfamiliar to Edward. Furthermore, he had as yet no independent power-base of his own from which to draw support. His inheritance was not a straightforward one. Aged about 37 on his half-brother's death, Edward would need powerful support if he was to rule effectively.

According to most of the sources, such support came in the person of Earl Godwin of Wessex who took the lead in persuading his fellow magnates to accept Edward as king. In fact, there was no other obvious candidate in 1042, but Godwin was determined nevertheless to assert himself and take the lead; perhaps so that he could put himself in a position to dominate the new, inexperienced king or, perhaps, to convince Edward of his loyalty. After all, Edward may have regarded the earl of Wessex with suspicion in 1042. Godwin's father, Wulfnoth, had betrayed Edward's father, Aethelred, in 1009; Godwin himself was deeply implicated in the murder of Edward's brother, Alfred, in 1036, and the earl had spent his life fighting for the Danish kings, to whom he owed his fortune and status. The *Vita Edwardi* records the present made to Edward by Godwin at the start of the reign of a great ship, and this is likely to have been a peace offering of some sort.[1] At the same time, Edward may have felt the need to cultivate Godwin's support, not just because he was the most powerful of the English earls, but also because of his Danish links. Through his wife, the earl was a kinsman of Sweyn Estrithson, king of Denmark. Sweyn was struggling in 1042 against King Magnus of Norway, who almost certainly had his own designs on the English throne; so Edward had a vested interest in Sweyn's victory and needed him as an ally. Godwin was thus an important point of common reference for the two kings.

Distasteful as both men might have found such an idea, therefore, king and earl needed each other in 1042–3. Nevertheless, that Edward was not crowned until Easter 1043 may suggest that a good deal of horse-trading took up the ten months or so after Harthacnut's death. The earls of Mercia and Northumbria, Leofric and Siward, retained their positions, and Godwin's two eldest sons, Sweyn and Harold, became earls of Herefordshire and East Anglia respectively in or shortly after 1043. Godwin's nephew, and Sweyn of Denmark's brother, Beorn, was granted an earldom in the east midlands in 1045 and, to set the seal on the relationship, Edward married Godwin's daughter Edith in 1045. The next king, it was assumed, would be of Godwin blood, and the fortunes of the family looked secure.

Another consequence of the pre-coronation bargaining may have been the humiliation of Edward's mother, Queen Emma, in 1043. Some time shortly after his coronation Edward, in company with Earls Leofric, Godwin and Siward, rode to Winchester where Emma was living. There they 'deprived her of all the treasures which she owned . . . because she had formerly been very hard to the king, her son, in that she did less for him than he wished both before he became king and afterwards as well'.[2] Perhaps this was Edward's initiative, but the great earls would also have stood to benefit if Emma was removed from the political scene. She had meddled before, and one price of their loyalty to Edward could have been his promise that he would distance himself from his mother. She eventually died at Winchester in 1052 and was buried there alongside her second husband, Cnut.

The marriage of political convenience between Edward and Godwin first showed signs of strain in 1046, when the earl's eldest son, Sweyn, was disgraced. Whilst campaigning on the Welsh border (part of his normal responsibilities as earl of Herefordshire), Sweyn abducted Eadgifu, the abbess of Leominster. According to the *Anglo-Saxon Chronicle*, 'he ordered the abbess . . . to be brought to him and kept her as long as it suited him'. John of Worcester suggests that there was an element of romance to the story by alleging that Sweyn wanted to marry the lady in question and that the king refused him permission to do so. More likely, he was interested in the lands of her abbey within his earldom. Either way, his behaviour was intolerable and, having surrendered his captive, Sweyn went into exile, first in Flanders and then in Denmark where, the *Anglo-Saxon Chronicle* mysteriously states, 'he ruined himself'.[3]

Godwin was unable to do anything to prevent Sweyn's exile; the earl's power in England was not absolute. The limits of Godwin's influence were also evident in 1047 when he tried to persuade Edward to send ships to help Sweyn of Denmark, who was struggling in his war against Magnus of Norway. The earl's suggestion was dismissed as, according to the *Anglo-Saxon Chronicle*, it seemed a 'foolish plan to everybody'.[4] Even though Edward would probably have preferred to see Sweyn triumph over Magnus, the king was apparently happy on this occasion to let the Scandinavian kings thrash things out between themselves. In the event, any threat to England from Magnus was removed by his death in October 1047. He was succeeded by Harald Hardrada, a Viking warrior with a legendary reputation.

The relationship between Edward and Godwin was perhaps further undermined in 1049 when Edward received a request for naval assistance from the emperor, Henry III, in his campaign against Baldwin, count of Flanders. Edward was probably pleased to have the opportunity to take action against Baldwin, who regularly allowed his harbours to be used by Scandinavian pirates who preyed upon English ships in the North Sea. More importantly, Flanders was the regular first port of call for exiles from the English court. Queen Emma had gone there in 1036 and in 1046 Sweyn had fled to Baldwin's court before going on to Denmark. Edward never had to use the fleet which he gathered at Sandwich in 1049, as Baldwin and the emperor came to terms, but the pointedness of the stance he adopted towards a friend of the Godwins cannot have gone unnoticed by the earl and his followers.

After Sweyn Godwinson's exile, his lands in England were shared out between his brother, Harold, and his cousin, Beorn. Not surprisingly, they were dismayed to see him return to England in 1049. However, Sweyn appears to have expected them to help him regain the king's favour. Harold and Beorn initially refused to do this, but Beorn later prevaricated with fateful consequences. On meeting with Sweyn, he was abducted and murdered. Sweyn had thus added a crime of international significance (Beorn was the king of Denmark's brother) to his already lengthy list of previous convictions. Edward and his counsellors declared him *nithing*, an outcast irrecoverably disgraced, and he fled into exile once more. His lands were given to the king's French nephew, Ralph of Mantes.[5] In 1050, however, Sweyn returned to England again and, re-markably, was pardoned by the king. This event has usually been seen as further evidence of Edward's vulnerability and weakness in the face of Godwin power. On the other hand, Sweyn's pardon may have been intended in part to abate the tension which probably existed between Godwin and the king by this stage; or, indeed, perhaps Edward thought that Sweyn's return might sow further dissension amongst his wife's kin. Whatever the reasons behind Sweyn's pardon, it is clear that, by 1050, Edward had shown himself capable of acting independently and against the interests of his father-in-law. But however strained their relationship was by then, it was as nothing compared with what was about to happen.

1051–1052

In 1051, Edward tried to rid himself of the Godwins for good and he almost succeeded. The spark which lit the fuse appears to have been the death of Archbishop Eadsige of Canterbury in October 1050. The monks of Canterbury elected one of their number, a relative of Godwin's named Aethelric, as Eadsige's successor. However, the king was determined not to allow such an important appointment to slip out of his control and he nominated the bishop of London, Robert of Jumièges, a Norman and an old associate of the king, to the post. What happened next is unclear and accounts differ as to what led to Godwin's eventual disgrace. Robert of Jumièges, anxious for influence within Kent, may have poisoned Edward's mind against the earl. Alternatively, Godwin lost Edward's favour because of the way he responded to a fight which took place in Dover between Godwin's men and the men of Eustace, count of Boulogne, Edward's brother-in-law. When Eustace complained to the king about the incident and Edward ordered Godwin to go to Kent and discipline his people (Kent was part of Godwin's earldom of Wessex), the earl refused. Godwin and his eldest sons were then summoned before the king to explain themselves, but before they reached London in September 1051 they became convinced that Edward was determined to make impossible demands of them and refuse them a fair hearing. Their only option was to flee abroad, Godwin, Sweyn, Tostig and Gyrth to Flanders, Harold and Leofwine to Ireland. As for Queen Edith, she was sent to live as a nun at Wherwell in Hampshire. The triumphant king immediately set about dismantling the Godwins' power-base. Aelfgar, son of Earl Leofric, was granted Harold's earldom of East Anglia and the Godwins' lands in the south-west were granted to another of Edward's loyal supporters, Odda of Deerhurst. Wessex was probably retained by the king himself. And according to more than one source, after the Godwins left England, Duke

William of Normandy visited the king and was fêted by him.[6] Whether Edward made William his heir during this visit is far less clear.

If Edward thought the Godwins had gone for good, though, he was being unrealistic. Godwin tried to send conciliatory messages to the king from Flanders, but they fell on deaf ears and an armed return was inevitable. In June 1052 Godwin landed in Kent and then sailed on to Sussex; but he returned to Bruges before he was confronted by the English defenders. Perhaps this was just a preliminary trip to assess the amount of support Godwin still retained within his earldom. Meanwhile, Harold and Leofwine had crossed from Dublin and ravaged in Somerset and Devon. Eventually they met up with their father, who had left Flanders again, on the Isle of Wight, probably in August. Together, they then sailed around the coast to Sussex and on to Kent. Finally they began their voyage up the Thames and towards London, where the king, with a large naval and land force, was awaiting their arrival. On his arrival in Southwark, Godwin sent messengers to the king asking for the restoration of all that he and his sons had been deprived of in the previous year. Edward refused and appears to have been prepared to fight. However, he found that he had little support for such a course of action, and the prospect of civil war was too much for those advising him, in particular Earls Siward and Leofric: 'it was hateful to almost all of them to fight against men of their own race', says the *Anglo-Saxon Chronicle*, 'and also they did not wish the country to be laid the more open to foreigners through their destroying each other'.[7] In the end a truce was negotiated and terms of settlement were agreed. The Godwins, including Queen Edith who returned to court, were restored to their lands and titles and many foreigners, Robert of Jumièges amongst them, who were widely blamed for having provoked the crisis in the first place, fled the country after having been outlawed. Robert was replaced as archbishop of Canterbury by Stigand, who was already (and continued to be) bishop of Winchester.

1053–1062

Edward's attempt to free himself from the control of Godwin and his kin had failed. Indeed, the king was perhaps more compromised than ever. The earl and his sons had been restored to their former positions of power, Edith had returned to the king's side, and the king's Norman supporters had been forced to flee the country. As a result, after 1052, Edward's room for independent action was severely circumscribed. Much of his time after this point was taken up with hunting and supervising the construction of his new abbey at Westminster. Although Edward was still an active king in the last decade or so of his reign, it is arguable that meaningful control of the realm rested with others. Earl Godwin's personal triumph was short-lived, however; he died in April 1053 after having celebrated Easter with his sons and the king at Winchester. Suitably, he was buried near his great patron, Cnut, at Winchester. Into Godwin's shoes as earl of Wessex stepped his son Harold, and he was to dominate the rest of the reign. Hitherto, Harold had been earl of East Anglia and, presumably in an attempt by Edward to maintain some parity of power between the great clans, his position there was taken by Aelfgar, the son of Earl Leofric of Mercia.

Events in northern England now began to assume an ominous importance. In the summer of 1054, the king ordered Earl Siward to march into Scotland, remove its king, Macbeth, and install Malcolm, the son of King Duncan (who had been killed by Macbeth in 1040), as the new king. Despite being assisted by Normans who had fled to Scotland in the aftermath of 1052, Macbeth was defeated and fled. In the same year, according to the *Anglo-Saxon Chronicle*, Bishop Ealdred of Worcester travelled to the court of Emperor Henry III in Cologne. John of Worcester explains that he was on a royal mission to make contact with Edward 'the Exile', the son of Edmund Ironside, Edward's half-brother, who had died in 1017. The younger Edward was now in Hungary, and it was Ealdred's task to bring him back to England, 'for the king had decided to make him his heir to the kingdom'.[8] Edward finally returned to England in 1057 but he died before seeing the king and left in England his son, Edgar, who would pursue his own claims to the throne in due course.

Meanwhile, in 1055 the dominant figure in the north, Earl Siward, had died. Who should succeed him was a question of crucial importance, given the extent to which the earl was relied upon to prevent Scottish and Scandinavian incursions into England. Siward's eldest son and his nephew had both been killed on the Scottish campaign of 1054 and his remaining son, Waltheof, was very young and incapable of governing. So the king had to make a decision and, fatefully, his choice as the new earl of Northumbria was Tostig, Earl Harold's younger brother. This choice has eluded convincing explanation ever since it was made, but it is often used as yet further evidence of King Edward's weakness in the face of Godwin might and of his political ineptitude. Overnight, the already far-reaching power of the Godwinsons was massively extended and the balance of power within England was shifted decisively in their favour.

Soon after Tostig's appointment, Earl Aelfgar of East Anglia, Leofric's son, was exiled. He was probably unhappy that northern England had been added to the Godwinsons' sphere of influence; alternatively, he may have had designs of his own on the northern earldom which were disappointed. In exile he joined forces with the ruler of north Wales, Gruffudd ap Llywelyn, and raided into Herefordshire. However, by 1057 Aelfgar had been received back into the English political community. In the autumn of that year, his father, Leofric, died and Aelfgar succeeded him as earl of Mercia. The Godwins also extended their power. When Earl Ralph of Hereford died in December 1057, Harold himself took control of his lands. Meanwhile, Harold's brother Gyrth took over from Aelfgar in East Anglia and another brother, Leofwine, was granted an earldom in the south-west. By 1058, then, all of England, with the exception of Mercia, was covered by earldoms in Godwinson hands. One family dominated English affairs like never before, and the land, wealth and patronage at their disposal arguably made them more powerful even than the king. Whether Edward acquiesced willingly in this state of affairs, encouraged it or felt he had little choice but to accept it are questions on which historians still disagree. However, it is certainly fair to say that a masterful king would never have allowed such a situation to arise.

Affairs in England were generally quiet between 1058 and 1062. Little is recorded in the *Anglo-Saxon Chronicle*, but the *Vita Edwardi* does describe a visit by Earl Tostig to Rome in 1061–2.[9] That he was able to make this trip at all and spend considerable time away from his earldom is suggestive of the confidence he and his brothers felt about the strength of the hold they had on England by the early 1060s. With the death of Earl Aelfgar of Mercia some time in or around 1062, that confidence must only have increased further. However, King Malcolm of Scotland did take advantage of Tostig's absence to launch a highly effective invasion of northern England during which he got as far south as Lancashire.

1063–1066

After Aelfgar's death, Mercia stayed in the hands of the Leofricsons and Aelfgar's eldest son, Edwin, became the new earl. However, Earl Harold was not slow to try to take advantage of this new situation by leading campaigns against Gruffudd ap Llywelyn in Wales. Gruffudd, of course, was Earl Aelfgar's old ally, and security on the Welsh border was traditionally the concern of the Mercian earl. Harold, therefore, was arguably encroaching on Edwin's newly-acquired authority when, late in 1062, he made a raid on Rhuddlan in north Wales and when, in the early summer of 1063, he and Tostig launched a full-scale campaign designed to oust the Welsh prince. Whilst Harold sailed along the coast of south Wales ravaging as he went, Tostig invaded from the north. Eventually, in August, seeing the direction in which events were going, Gruffudd's own men killed their leader and delivered his head to Harold.

Some time after these events, in 1064 or 1065, Earl Harold travelled to France. This trip continues to be highly controversial. It is not clear precisely when it took place, and some historians have been reluctant to accept that it took place at all.[10] And assuming that Harold did cross the Channel at some point around this time, it is even less clear why he went. The Norman sources are keen to stress that Harold went to visit

Duke William of Normandy and to confirm the offer of the throne made to the duke by King Edward in 1051; less partial sources suggest that Harold went for reasons of his own. The Canterbury monk, Eadmer, for example, writing after 1090, states that Harold visited Normandy to procure the release from captivity of two of his relatives, namely Wulfnoth (Harold's brother) and Haakon (his nephew).[11] These must have been the same relatives who, William of Poitiers tells us, were handed over when Edward originally made his promise of the throne to Duke William in the early 1050s. Eadmer also states that Harold was unaware that Edward had ever offered the throne to William until the latter himself revealed to his guest that this offer had been made whilst Edward was still an exile in Normandy. So perhaps Harold's intentions in visiting William were different again. It is not impossible that Harold had set out with his own agenda, namely to ascertain the degree of support he would receive from northern France if he made a bid for the throne on Edward's death. For the Norman historians writing after William's victory at Hastings, however, it was essential to portray Harold as an illegitimate usurper who had no valid claim to the English throne. They did this by portraying him as a disloyal perjurer. William of Jumièges states that Harold was sent to Normandy by King Edward and that, once at William's court, he 'swore fealty concerning the kingdom with many oaths'. William of Poitiers goes even further. In a public ceremony, almost certainly similar in form to the one depicted on the Bayeux Tapestry, Harold swore to act as William's agent in England pending King Edward's death and to support William's claim to the English throne thereafter.[12] He also promised to place various important military strongholds (not least Dover) in the hands of William's men, presumably to serve as bridgeheads in anticipation of William's eventual arrival in England. In return for all this, William confirmed Harold in his lands and powers.

Once back in England, in the spring of 1065, Harold embarked on a campaign in south Wales. More significantly, in October 1065 a rebellion broke out against Earl Tostig in Northumbria. Although the *Vita Edwardi* suggests that Earl Harold played a part in deliberately provoking the revolt, local grievances seem to have been at its root. Tostig's subjects may have been unhappy about his failure to protect them from Malcolm of Scotland's invasion in 1061. More specifically, according to John of Worcester, Tostig's rule in the north was brutal and cruel: he was responsible for the deaths of two prominent Northumbrian noblemen, whilst his sister (Queen Edith, no less) had ordered the killing of the Northumbrian thegn Gospatric 'for her brother's sake' at the king's Christmas court in 1064. His rule was also oppressive for other reasons: he had taken 'an immense tax . . . wrongly', and even the pro-Godwin *Vita Edwardi* concedes that he had repressed the Northumbrian nobility 'with the heavy yoke of his rule because of their misdeeds', and that he was prone to act unjustly in order to gain the property of others for himself.[13] The rebels chose a new earl, Morcar, the brother of Earl Edwin of Mercia, and marched south where Harold came to negotiate with them. Harold returned to the king with the news that the rebels were determined to keep their new earl and force Tostig out; Edward acceded to their demands and Harold returned to Northampton to tell the northerners that his brother was no longer their earl. Harold does not appear to have tried very hard to stand up for Tostig, who went into exile in Flanders with his family nursing a burning grievance against the perceived disloyalty of his brother. At about this time, too, Waltheof, the son of Earl Siward who had died in 1055, became earl of Northamptonshire and Huntingdonshire.

The northern revolt was a severe shock to the old king, and by Christmas 1065 he was ill; so ill in fact that he was unable to attend the consecration of his new church at Westminster on 28 December. Whether he was too ill to make arrangements for the succession is another area of dispute, but the sources suggest that, just prior to his death, he did nominate Harold as the next king. In any event, he died on 5 January 1066. On 6 January, in the morning, he was buried in his new church, and later that same day, Earl Harold of Wessex was consecrated and crowned there.

Harold II, January–October 1066

To Stamford Bridge

Harold's reign is a neglected one, and it is hard to hack a way through the thicket of Norman propaganda to see what sort of king Harold was and how he set about dealing with the problems he faced in 1066. One thing is certain, however: although these problems were far from insignificant, when Harold became king his position was a strong one. He had every reason to think that he would rule for a long time to come.

Harold spent the first phase of his reign, immediately after his coronation, in northern England. He was probably taking pains to reassure the leading men of Northumbria that the settlement of the previous year still held good, and that Tostig would not be allowed to return. This is also one point at which Harold could have married Alditha, the sister of Earls Edwin and Morcar. Having secured the loyalty of the leading men of the north, Harold had returned to Westminster by Easter, and there he held court. It was shortly after Easter, too, that Halley's Comet appeared over England. Visible for a week from 24 April, the comet was depicted in the Bayeux Tapestry and spoken of in the *Anglo-Saxon Chronicle* and by William of Jumièges; but what contemporaries really made of it at the time is hard to say.[14] It would certainly have been perceived as an omen, but whether it was a good one or a bad one remained to be seen.

In May, Tostig returned to English shores, and landed on the Isle of Wight (as his father had done in 1052), where he had lands and followers. He was accompanied by a fleet of uncertain size which had been supplied to him by Count Baldwin of Flanders. It is unclear whether this was intended as a full-scale invasion; more likely, the enterprise was designed to ascertain the degree of support Tostig might expect if he reasserted himself more forcefully. He raided along the south coast, but appears to have gathered little momentum or support. And when he heard that his brother, the new king, was advancing against him, he turned northwards, presumably to regroup and reassess his options. Tostig made some forays into Lincolnshire as he travelled up the eastern coastline and down the river Humber, but he was eventually seen off for the time being by Harold's new brothers-in-law, Earls Edwin and Morcar. They dealt, decisively it seems, with Tostig and his men, and Tostig fled as a result to Scotland, to the court of his old ally, King Malcolm. He remained there, brooding and plotting, for the rest of the summer.

Tostig's flight left the new king able to deal with what he probably perceived as a far more serious threat, the one posed by William of Normandy. If William of Jumièges is to be believed, on hearing news of King Edward's death and Harold's seizure of power, William sent envoys to Harold in England 'exhorting him to withdraw from this madness and keep the faith which he had sworn'. For his part, according to the *Anglo-Saxon Chronicle*, Harold 'assembled a naval force and a land force ['a large fleet and a horsed army', according to John of Worcester] larger than any king had assembled before in this country, because he had been told that count [*sic*] William from Normandy, king Edward's kinsman, meant to come here and subdue the country'. Indirect evidence in support of this is given by William of Poitiers, who has those of Duke William's followers who opposed his invasion stress the size of Harold's fleet, his wealth and the extent of the military resources generally at his disposal. If Harold was able to gather such forces around him, it is clear that he had plenty of English support.[15]

Harold kept his troops on stand-by along the Channel coast for the whole of the summer, anxiously awaiting the anticipated Norman invasion.[16] By the beginning of September, however, no such invasion had been launched. Then, by 8 September the *Anglo-Saxon Chronicle* says, 'the provisions of the people were gone, and nobody could keep them there any longer. Then the men were allowed to go home, and the king rode inland.' In other words, Harold was forced to disband his forces because he was no longer able to feed and supply them. It was singularly unfortunate for the king, therefore, that just as his forces were breaking up, news did arrive of an invasion, not on the south coast by the Normans, but in the north-east by Tostig and, more significantly, Harald Hardrada, King of Norway. Tostig had probably contacted King Harald during his Scottish exile and Harald, an experienced and battle-hardened warrior with a large fleet at his disposal (300 ships according to the *Anglo-Saxon Chronicle*; 500, according to John of Worcester), probably liked his chances, especially in view of the fact that English eyes were directed towards Normandy. Had he wanted to, Harald could have staked a claim to the English throne on the basis of an agreement allegedly made between Magnus of Norway (Harald's nephew) and Harthacnut in about 1040, but he probably did not concern himself with such legal niceties. England was rich and, so he probably thought, there for the taking.

News of the northern invasion came as a complete surprise to King Harold. Tostig and Harald met up at the mouth of the river Tyne. Their joint forces then sailed down the coast and up the rivers Humber and Ouse towards York. Meanwhile, King Harold rushed northwards 'day and night as quickly as he could assemble his force' to confront the invaders. This suggests that Harold recruited as he travelled, and that he could recruit any troops at this stage is further testimony to the support he enjoyed across England. However, before he reached York, the first of this year's three battles had already taken place (on 20 September) outside York at Gate Fulford between the invaders on one side and the forces of Earls Edwin and Morcar on the other. The battle appears to have been brutal, long and bloody. There were heavy casualties on both sides, but eventually Tostig and Harald won the day and took control of York.

Harold arrived in Yorkshire on 24 September, only four days after the battle. By 25 September the bulk of the invasion force was encamped at the village of Stamford Bridge, to the north-east of York. Harold advanced through York on the 25th, came upon the invaders 'by surprise' and immediately engaged them in battle. Hardrada and Tostig were almost certainly unprepared, but they still managed to put up strong resistance, and the fighting lasted most of the day. Eventually, Hardrada and Tostig were both killed, along with many of their followers. Stamford Bridge was a crushing, decisive victory for Harold, and the high point of his reign. Two potential threats to his rule (Tostig and Hardrada) had been removed at a single stroke, and Harold had confirmed his military reputation and justified his elevation to the throne earlier in the year. Unfortunately for Harold, however, it was precisely at this point, after nearly four months of waiting, that the wind in the English Channel changed in the Duke of Normandy's favour. Whilst Harold was still in the north, William's fleet landed at Pevensey in Sussex on 28 September 1066.

The Hastings campaign

William's invasion preparations had been thorough. According to William of Poitiers, on hearing of Edward the Confessor's death, the duke called a meeting of his leading magnates at which many of them expressed their misgivings about an invasion. Such a plan was 'too hazardous and far beyond the resources of Normandy'. Moreover, they said, Harold was rich enough to recruit powerful assistance, he had 'a numberless fleet with expert crews' and 'the wealth and therefore military resources of his country far exceeded' those of Normandy.[17] Their caution was not misplaced; William's plans would involve the construction of a large fleet, a risky sea crossing and an opposed landing in a hostile country. Success was far from guaranteed.

Despite these objections, William managed to convince his magnates to fall in with his plans. This says much for his own determination and strength of character, and for the rewards he offered. William of Poitiers tells of the 'generous provision' he made for those who came with him, and also of the promises he made of riches to come. Indeed, William had one advantage over Harold: he could promise to make gifts of the lands he conquered: 'Without doubt he will overcome who is prepared to bestow not only his own property but that of his foe'.[18] And certainly England, if conquered, had much to offer: its wealth was almost proverbial and William's followers were soon persuaded that the risks were worth taking.

Unlike Harold, William had no ready-made fleet upon which to call. He had to rely on his vassals to provide him with some ships and build the rest from scratch. The Bayeux Tapestry shows this being done. William of Jumièges' assertion that William had a fleet of 3,000 vessels built can almost certainly be dismissed, but it does at least suggest that the fleet was large.[19] William also needed ground troops and again had to rely on his vassals to provide most of these. He recruited more volunteers from outside Normandy, from Brittany, Ponthieu, Flanders and even further afield. The fleet was probably ready to set sail in July, but adverse winds played a part in keeping it at home. Until they were able to set sail, William's troops had to be accommodated and fed; their horses, too, had to be provided for. William of Poitiers estimated that William fed 50,000 men at his own expense for the whole of this period, but this is almost certainly a wild exaggeration.[20] Nevertheless, the demands of feeding and providing for a large force of men and horses were huge.

According to William of Poitiers, Duke William also had influential support for his plans to seize the English throne. Both the emperor, Henry IV, and King Sweyn of Denmark backed him as, most famously, did Pope Alexander II, who also, we are told, supplied William with a papal banner 'behind which he might advance more confidently and securely against his enemy'.[21] But whether he had their official support or not, none of these new allies provided William with meaningful military aid. Of much more importance in the immediate context of September 1066 was William's ability to leave Normandy without fear of external attack. Had the duke of Normandy's two perennial foes, the king of France and the count of Anjou, been adults, William's difficulties would have been seriously compounded. In the summer of 1066, the political circumstances within northern France worked hugely to his advantage.

William's crossing of the English Channel was a complex amphibious operation. Its timing was also crucial. The fleet was probably ready to sail by early August 1066 at the latest, but it probably did not set sail until 28 September. William of Jumièges states that the fleet had been constructed at St Valéry-sur-Somme and that it sailed for England from there. However, most historians today prefer William of Poitiers' version of events which explains how the fleet, which had been constructed at the mouth of the river Dives in Normandy, was blown north to St Valéry whence it finally sailed for England.[22] But other explanations for this delay offer themselves for consideration. William must surely have known, through spies and informants, something of what was happening in England. Perhaps he moved his fleet north on hearing the news that Harold had disbanded his forces on 8 September; the crossing from St Valéry was much shorter than that from the Dives and William may always have planned to do this when the time was right. Furthermore, it is surely no coincidence that the fleet finally set sail when Harold was still in northern England dealing with Hardrada and Tostig at Stamford Bridge. William may even have known about their invasion in advance. He would not have known the outcome of Harold's northern campaign when he set sail, but he must have known that the south coast of England was largely undefended.

William of Poitiers' emphasis on the weather places the ultimate responsibility for the duke's fate in God's hands and gives further evidence of divine approval for William's plans. And indeed, it was in response to the duke's prayers, William says, that the direction of the wind finally changed. Immediately, the ships were boarded and during the night of (probably) 27–8 September they set sail.[23] William did not want to arrive in England before daybreak, and so he ordered the other ships to anchor close to him in the Channel until they saw a lantern lit on board his ship: that was the signal to sail on. However, William lost contact with the fleet whilst in mid-Channel and he had to reassure his shipmates that they would be found. Sure enough, the fleet regrouped and eventually landed, unopposed, at Pevensey. After landing and erecting a defensive earthwork within the walls of the old Roman fort, William quickly moved on to Hastings, where he threw up another defensive fortification. He also ravaged the surrounding countryside as he went. By devastating parts of Harold's Wessex heartland, it is likely that William planned to provoke Harold into battle. The duke also did not want to move too far inland for fear of being cut off from his supplies and his ships. Having probably heard about William's landing by 1 or 2 October, Harold moved with the impressive speed which was by now his trademark. The return journey from Yorkshire to London was nearly 200 miles long, and was most likely carried out between 2–3 and 9–10 October. When he arrived at London, Harold probably spent a couple of days organising his resources, gathering reinforcements and making his final plans. On 11 October at the latest, he set out on the 60-mile march to Hastings.

When Harold arrived at Hastings on Friday 13 October, his plan may have been to engage the enemy as soon as possible and by surprise. This had worked at Stamford Bridge, after all. Alternatively, he might have planned to bottle William up in his south-coast pocket, deprive him of supplies, wait for reinforcements to arrive and then strike the final blow. Whatever his plans were, he did not have the chance to put them into operation. William's scouts had warned their leader of Harold's approach, and it was the duke who in the event surprised the king 'before [Harold's] army was drawn up in battle array', the *Anglo-Saxon Chronicle* claims, in the early hours of Saturday 14 October.[24] Harold and his troops were still able to take up a strong defensive position, behind a tightly-packed shield-wall on a ridge above William's forces. Moreover, although John of Worcester states that Harold's forces were depleted after their exertions in the north, and that 'half his army had not yet come in' when the fighting at Hastings began, the two sides were probably evenly matched in terms of numbers at the outset.[25] No contemporary gives reliable figures for the numbers who fought at Hastings. It has been stated in the most recent and most detailed reconstruction of the battle that, on the English side at least, 'tens of thousands are a possibility'.[26] However, the generally accepted view remains that there were probably between 6,000 and 8,000 men on each side. Of course, it is impossible in the end to know what the actual figures were.

At the start of the battle, at about 9 o'clock in the morning, the onus was on William to attack. Initial assaults on the English by the Norman infantry had little impact, and William's mounted knights were left to charge uphill against a still well-organised and disciplined foe. These attacks were ineffective, too, and the first chink in either side's armour appeared on William's left as his Breton contingent, under their leader, Alan, turned and fled under pressure from the English right. Cries soon went up that William himself had been killed, and the duke had to tour the battlefield with his helmet raised to show his anxious troops that he was still alive. William had survived this moment of crisis, and it eventually led to his victory. For as the Bretons had fled, many on the English right had broken ranks to pursue them. They were soon cut off from their comrades, surrounded by enemy cavalry and cut down. The Normans now began to use this tactic of 'feigned flight' deliberately, and the English footsoldiers were drawn into the trap. Twice more William's forces attacked only to turn and flee as if routed. The English pursued them down the hill, on foot of course, where they were surrounded and killed. This inevitably led to a weakening of the shield-wall at the top of

DEBATE 1
Why did William of Normandy win the Battle of Hastings?

According to contemporaries, William the Conqueror won at Hastings because God wanted him to. English sources accept that they were being punished for their sinfulness; Norman sources depict Harold as a perjured usurper who got what he deserved. Historians have looked for earthly reasons for William's victory. The standard modern account of the battle suggests that the Normans won 'amongst other means by superior military techniques and by superior generalship', although the most recent analysis would agree with this only in part.[1] It is arguable that William was better-prepared for battle than Harold, whose forces had marched over 400 miles in a matter of weeks and already fought an exhausting battle. William by contrast landed unopposed with fresh, highly-motivated troops; he could wait for his enemy to come to him. Only guesses can be made about the numbers on each side during the battle, and information about how the armies were deployed is not completely trustworthy. However, the sheer length of the battle suggests that the two armies were well-matched. There were differences in technique and approach. The English fought on foot; the Normans used infantry *and* cavalry. The idea that the lack of cavalry on the English side was decisive still persists.[2] However, until their feigned retreats began to take a toll on the English forces, the Normans' more conventional charges had made little impact on the English defensive line. Therefore, the decisions taken during the battle by Harold and William must have been crucial. William was a more experienced battlefield commander than his opponent. If the Norman accounts of Hastings are to be believed, he was both an inspirational leader capable of rallying his troops when they thought he was dead, and a tactical genius who saw the potential for victory in the chaos of the Breton retreat. Perhaps Harold showed his inexperience by attacking before his forces were fully assembled. Perhaps he should have gambled on a full-blooded pursuit of the Bretons as they fled the field early in the battle. Ultimately, however, the battle was decisive because Harold died and because the Normans ruthlessly pursued the defeated English. William was fortunate, too: the wind changed in his favour at the ideal moment for a Channel crossing; during the battle he lost several horses whilst avoiding injury himself. Contemporaries would not have thought of him as lucky, however. Such events proved that William had God on his side.

1 Brown, 'The Battle of Hastings', p. 101, Lawson, *The Battle of Hastings, 1066*, pp. 217–20, provides a summary of this author's views.
2 See, for example, Carpenter, *The Struggle for Mastery*, p. 73.

the ridge. By late afternoon the English were on the back foot, and the decisive blow was dealt when King Harold was killed. Perhaps Harold was felled by a lucky arrow which hit him in the eye. However, it is more likely that the relevant scenes in the Bayeux Tapestry show him being first hit in the head and then cut down.[27] News of this calamity prompted his remaining forces to scatter and flee, and many were cut down as they tried to escape from the field. By the time dusk fell on the battlefield at about 5 o'clock, and after at least eight hours of fighting, it belonged to the Normans and Duke William.

The Interregnum, 14 October–25 December 1066

William had triumphed at Hastings, but only consecration could make him king. In the weeks immediately after the battle, indeed, it remained far from certain that the Norman duke would be able to realise his claim to the English throne. After his victory, William did not head straight for London. He allowed his army a few days' rest, and waited to see whether the English would come and submit to him. When they failed to appear, he began to move methodically around the south coast. After securing the surrender of the fortified town of Romney, he then made for Dover. Seemingly impregnable it may have been, but the garrison surrendered rather than run the risk of being punished for resisting. William was then kept at Dover for a week from 21 to 28 October as his army fell victim to dysentery. He made use of the delay by ordering the construction of a castle there. The next target was Canterbury, where William himself fell ill. The city's importance was both strategic and, as the seat of the archbishop, symbolic. It submitted to William at the end of October, at about the same time as the surrender of Winchester, where the royal treasury was housed.

From Canterbury, William turned west. However, he did not reach Southwark until late November and, when he finally got there, he did not attempt to cross the river. Within the city on the north bank of the Thames, resistance was being organised. Archbishop Stigand, Earls Edwin and Morcar and other high-status survivors of Harold's regime were rallying around Edgar *aetheling* as the native candidate for the throne. Rather than face them head on at this stage, William adopted a different strategy. Burning as he went, he marched his troops around the south and west of London through Surrey, Hampshire and Berkshire before finally crossing the Thames at Wallingford in early December. The ravaging was not mindless thuggery. It was designed to undermine the political and economic power-bases of the surviving members of the Anglo-Saxon élite and to demoralise the population. If William could show the retainers and followers of the English magnates that their lordship counted for nothing, they would not continue to support them.

At Wallingford, the first of the important submissions to William, by Archbishop Stigand, took place. Then, at Berkhamsted, Edgar *aetheling* himself, Archbishop Ealdred of York, Earls Edwin and Morcar and other leading men, submitted. For the *Anglo-Saxon Chronicle*, it was 'a great piece of folly that they had not done it earlier, since God would not make things better, because of our sins'.[28] The plan to pit Edgar *aetheling* against William had come to nothing, and the way was open for the latter to become king. At this point William took the counsel of his leading followers, all of whom urged him on towards his coronation in London. In advance of this, William sent a force into the capital to erect a fortress (this probably became the Tower of London), and by Christmas 1066, more than two months after his victory at Hastings, William was finally ready to be crowned. In Edward the Confessor's great church at Westminster on Christmas Day 1066, Archbishop Ealdred of York asked the assembled English if they would have William crowned and, according to William of Poitiers, 'all gave their joyful assent without hesitation'.[29] But all did not go smoothly. When the Norman soldiers assembled outside the abbey during the coronation heard the loud shout of acclamation from inside in a foreign tongue, they feared the worst, assumed treachery was afoot and torched the neighbouring houses. According to Orderic Vitalis, most of the congregation fled from the church in panic and confusion and the ceremony was completed by the bishops and clergy with the new king, the victor of Hastings and now the Lord's anointed, trembling from head to foot.[30]

Notes

1 *V.Ed.*, pp. 13–14.
2 *NC*, p. 59.
3 *EHD II*, pp. 107, 111; *JW* ii, p. 549.
4 *EHD II*, pp. 108–9.
5 *EHD II*, pp. 111–13.
6 *NC*, p. 51.
7 *NC*, p. 64.
8 *NC*, p. 67.
9 *V.Ed.*, pp. 34–7.
10 The Norman accounts of Harold's trip can be found in *NC*, pp. 13–14, 22–4.
11 *Eadmer*, p. 6.
12 *EHD II*, p. 267 (Plate XXVII).
13 *V.Ed.*, pp. 50–5; *NC*, p. 68.
14 *NC*, pp. 14, 69; *EHD II*, p. 270 (Plate XXXIV).
15 *NC*, pp. 14, 27–8, 69.
16 References in this and the following two paragraphs are all from the *Anglo-Saxon Chronicle* unless stated otherwise, and are taken from *NC*, pp. 70–1.
17 *NC*, pp. 26, 27–8.
18 *NC*, p. 28.

19 *NC*, p. 14; *EHD II*, pp. 272–5 (Plates XXXVI–XXXIX).

20 *NC*, pp. 26–7.

21 *NC*, p. 27.

22 *NC*, pp. 14, 28–9.

23 *NC*, pp. 28–9.

24 *NC*, p. 71. The principal narrative account of the Battle of Hastings, relied on here unless otherwise stated, is William of Poitiers': *NC*, pp. 31–5.

25 *NC*, p. 73.

26 Lawson, *The Battle of Hastings, 1066*, p. 150, after a careful discussion of the evidence.

27 *EHD II*, pp. 298, 300 (Plates LXXVI–LXXVII).

28 *NC*, p. 72.

29 *NC*, p. 37.

30 *OV* ii, p. 105.

2

Ruling the Kingdom, 1042–1066

'The Kingdom of England' was a relatively new creation in 1042. The kings of Wessex had steadily extended their influence over much of midland and eastern England during the tenth century, and they had even gone north on occasion to try to assert their authority there. In the process, they had imposed upon those areas they came to control structures and mechanisms of power which meant that their kingdom, by the mid-eleventh century, was arguably the most well-organised and best-governed in western Europe.

King and nobility

At the summit of the political mountain was the king himself. His office, exemplified by Old Testament models such as David and Solomon, was divinely-sanctioned, and he was set apart from ordinary men when he was consecrated with holy oils at his coronation. Edward the Confessor, indeed, was the first English king to be credited with healing powers, when he cured a woman with a disfiguring throat complaint and restored the sight of several blind men. These acts were more reflections of Edward's sanctity than his regality, but there was a spiritual dimension to the king's power which corresponded to his principal duties: protecting the Church and defending his people. The Church needed his help against heathens and exploiters; his people needed it against criminals and hostile armies. To fulfil his obligations, the theoretical powers in the king's armoury were extensive. All public authority was derived from him; only he could make laws which purported to apply across the whole kingdom; only he could mint coins; only he could raise taxation for national purposes; only he could raise armies for national defence. He controlled economic activity and trade to a significant extent, and he made foreign policy. By the second half of the eleventh century, too, there was developing the concept of a 'national peace' which it was the king's duty to keep and preserve.

In practice, matters were not as straightforward as this, and there were significant practical restrictions on the king's theoretical powers. By 1042, for example, succession to the throne was still determined by more than hereditary right. If the dying king left a son, he had a good chance of succeeding his father, but if he was young or there were rival candidates, he might find it difficult. And there was no chance at all of becoming king without the support of the English nobility and the English Church; in other words, without the support of the people who mattered politically. It was the clerical and lay élite, dominated by Earl Godwin of Wessex, which secured Edward's elevation to the kingship in 1042; and, whether Edward nominated him as his successor or not, according to John of Worcester it was 'the magnates of the whole realm' who elected Harold king in January 1066.[1]

A new king, having overcome this hurdle, might also have to deal with a problematic inheritance. Edward the Confessor, for example, knew little of England and its ways in 1042 (he may not even have spoken the language very well); he had no landed power-base of his own and no entrenched supporters. He also had to deal with a political system, created largely by King Cnut, in which the cumulative landed power of the great earls dwarfed that of the king. This meant that, during the 1040s, he was forced to get support where he could, and thus he was forced into the steely grip of Earl Godwin. The only blot on Harold's otherwise textbook inheritance in 1066, by contrast, was his lack of a blood relationship with the former ruling dynasty. This was important, of course, but with the support of the nobility and the Church, his military reputation, network of followers and huge landed wealth he could act assertively and independently from the start.

The personality of the king was a crucial factor, too, in determining his chances of ruling effectively and independently. A king was supposed to be pious and generous. He was also expected to be a successful military leader and an impartial judge. In essence he had to be able to inspire loyalty or instil fear, depending on the circumstances. Harold, the founder of a great church at Waltham in Essex, had his pious side, and he was generally acknowledged as intelligent and a great warrior. He also had the landed resources at his disposal which potentially made him a munificent and attractive lord. The readiness with which the English lay and ecclesiastical magnates turned to him on Edward's death is good evidence of the respect he was able to command. By contrast, whilst Edward the Confessor was certainly pious, even saintly, there is little evidence of his qualities as a warrior. His reign was largely peaceful, and when fighting was required, he preferred to let others do it for him, Earl Siward in Scotland in 1054, for example, and Harold in Wales in 1063. And when he did express a desire to fight himself (in 1052 when the Godwins returned to England or in 1065 during the Northumbrian revolt), he could not get his leading subjects to support him. There is also little evidence that Edward had the ability to act decisively when it mattered on other occasions. This was particularly apparent in relation to the succession. A prudent king would try to make it clear whom he wanted to succeed him. His wishes were not always put into effect, of course, and succession disputes were far from unusual in Anglo-Saxon England. But whilst there was nothing the king could do to help his nominee after his own death, he could at least try to address the issue of succession whilst he was alive. This would calm the nerves of the political élite, which hated uncertainty; and it was in the king's interest, too, as he could nominate the individual whom he saw as best-equipped to carry on his good work. Edward had no children, but whilst this made his choice more difficult, it did not make it impossible. However, for over fifteen years Edward appears to have vacillated between several different candidates. In 1051, in the aftermath of the Godwins' exile, he may have nominated Duke William of Normandy. Then later, in 1054–5, he recalled Edward 'the Exile' to England for reasons which must have concerned the succession. When the latter died, perhaps his son Edgar became Edward's choice. Then, in 1064–5, Edward may have sent Earl Harold to Normandy to restate the offer of the throne he had made to Duke William over a decade before. Finally, on his death-bed, Edward probably nominated Harold himself as the next king. He was a good choice in many ways, as has been seen, but there was bound to be trouble if William and Edgar were going to stand up for their own claims to the throne. Edward's inability to resolve the succession question during his lifetime created unnecessary tensions and rivalries which led, in the end, to the collapse of Anglo-Saxon kingship.

Inheritances and personalities aside, on a structural level, too, royal authority in the mid-eleventh century was not as extensive as it might at first sight appear. The king was restricted in carrying out what he might wish to do by his duty to listen to and heed the advice of his leading subjects, collectively his *witan* ('wise men'). The course of politics at the highest level was a reflection of the way the king dealt with his most powerful men, his earls and his thegns. He needed their support if the country was to be well-governed and if they were to fight willingly with him in wartime. At the same time, they needed him to legitimise and extend their power. Ultimately, it was up to the king to decide when he took counsel and from whom; but if he ignored those who saw them-selves as his natural advisers, or favoured some at the expense of others, he might be storing up problems for himself. There was also more to the king's relationship with his great men than the giving and receiving of advice. The king gave judgments in disputes between or concerning his great men: any perceived partiality here might give rise to grudges and grievances. Earl Aelfgar's reaction to Edward's appointment of Tostig as earl of Northumbria in 1055 shows how fine a balance the king had to maintain between the competing claims of rival aristocratic families.

A strong king was able to dominate and control his nobility. A weak king, on the other hand, would be dominated and controlled by them. Whether a king was strong or weak depended on the sort of man he was, but perhaps even more on the amount of resources he had at his disposal. In eleventh-century England, land was the ultimate source of wealth and political power. With it, a careful king could reward his followers and command their loyalty. The king was the principal source of patronage in the kingdom. The way he distributed land, offices, honours and rewards was crucial in determining the way his powerful men regarded him. However, he did not have a free hand. The late Anglo-Saxon kings had more land and exercised power more effectively in some parts of the country than in others. The bulk of the royal lands were in the south, within the old kingdom of Wessex; by contrast, in remote northern England, the king had fewer estates and whilst his authority was acknowledged on paper, it counted for relatively little in reality. Even in southern England, Edward the Confessor was not personally as strong as his leading subjects, Earl Godwin and his sons, because he held less land and had fewer personal followers than they did. What is more, the lands Edward did hold tended to be within the earldom of Wessex, the area most closely controlled by Godwin and then Harold as earls. The vast extent of the Godwins' landed empire is revealed by the Domesday survey, undertaken in 1086–7 by order of William the Conqueror. According to Domesday, the estates of the Godwins (Harold, Tostig, Gyrth, Leofwine and Edith) in 1066 were concentrated in the south and east of England. However, they were not confined to these areas, and the family's holdings were more widely scattered and extensive than those of any of their rivals, principally the descendants of Earl Siward of Northumbria (d. 1055) and of Earl Leofric of Mercia (d. 1057), and the king himself. The Godwin family estates were valued at around £7,000 in 1066, with Harold's own share about £5,000. By contrast, the estates of Leofric's family were worth £2,400 and Siward's £350. The king's lands were valued at about £5,000. Such great wealth so widely spread allowed the Godwins to recruit and find support across England. Domesday Book records the names of hundreds of Godwin retainers scattered across eighteen of the twenty-six English shires, often powerful men in their own right of great regional importance. The Godwins and their followers probably controlled about a third of all the land in England in 1066. The Church controlled another third, leaving just one more third for all the other landholders, including the king. Thus, the unrestrained growth of the family's power gave the Godwins a huge amount of land and an immense following. This only served to increase their power and influence further.

Earl Godwin was already England's richest earl when Edward became king. But it was the king himself who furthered the process whereby Godwin's sons had come to dominate England so conclusively by the 1060s. He granted them other earldoms in the 1040s and created new ones for them, too. He also installed them in power in areas where, politically speaking, the creation of a counter-balance to their authority elsewhere might have been more prudent; making Tostig earl of Northumbria in 1055 is the obvious example. He even married one of them. Why Edward favoured the Godwins to this extent has always preoccupied historians. Given the nature of his inheritance, he may not have had any choice but to go along with what they wanted. However, whether he was a fool or a realist, the implications for the king of such power resting in the hands of one family and its supporters were alarming. He needed powerful men to govern the kingdom region by region, and to protect it from foreign invasion, and much of the land held by Edward's great nobles lay in exposed and vulnerable coastal or frontier areas. Nevertheless, the dominance of the great families, and of one family above all others, must have led to the alienation and diminution of royal authority by 1066. When Harold became king, of course, the situation was turned on its head. He was able to bring together under his sole authority his family lands and the royal lands, along with all the other powers and privileges he inherited from Edward. To this he could add the mystical and awesome authority of consecrated kingship itself. Overnight on 5–6 January 1066, the king of England was placed in a position from which he could dominate England in practice as well as in theory.

The crisis of 1051–1052

The extent to which Edward's authority was compromised by Godwin power and influence was made most apparent by the events of 1051–2. Edward may have chosen this moment to try to rid himself of the Godwins because his marriage to Edith had failed to produce an heir. Alternatively, his target from the start may have been the earl of Wessex himself. However, whether or not the king deliberately engineered the Godwins' disgrace and exile, his success in 1051 was short-lived. The Godwins were too well-entrenched across England to be permanently kept out and, when they returned in 1052, Edward was powerless to persuade the other earls and magnates to oppose them by force. Godwin and his sons were reinstated, those whom Edward had appointed in their places were removed from office and Edward's Norman supporters, including Robert of Jumièges, were exiled. The king had been humiliated, and he never attempted to take on the Godwins again. Indeed, after 1053 even more power seems to have been lost by the king to his most influential subjects. Once Harold had become earl of Wessex on his father's death in 1053, he came increasingly to dominate royal government and administration. John of Worcester described him as *subregulus* ('underking') at the time of King Edward's death, and the author of the *Vita Edwardi* called him Edward's *nutricius* ('governor').[2] And certainly, by the closing years of the reign, it is arguable that he was acting more like a king than a leading subject. He dealt decisively with Gruffudd ap Llywelyn in Wales in 1063, for example. During the Northumbrian revolt, he negotiated with the rebels and, for his own reasons, perhaps, was responsible for persuading Edward to accept the removal of Tostig and the appointment of Morcar as earl of Northumbria. And during Edward's final illness in 1065, there is little doubt that Harold, probably assisted by his sister, Queen Edith, was effectively in charge of the country. Any analysis of Harold's trip to Normandy in 1064–5, moreover, should take account of the immense power the earl of Wessex wielded at the heart of royal government by that time. Of course he may have visited William as Edward's messenger; but it is just as likely that he went there to put into effect his own plans.

Royal government

Times of crisis apart, everyday royal government in the mid-eleventh century was a personal business with which the king himself was probably nearly always involved to some extent. The king was more or less always on the move. Like any other lord, he wanted to visit his lands to ensure that they were being run properly. He also needed to move in order to attend councils, ecclesiastical assemblies and other important meetings. Edward the Confessor certainly, and probably Harold too, also wanted to hunt, and different hunting-grounds offered different challenges. The arrival of the royal court in a particular area also brought the local community into contact with the king and allowed it to see his authority demonstrated up close: subjects could be impressed by the splendour and glamour of his court, and they could also put their grievances and requests to him. More pragmatically, the king had to keep moving between his estates in order to collect and consume the food-rents that were due to him from his tenants. They were his basic means of sustenance.

No king was doing his duty unless he was firmly 'hands on', addressing significant questions of foreign and domestic policy, perhaps, or dealing with the trivial grievance of a low-status suitor. There was no distinction drawn between the person of the king and the institution of the crown, or between the private and public faces of the monarch. Consequently, there was no limit to the types of business with which he might have to deal. It is probable, therefore, that, during his waking hours, the king was almost always part of a group. Closest to him would be the members of his immediate family, but nearby, too, would be the members of his wider *familia* or household. Central to this would be the domestic servants of the king and queen, men (overwhelmingly but not exclusively) who were responsible for the food, drink, clothing, money, valuables and intimate personal needs of their royal master and mistress. Working alongside them would be the royal priests and clerks, whose principal function was to administer to the spiritual needs of the royal entourage, but who also, being literate, would have been responsible for reading and writing royal documents. Also with the king at most times would have been a group of military men, a bodyguard of sorts, his *housecarls*. They would protect the king if necessary, but they would also provide the core of the royal army in times of war and hunt with him in times of peace.

Although the size of this inner core of royal servants would have varied from time to time, it probably formed a semi-permanent staff around the king. In addition, there would always have been others at court who made up the extended part of the royal household. Individuals seeking the king's assistance in a legal dispute, or those hopeful of an office or the grant of a privilege would have sought out the king and his servants. More significantly, the great lay and ecclesiastical magnates, earls, thegns, archbishops, bishops and abbots, would have been in regular attendance on the king, and more would have been present than usual at the great religious festivals of the year when the king would have solemnly celebrated the holy day and then feasted splendidly with his expanded entourage. It may have been Edward the Confessor, too, who began the practice of holding regular meetings at the major religious festivals of Christmas, Easter and Whitsun where he formally 'wore his crown' in view of his subjects.

The great men, the earls and bishops in particular, needed to be close to the king in order to maintain their political profile, benefit from royal patronage and keep pace with the news and gossip. But they also claimed the right to act as the king's chief advisers, and they expected him to listen to what they said. They were the king's *witan* and when they met together with the king they formed the *witenagemot* ('meeting of the wise'). This was not an organised institution with fixed meeting-times or membership. Nevertheless, it was powerful and influential; it expressed the collective will of the political nation and, particularly at times of present or impending crisis, the king could not afford to ignore it. New laws would be thrashed out and proclaimed there, grants of land would be authorised, disputes would be judged and settled, and appointments to important lay and ecclesiastical offices would be discussed and ratified. The power and influence of these men acting together was demonstrated in 1051 when they tried to iron out the differences between Edward and

Godwin, and in 1052 and 1065 when they refused to back Edward against the Northumbrian rebels. It would have been the *witan*, too, who approved Harold's elevation to the kingship in 1066.

The kings almost certainly had favourites amongst their family and counsellors, those whose advice they preferred or found most acceptable. Edward the Confessor, indeed, has traditionally been seen as having shown excessive favour to Normans, whom he brought with him from France in 1042, and whom he attempted to impose on English government at the expense of his native English subjects. Such a view now no longer bears much scrutiny, even though it has near-contemporary support. The *Vita Edwardi* states that when Edward came to England in 1042, 'quite a number of men of that nation [Normandy], and they not base-born, accompanied him. And these, since he was master of the whole kingdom, he kept with him, enriched them with many honours, and made them his privy counsellors and administrators of the royal palace.'[3] However, apart from Robert, who became bishop of London in 1044 and archbishop of Canterbury in 1050, and Ralph of Mantes, Edward's nephew by his sister's marriage, who had become earl of Hereford by 1050, there is little trace of these Normans. Neither the witness lists to Edward's charters (which show who was present at the royal court when the charter was granted) nor Domesday Book (which records who held land across most of England at the time of Edward's death) suggest that Norman influence at Edward's court was strong or that he lavishly endowed Normans with lands.

Below the level of the king and his *witan*, and within the semi-permanent core of the royal household, a rudimentary royal bureaucracy was operated by some of the king's servants. However, there is no compelling evidence from this period for the existence of separate 'departments' of royal government, of a treasury or a chancery staffed by professional servants. The king would have kept ready cash with him in order to defray his immediate expenses. Household servants would have been responsible for making payments and, presumably, for keeping receipts of some sort. The collection, counting and storage of geld, though, was on a different scale entirely and would have required a system considerably more sophisticated than this. That writing was important within that system is clear, and some system of written record making and keeping had developed by 1066. Several so-called 'geld rolls' have survived, written in English, which outline liabilities to pay geld in south-west England and Northamptonshire. These were written after 1066 and relate to gelds levied in the 1070s and 1080s, but historians have suggested that they represent the survival of an Anglo-Saxon system. The king and ecclesiastical lords, moreover, would almost certainly have kept written records detailing their property and stock.

However, the two most important forms of written royal record of the period were the charter and the sealed writ. Charters were solemn documents, written in Latin, recording a grant of land or privileges to an individual or a church by the king. They were drawn up according to strict conventions, and much of their content is formulaic. Charters were valued and kept by those to whom lands and privileges were granted because they functioned as title-deeds to the property they conveyed. They are important to historians because, amongst other things, they show the king's powers of patronage in action and they reveal, through the list of witnesses to the transaction which each charter contains, who was active in and around the king's household at the time of the grant. Whether royal charters were written by members of the king's household or by the recipients of the grants is a matter of continuing debate. The sealed writ was a less formal document than the charter. Ninety-nine survive from the reign of Edward the Confessor, either as originals or copies. They were written in English and authenticated by an impression of the king's seal. They were addressed to particular individuals or officials (usually the sheriff), and recorded a grant of land made by the king or his confirmation of a previous one. It is possible they conveyed other types of order or instruction, too, but their primary purpose at this time was to act as title-deeds to property. Designed to be read out and publicised through the shire court, the writ was a very effective instrument in the exercise of royal authority. Under Edward the Confessor, the royal priest Regenbald is described in the witness list to one charter as 'keeper of the king's seal' and, in another, as 'the king's chancellor'. He clearly had a special responsibility for supervising the production and authentication of royal documents within the king's household.

Whilst writing was clearly important, the sophistication of late Anglo-Saxon government in this context should not be exaggerated. It is not known how many documents were produced, because so few have survived. There are fewer than 2,000 writs and charters for the whole pre-conquest period, and at least some of these are later forgeries; as has been seen, only about a hundred survive from Edward the Confessor's reign, and only one from Harold's. Most transactions would have continued to be carried out in the traditional ways, that is orally and through some symbolic ceremony or other. In Clanchy's words, 'Certainly the Anglo-Saxon vernacular writ, as it existed in the reign of Edward the Confessor, was the root from which later varieties of royal charters and letters grew ... [but] it seems unlikely that England was governed by a bureaucracy using documents in its routine procedures before 1066'.[4]

Local government

Directly below the king in terms of authority were the earls. This office derived ultimately from that of the *ealdormen* of ninth-century Wessex, most of whom had been responsible for enforcing royal rights and carrying out royal orders within an individual shire. By the end of the tenth century, however, individual ealdormen had become more powerful and tended to control several shires at once. Under Cnut, they came to be called earls (from the Old English *eorl* which roughly translates as 'noble'), and it was during his reign that Leofric, Siward and Godwin appear as holders of these posts. The number and size of the earldoms was not fixed, but at the start of Edward's reign there were four principal ones: Wessex, Mercia, Northumbria and East Anglia. The powers of the earls were not clearly defined either. In effect, they functioned as represent-atives of the king in the shires under their control. The king could not exercise his authority everywhere in person, and he needed men who kept the peace, exercised justice and raised armies in his name. An earldom was a reward for a particularly highly esteemed subject of the king, and tenure of an earldom only served to make the earls themselves richer (they kept for themselves a third of the profits of royal justice in the shire courts, for example). However, whilst they exercised a good deal of auto-nomy in carrying out their duties, they were not independent rulers. They could not mint their own coins or hold their own courts. An earl owed his position to the king, and, in theory at least, held it only for as long as the king wished. But they were the king's chief counsellors and his most powerful subjects; he needed to retain their support if he was to exercise meaningful authority across the country.

Below the earls, and dominating local society before 1066, were the thegns. They have been described as 'the county gentry of Anglo-Saxon England', but their status as substantial landholders (nobody could qualify as a thegn unless he held at least five hides of land, and many held far more than this) really made them members of the aristocracy.[5] Along with that status went both military and administrative responsibilities. The most highly-favoured might serve in the king's own household, others in the household of a more powerful lord; but more usually they gave judgment in the shire courts and formed the stiff backbone of the royal armies. The king needed to control them, therefore, as 'collectively, the thegns were the very fabric of social and political order . . . and it was the king's ability (or otherwise) to command their support which deter-mined his ability (or otherwise) to pursue a particular course of action. Kings gained much from their royal office, and ealdormen [later, earls] had much to gain from exploiting their own positions of power; but in the final analysis it was the thegns who counted.'[6]

There may have been up to five thousand thegns in all in 1066, by which time all of England, with the exception of the region north of the river Tees to the east of the Pennines and the river Mersey to their west, and the anomalous area of Rutland, was divided into shires, each under the control of a 'shire-reeve' or 'sheriff'. The sheriff, usually a local thegn, was the earl's deputy in his particular shire, but he was also the king's principal representative on the ground with day-to-day responsibility for supervising the collection of taxes, presiding over the shire court, and raising and perhaps leading military forces when required to do so. He also administered the king's lands in his shire and collected their revenues. The sheriff than kept the latter in return for paying the king a fixed amount every year (the 'farm'). The shires were in turn subdivided into hundreds (in southern England) and wapentakes (in the Danelaw), which were administered by reeves. Each hundred had its own court, which met once a month. Below the level of the hundred was the vill, each of which had its own reeve as well. Not all shires, hundreds or vills were alike by any means, and there were plenty of regional customs and variations within this system, but it was sufficiently uniform and regular to give at least a degree of organisational cohesion to English local government in the mid-eleventh century.

Royal wealth

The king derived his income from many sources. He made money from the legal system, and from his attempts to regulate internal and foreign trade. Merchants paid tolls, for example, and trading communities might pay lump sums for the privilege of being exempt from such dues. Certain trading activities could only take place at designated royal centres with royal officials overseeing the transactions. More importantly, though, the king made money from his lands. He received the annual farm from the sheriff of each county, but he also made money from the lands he kept under his own direct control (his 'demesne'). Much of the king's demesne would have been leased out in return for rent, payable in cash, foodstuffs or services. Surplus produce could be sold by the king's agents at local markets. He therefore had a financial interest in the development of both the urban and rural economies.

More impressively and quite uniquely at the time, however, the administrative division of England into shires and hundreds facilitated the levying of a land tax, or geld, across most of the country. The tax had originally been levied in the early eleventh century and used to buy off the Danish invaders and protect the kingdom against fresh attacks. It was controlled at the centre and administered locally by the sheriff. It was assessed on property, more specifically 'on the hide'. The hide was the basic unit of land measurement in Anglo-Saxon England; it originally represented the amount of land required to sustain a family for a year. The size of the hide was not fixed, but varied according to the value and resources of the land involved. Geld was usually collected, perhaps as often as annually, at the rate of two shillings per hide. It has been estimated that the normal yield from such a tax would have been about £6,000, but it was also capable of raising much larger sums. According to the *Anglo-Saxon Chronicle*, between 991 and 1012 £137,000 was paid by the English authorities to ward off the attacks of Danish invaders, and another £82,500 was raised by Cnut in 1018 after he had become king. The sheer scale of the effort involved in raising such sums so often provides further reason for thinking that the pre-conquest kings had at their disposal an extensive set of written records concerning their kingdom which has now been lost.

Linked to the king's wealth and England's system of taxation was the coinage. By 1042, the English coinage was superior to any other in northwest Europe, and the system for administering it was well-established. The minting of coins was a royal monopoly. Dies were produced in London and silver pennies of standard design were then produced by some sixty mints, staffed by royally-licensed moneyers, located across southern and central England (the only northern mint was at York). The pennies were of relatively high value in themselves and they were cut into halves (halfpennies) or quarters (farthings) to provide smaller change. The high quality and geographical spread of the coinage are important indicators of how far royal power was acknowledged across the kingdom; and the king's image and title on the coins were visible manifestations of royal power. But the importance of the coinage to the king was more than symbolic. He made money from it, too. Local moneyers would pay to acquire their centrally-struck dies, and at least every three years during the eleventh century a new coinage was issued, at which time weights and designs might be altered. Only coins of the current type were legal tender; so when the designs changed, old coins had to be brought to royal centres and exchanged for new ones. For this privilege, people might pay as much as 15 per cent of the value of their old coins. Some of this would be kept by the moneyer, but the bulk would be pocketed by the king.

Military organisation

The military capabilities of late Anglo-Saxon England appear to have been impressive. The defeat of the Vikings and the conquest of the Danelaw in the ninth and tenth centuries were remarkable administrative and military feats. Later, in the 1040s, both King Sweyn of Denmark and the emperor, Henry III, were keen to obtain English military assistance. Moreover, Edward the Confessor, through Earl Harold's efforts, was able to reduce the Welsh to subjection with apparent ease in 1063, and this followed Earl Siward's victory against the Scots and their Norman allies in 1054. Perhaps the greatest achievement of all was Harold's northern campaign of 1066. Of course, there were defeats, too: England was, after all, conquered by foreign invaders twice during the eleventh century. And on a smaller scale, during the reign of Edward the Confessor, there were frustrating campaigns against the Welsh to set alongside Harold's victory of 1063. In 1052, for example, Gruffudd ap Llywelyn raided

Herefordshire and defeated local forces near Leominster, and in 1055, along with the exiled Earl Aelfgar of Mercia, he overcame local troops who had been made to fight on horseback by their French earl, Ralph of Mantes, and sacked Hereford. However, that the English system was able to cope with and recover from such reverses is good evidence of its resilience and its sophistication.

But where did the men who fought in these campaigns come from? It has been suggested that this period 'saw the mobilisation of the country and its resources for war to an extent that was not to be repeated until the total wars of the twentieth century'.[7] Unfortunately, however, there is little firm evidence which clearly demonstrates how Anglo-Saxon armies were raised and organised. There was no standing army as such, although the household retainers permanently with the king and each great magnate would have formed the core of any national force. They might be called *housecarls* in the sources, but this Scandinavian term does not denote any difference of function or status from the English thegn. All household troops were provided by their lord with food, lodging and wages. They would hope to receive land in due course. Below this level was the bulk of the national army, or the *fyrd*. The 'common burdens' of bridge and fortress-work and service in the *fyrd* were imposed on all freemen by English kings in the eighth century. Military service was also due from those who had been granted 'bookland' (that is, land granted in perpetuity, not loaned) by the king. How much service largely depended upon the size of the estate in question. Obligations were based upon the hideage assessment of each estate: in Berkshire before 1066, for example, it was understood that every five hides would provide one soldier for the army or one sailor for the fleet who would serve at his own expense for sixty days. This system or something like it may have operated more widely across England. If England in 1066 was comprised of roughly 80,000 hides, as has been suggested, then this would represent no fewer than 15,000 men on the basis of the Berkshire obligation. In practice arrangements were probably more flexible than this. Holders of larger estates, for example, might be expected to bring a quota of followers calculated either according to so many men per hide or on the basis of an individual arrangement. Much smaller forces might be summoned to act within specific areas.

The late Anglo-Saxon military system has come in for criticism from historians in the past, who have been keen to emphasise the modernity and sophistication of the Norman military machine. The fact that King Harold had to disband his forces in September 1066, for example, has been taken as evidence of the problems inherent in the system. In fact, Harold did well to keep his force in the field as long as he did. What is more, he was able to call out the *fyrd* at least three times in 1066, and even if his army was not as large as it might have been at Hastings, and

DEBATE 2
How effective a king was Edward the Confessor?

According to his most recent biographer, 'In modern times [Edward the Confessor] has generally been regarded with mistrust, as a devious and ambiguous man, a dubious patriot, a weak and irresponsible king, a doubtful saint'.[1] It is certainly easy to criticise Edward. His failure decisively to resolve the problem of the succession had disastrous consequences for the Old English monarchy, and throughout his reign he lacked the masterful charisma required of a successful king. Indeed, Edward's failure to manage his nobility is the principal charge against him. He was controlled by Earl Godwin of Wessex during the first half of his reign, it is alleged, and he was little more than a figurehead after 1052 as he left the task of governing England to Harold Godwinson and spent his own time hunting and building Westminster Abbey. What is more, his critics say, Edward recklessly sponsored the expansion of Godwin power. According to Fleming, 'If the Confessor approved of the family's rapid aggrandisement and its vast network of allies, he was a fool; if he acquiesced he cannot have been in full control of his kingdom'.[2] However, even Fleming accepts that Edward's position on becoming king was a difficult one, and Nick Higham has emphasised that 'Edward's foreignness and comparative friendlessness in England in 1042 . . . required that he ruled very cautiously and very much by consensus, initially at least'.[3] Thereafter, in 1051, Edward did at least *try* to get rid of the Godwins, and if he never attempted anything similar again, perhaps he was being realistic rather than feeble. Edward's indulgence towards the Godwins may not have been completely imprudent either: many of the lands he gave them were in sensitive coastal areas, and the peace England enjoyed during Edward's reign may be attributable in part to the way he delegated military responsibilities to his leading subjects. Nevertheless, whilst Edward's England was prosperous and well-governed, the king's own responsibility for this was limited. Edward faced considerable problems, but he was neither a strong character nor an able politician. When he died, he had just failed yet again to impose his will on his subjects, this time during the Northumbrian revolt of 1065. It is arguable that the English monarchy was weaker in 1066 than in 1042. Perhaps only the accession of Harold II, with his vast resources, extensive following and martial reputation, saved it from continuing decline.

1 Barlow, *Edward the Confessor*, p. 286.
2 R. Fleming, *Kings and Lords in Conquest England* (Cambridge, 1991), p. 102.
3 Higham, *The Death of Anglo-Saxon England*, p. 119.

even if it contained no cavalry, it was still nearly too much for the Normans. The strain under which the system operated in 1066 was huge, and that it almost overcame the problems it faced is surely testimony to that system's strengths, not its weaknesses. The military system Edward the Confessor and Harold had at their disposal was 'well-organised, well-equipped and a reflection of the intelligence and power to be found in other aspects of the late Anglo-Saxon state'.[8]

Conclusion

The best evidence of the overall sophistication and coherence of late Anglo-Saxon government is, perhaps paradoxically, Domesday Book, compiled at the end of William the Conqueror's reign. More will be said about Domesday in Chapter 6, but it is worth emphasising here that all of the work of the survey was carried out in 1086 using the Old English administrative system and the available records of Old English government. To facilitate the survey, the country was divided into seven or eight separate circuits, each made up of a group of shires. The great landholders organised their information by subdividing their lands into hides, and their returns to the government contained information which they must already have had written down for their own purposes. Next, local people from each hundred or wapentake were formed into juries and gave evidence at the shire court as to the accuracy of the returns which had been submitted. The survey was probably completed as early as August 1086, a remarkable achievement for such an ambitious project, and further evidence of 'the responsiveness of the inherited territorial framework of county and hundred'.[9] Hides, shires, hundreds, wapentakes, juries: these Anglo-Saxon creations were still central to the organisation and administration of England twenty years after Hastings, and they remained so for centuries after that. And the fact that the shires survived until 1974 as the basic units of local government in England speaks volumes for their toughness and effectiveness as an institution.

Notes

1 *NC*, p. 69.
2 *NC*, p. 69; *V.Ed.*, p. 79.
3 *NC*, p. 83.
4 Clanchy, *From Memory to Written Record*, pp. 31–2.
5 Carpenter, *The Struggle for Mastery*, p. 66.
6 Keynes on 'Thegns' in the *Blackwell Encyclopaedia of Anglo-Saxon England*, pp. 443–4.
7 Lawson, *The Battle of Hastings, 1066*, p. 160.
8 Ibid., p. 123.
9 Bartlett, *England under the Norman and Angevin Kings*, pp. 194–5.

3

The Kings and the Law, 1042–1066

One of the principal duties of a medieval king, contemporaries thought, was the protection of his people. On one level this meant defending them from invasion and being successful in war. On another, it meant giving good justice, punishing wrongdoers and keeping the peace. This in turn meant that the king was expected to be both a lawgiver, obliged to keep good laws and abolish bad ones, and a judge with the task of giving judgments for, against and between his subjects. According to the *Vita Edwardi*, for example, 'This goodly king abrogated bad laws, with his *witan* established good ones, and filled with joy all that Britain over which . . . he ruled'. And according to John of Worcester, on becoming king in 1066 'Harold immediately began to abolish unjust laws and to make good ones . . . But he treated malefactors with great severity, and gave general orders to his earls, ealdormen, sheriffs and thegns to imprison all thieves, robbers and disturbers of the kingdom.'[1] That the king's right to exercise authority through the making and enforcing of laws was acknowledged and accepted by his subjects provides another example of the power and extensive reach of the late Anglo-Saxon kings.

Codes and cases

The king's position as lawgiver added an extra dimension to his authority, as the power to make or at least declare the law was one of those prerogatives which set kings apart from other men. Not surprisingly, therefore, the Anglo-Saxon kings were enthusiastic legislators. The tenth century had been the great age of royal law codes, ideological statements of practice and principle, whose purpose was to place the kings in a long line of ancestral, biblical judges. Following the examples of great

Anglo-Saxon kings such as Ine of Wessex and Offa of Mercia, and of Old Testament kings like Solomon, Alfred and Edward the Elder issued codes of laws, Athelstan at least three and perhaps four; three survive from Edmund's reign. Cnut's law codes eventually became the epitome of English law after 1066. Neither Edward the Confessor nor Harold, as far as we know, issued codes of his own. In Harold's case, he probably never had the time. As for Edward, 'perhaps his reputation for justice rested on his judgements and pronouncements by word of mouth'.[2]

The law codes were not just royal propaganda. Their detailed provisions, concerning crime, law enforcement and remedies in particular, were supposed to be implemented. After all, the making *and* enforcement of laws are both functions of power, and of strong and effective government. The more a king could have his laws implemented, the more powerful, and rich, he would become. How far such laws were applied in practice before 1066 is unclear; the surviving evidence, principally in the form of writs, charters, wills and records of individual lawsuits, is considerable, but fragmentary and elusive. Nevertheless, it appears very likely that by the middle of the eleventh century, certain types of criminal case ('royal pleas' or 'pleas of the crown') could only be tried by the king or by his judges – offences such as murder, treason, arson and rape. There was also evolving rapidly the idea of a national 'peace' which it was the king's duty to maintain and preserve. If someone was accused of doing something which breached the king's peace, once again he could only be tried by a royal judge. And another aspect of this development was the obligation placed on all adult males over the age of 12 to take an oath of loyalty to the king, which contained a promise not to commit theft. These related concepts, 'royal pleas', 'the king's peace' and the loyalty oath, reflected the developing view that it was the king's duty to deal with disorder and socially unacceptable behaviour. The first two in particular were by no means fully formed by 1066, but neither were they innovations of the post-conquest period.

Courts and communities

Moreover, by 1042 there was in place the outline of a kingdom-wide legal system, organised from the centre with the king at its head. Central to the operation of this system were the courts, the most important of which was the king's own. Here, in company with them, the king would hear disputes between his great men and make his judgments with their advice. He would deal with smaller business, too, from individual petitioners and suitors to his court. He would ratify land transfers, pronounce on the law and give an example to his agents, the earls, sheriffs and other important men whose job it would be to enforce royal authority in the localities.

Below the level of the king's court were the courts of the shire and the hundred (or wapentake). Each shire had a court which met twice a year, and it was presided over either by the earl or, probably more usually, by the sheriff. It was the principal forum for the exercise of royal justice in the localities. The important men of the shire, landholders both lay and ecclesiastical, would usually attend. It was where local land disputes were heard and royal rights proclaimed and enforced. The king himself might send cases to the shire court to be heard there. Cases of theft and violence would be dealt with, too, especially if they were cases of the type which could only be heard by the king or his judges. But the twice-yearly meetings of the shire court were more than purely judicial occasions. They were assemblies of the political community of the shire. Royal pronouncements would be made there; royal grants of land, embodied in charters or writs, would be announced; local land transfers would be arranged and confirmed; news and gossip would be shared; networking would go on. Each hundred or wapentake had its own court, too, which met more frequently than the shire court, probably once a month. Presided over by a reeve, according to the twelfth-century legal tract known as *The Laws of Edward the Confessor*, hundred courts 'deal with cases between vills and neighbours, and according as there are fines, compensatory payments and agreements, about pastures, meadows, harvests, disputes between neighbours and many things of this kind which frequently arise'.[3] The operation of the shire and hundred courts, public occasions where authority was exercised on the king's behalf by his agents, meant that royal control over the lives of ordinary people was being extended, primarily through the operation and application of the law. The hundred court, indeed, with its monthly meetings, must have provided most people with their primary experience of royal government in action.

The implications of these developments should not be overstated. There was as yet no such thing as 'the Common Law of England' in the sense of a set of laws applied universally and consistently by equivalent tribunals throughout the kingdom, and overseen by a dominant central authority. Late Anglo-Saxon kings were strong, but there were limits to their coercive authority. On an everyday level, for most of the king's subjects, the substance of law, especially that relating to land, was based on local custom and tradition, and its enforcement was locally controlled. The established laws varied considerably between neighbouring areas, and especially between different parts of the kingdom. Cnut's law code had recognised that differences existed between the laws of Wessex, Mercia and the Danelaw, and the so-called *Laws of Henry I*, written in about 1115, did the same. What these differences were is difficult to say. The right to take the profits of justice was sometimes in private rather than royal hands, moreover, although such a right would have been granted to an individual or an institution by the king. Sometimes whole hundreds or groups of hundreds were placed in private hands by the king. Great noblemen and churches had benefited in this way before the 1040s, for example, and thus, by 1066, the abbey of Bury St Edmunds had jurisdiction over $8^1/2$ hundreds in Suffolk and the church at Ely over $5^1/2$ hundreds in the same county. Often included in these grants of land were jurisdictional rights, too, expressed in such exotic terminology as 'sake and soke', or 'toll, team and *infangentheof*'. The precise meaning of these phrases is obscure, but they imply the right to exercise certain rights. If someone was granted *infangentheof*, for example, that person had the right to apprehend and summarily execute a thief caught red-handed on his lands. There were limits to these rights, however: royal pleas remained the king's exclusive preserve, for example, and could only be heard by him or his representatives.

Nevertheless, there were restrictions on the extent to which the king and his agents could administer a system of justice across his kingdom. This was clearer still where the policing and prosecution of crime were concerned. There was no national police force in the eleventh century, and unless a criminal was caught in the act, he would probably escape or remain undetected within his vill. Therefore the local community had to rely on its own members to police each other through the system of tithings or 'frankpledge'. A tithing was a group of ten or twelve freemen who acted as mutual guarantors that they would not commit offences, and that they would produce the guilty party if an offence was committed by one of their number. Evidence for the way tithings worked before 1066 is scarce, but by the early twelfth century it is possible to see the system working in some detail and it is unlikely that it had been changed significantly after the conquest. If the members of a tithing failed to fulfil their duties, they were punished financially. If an offence was committed and it was found that the offender was not in a tithing, the whole vill would be fined for having failed to regulate itself properly. Certain areas and groups were never included in this system, and there appears to have been no such structure at all in the northern and western border counties. But, these exceptions apart, by the mid-eleventh century it was established that every freeman over a certain age (probably 12) had to belong to a tithing.

To fulfil its responsibilities properly, a tithing had to exercise various duties. It had to maintain a general watch on local affairs, it had to raise the alarm on the discovery of an offence and make arrests, and it had to keep captured offenders in custody. It was also the duty of all members of the tithing to ensure that their fellow members did not commit crimes. Ultimate responsibility for the regulation of the frankpledge system rested with the sheriff. Twice a year he toured his shire and held special sessions of each hundred court. There he checked that the tithings were complete and properly manned, and it was probably at these sittings of the hundred that the tithings presented those they had been holding in custody. Whilst the tithing system was operated by local men, therefore, its supervision rested ultimately with the king and his officers: in other words, if the king could not police his kingdom in person, he could at least make sure that others were doing it for him.

Trial and punishment

Once cases arrived in a court, there had to be a trial of some kind. Prosecutions would be brought by individuals, who undertook to prove their allegations, or communally through the tithing. If guilt or innocence were unclear a form of proof had to be decided upon. If there was written evidence, a relevant charter in a dispute over land, for example, then that could be relied upon. However, verbal agreements about land were probably more common than written ones; such evidence, especially for litigants from lower social backgrounds, would have been rare. Alternatively, there may have been witnesses to the events in question. Their oral testimony was certainly valuable. However, where an accused denied his guilt, there were two main methods of proof: oath and ordeal. Both introduced God and the supernatural into the final judgment. Oaths could be given alone or with the backing of an appropriate number of 'oath-helpers', who swore as to the good character of the accused and the likelihood that he was telling the truth. However, not everyone was deemed fit to prove their innocence by oath (they were not 'oath-worthy'). A person of high social status would usually be deemed more oath-worthy than someone of lower standing, and slaves and the unfree could not take oaths at all. A stranger accused of crime in an area where he was unknown would be unable to swear alone and would find it difficult to recruit oath-helpers to support him. Similarly, an accused of ill-repute would not be able to swear alone, and would have needed supporting oaths to reinforce his own. In such circumstances, people may have been reluctant to risk their own standing in support of someone whose wrongdoing might cast doubt upon their own honourable reputation.

As for the ordeal, in England both before and after 1066 it was used far more in criminal cases than in civil ones and, it seems most likely, where oath-taking was not an option for some reason. The ordeal was a ritualised appeal for divine judgment and it took two main forms. In trial by cold water, the accused was lowered into a pit full of water which had been blessed by a priest. Guilt was established if he floated, on the basis that holy water would not receive a sinner by allowing him to sink. In trial by hot iron, the accused had to carry a piece of red-hot iron for three paces. The burnt hand was then bound and examined three days after the trial. If the wound was infected, guilt was certain; if it was clean, he was innocent. There is no reason to doubt that, for most people, the outcome of the ordeal was a reliable demonstration of God's preference for one party or another. But almost certainly, the mere prospect of the ordeal would have been enough to push many accused towards confession.

On a finding of guilt, an appropriate sentence had to be imposed. For serious offences (murder, treason and arson, for example) the death penalty was available. However, execution was probably only resorted to when financial compensation was deemed inappropriate or insufficient. For more often than not, it seems, punishment came in this form. If property rights had been infringed, money was paid by the wrongdoer. But this system of compensatory justice also extended to criminal penalties. The victim of a crime would be paid if his belongings had been stolen or damaged, but he would also be paid if he had been physically injured. The amount of compensation would depend on the position and extent of his wounds, and there were complex tariffs setting out the value of specific wounds. Deals would have been struck between the parties as well. All freemen, moreover, had a monetary value placed upon their lives, a *wergild* (literally 'man price'). This was payable in several different types of case, but it was awarded principally to the family of a person who had been killed, and was paid either by the killer or his kin to avoid the carrying out of a feud or vendetta by the dead victim's kin. The amount payable in a particular case depended on the rank of the victim. The king's *wergild* was largest of all. It is impossible to determine how extensively this system of financial penalties was in operation across England between 1042 and 1066. There have been suggestions that its importance was declining as kings sought to enforce more direct control over the workings of the courts. But by 1066 the shift from compensatory justice to punitive justice had certainly not been completed.

Conclusion

The legal system of late Anglo-Saxon England was more of a patchwork quilt than a seamless robe. Laws varied from place to place, their consistent enforcement was virtually impossible, and parts of the country remained un-shired, un-hidated and forever excluded from the tithing system. Nevertheless, the basic structure of a national legal system had been established by 1066, and the seeds of the English Common Law had been planted. Of course, there would be significant developments in the substance and the form of the Anglo-Saxon system during the Norman and Angevin periods. But the courts of the king, the shire and the hundred would remain the principal courts of the kingdom for the rest of the Middle Ages; and notions of the king's peace and cases which only the king could hear remained central to legal practice after 1066 and far beyond. By 1066, then, there were still limits to the king's authority as supreme judge and lawgiver. However, future developments would be forged on the anvil of a long-established English system.

Notes

1 *V.Ed.*, p. 13; *EHD II*, pp. 225–6.
2 Wormald, *The Making of English Law*, p. 128.
3 Bruce R. O'Brien, *God's Peace and King's Peace: The Laws of Edward the Confessor* (Philadelphia, 1999), p. 187.

4

The Kings and the Church, 1042–1066

Kings were unique amongst laymen because their office was divinely-sanctioned. Others had land, money and followers, but the king alone became God's deputy when he was consecrated with holy oil at his coronation. In return for elevating him above ordinary men, the Church expected to be protected and defended by the king against exploiters and enemies of Christ. The king and his Church were therefore supposed to work in harmony with each other so as to allow God's work in the world to be done in peace and without disruption. In practice, however, the archbishops, bishops and abbots of pre-conquest England were often figures of political rather than religious significance. They were appointed by the king and many came from the ranks of the royal household and advised him closely on political events. Once in their dioceses, they controlled land and had financial, judicial and military obligations to their royal lord. The kings of late Anglo-Saxon England governed the Church largely unimpeded, therefore, and, in their turn, leading church-men played an essential role in the government of the kingdom. So, after a general assessment of the condition of the English Church under the last two Anglo-Saxon kings, it is from a political and governmental perspective that their relationship with that Church will be analysed.

The late Anglo-Saxon Church

England had been divided into two ecclesiastical provinces, Canterbury and York, each with its own archbishop, since the sixth century. In theory neither archbishop was supposed to have precedence over the other. However, because the archbishops had authority over the bishops within their provinces, and because the south of England was in general richer than the north, Canterbury held sway: in 1066 there were twelve

English bishoprics including Canterbury and York, but only two of these were in the northern province. A peculiarity of the English system by this time, too, was the existence of 'monastic cathedrals' at Canterbury, Worcester, Winchester and Sherborne, alongside 'secular' ones elsewhere. The former were staffed by monks who lived secluded in their cloister, and the latter by canons who were supported by the revenues from the churches they ministered to outside their cathedral precincts. Monastic cathedrals had their origins in the second half of the tenth century, when many monasteries had been founded or refounded as part of a deliberate drive to restore monastic observance in England after the Viking attacks of the ninth century. By 1066, there were some forty-five monasteries in England in addition to those which were the seats of bishoprics. The leading reformers a century before had been the monks Dunstan, Aethelwold and Oswald, who were to become respectively archbishop of Canterbury (959–88), bishop of Winchester (963–84) and bishop of Worcester/archbishop of York (961–92/971–92). Their reforming programme had been supported by the English kings, in particular Edgar (959–75), and from this time monks were chosen as bishops in England much more often than was generally the case elsewhere in western Europe.

By the eleventh century, each bishopric was gradually being divided more formally into smaller units. These were eventually to become the parishes of medieval and modern England, although the process of development was far from complete by 1066. Nevertheless, most villages would have had a church of their own by 1042. These local churches may have been established by the bishop or even the king, but most would have been set up by the local nobleman, who would reserve the right to choose the priest who administered to the basic spiritual needs of his congregation – baptisms, marriages, confession, burial, regular services. The local church itself and the right to appoint its priest were regarded by those who controlled them as pieces of real property belonging to them as of right, and over which nobody else, even the local bishop, had any control.

How well this system dealt with the spiritual needs of the English people in the years immediately prior to the Norman Conquest is a matter of some debate. Norman writers in the years after 1066 had a vested interest in portraying the Old English Church, personified by the much-maligned Archbishop Stigand of Canterbury (1052–70), as backward and corrupt. The English people were sinners, after all, and William's victory at Hastings was God's judgment on them. Post-conquest English writers were not immune from such sentiments, either. William of Malmesbury, for example, was convinced in the mid-1120s that the Normans 'revived by their coming the practice of religion which everywhere was lapsing'.[1] William, of course, was writing with hindsight and after William I in particular had made some important changes to the way the English Church was organised, and to its personnel. By the time William wrote, moreover, a movement for reform within the western Church had been under way for nearly seventy-five years and its principles were well-established. From the late 1040s onwards a line of reforming popes had set out to eliminate abuses within the Church, in particular simony (the buying and selling of ecclesiastical offices) and clerical concubinage (the keeping of wives or mistresses by priests), and to reduce the amount of lay interference in Church affairs. Indeed, the papacy gave its support to Duke William's invasion in 1066, and provided him with a papal banner to carry in battle, partly in the hope that the Normans would bring the English Church more into line with the reforming trends of continental Europe. And finally, William of Malmesbury, a monk himself, would have had in mind when writing the great reforming examples of Saints Dunstan, Aethelwold and Oswald and their stress on the pursuit of monastic ideals. Against this backdrop, and at such a distance, the shortcomings of the pre-conquest Church must have seemed very apparent to William, and it is probably fair to describe the period between 1000 and 1066 as 'the slack water between two tides of reform'.[2]

Nevertheless, there is a strong case to be made that if the late Anglo-Saxon Church is judged by the standards of its own time rather than by those of the 970s or 1120s, it compares well with other western European Churches. Bishop Leofwine of Lichfield (1053–67) was married, but it is hard to find other such high-profile examples. At a lower level, many parish priests would have had wives or mistresses and children, but in the third quarter of the eleventh century such conduct would have been prevalent across Europe. Most English parish priests, moreover, were almost certainly not well-educated, but there is no reason to doubt that they carried out their duties responsibly. Simony does not appear to have been widespread either. Stigand was accused after 1066 of having bought offices and churches, but such charges might be expected from those who sought to discredit him for their own political purposes. And rumours about Abbot Spearhafoc of Abingdon may have prevented him from becoming bishop of London in 1051. Stigand was also a pluralist in that, from 1052, he was simultaneously bishop of Winchester and archbishop of Canterbury. And there were other noted pluralists, too. Earl Leofric's nephew and namesake was simultaneously abbot of Burton, Coventry, Crowland, Thorney and Peterborough. Herman was bishop of Ramsbury and Sherborne from 1056. Between 1055 and 1058, Ealdred, bishop of Worcester, also administered the dioceses of Hereford and Ramsbury, and, when he became archbishop of York in 1061, he was only prevented from jointly holding the archbishopric along with Worcester when the pope refused him permission to do so. It had become traditional by this time for these two sees to be held together; no less a figure than St Oswald had done this, for example, less than a century before. However, the pope's decision in 1061 gave a clear signal that such practices were no longer acceptable in the eyes of the reform papacy. But such a signal was still novel, and it was still not long since one of the greatest of the reforming popes, Leo IX (1049–54), had retained his diocese of Toul after succeeding to the see of St Peter.

Therefore, the Old English Church was probably no more corrupt than its continental counterparts. Indeed, it even displayed signs of vitality. As will be seen, pre-conquest England was no isolated backwater in ecclesiastical terms. The king was not averse to recruiting his bishops from abroad, and contacts with Rome were regular if not frequent. Laymen went on pilgrimage, most notably Sweyn Godwinson to Jerusalem after his family's exile in 1051, and his brothers Harold and Tostig to Rome in 1061. In a different context, William of Malmesbury's judgement in the 1120s that, after the Norman Conquest, 'throughout the land you might see churches rising in every vill, and monasteries in the towns and cities, built in a style unknown before' does not preclude the possibility that churches of all kinds were being built in wood and stone in England before 1066.[3] Evidence of such activity at a local level is inevitably lacking, but 'a strong inference from many parts of the country that this was a time when there was a significant increase in the number of manorial churches' has recently been drawn.[4] And there is more hard evidence for the building or redevelopment of great churches. Aelfwold, bishop of Sherborne (1045/6–58), rebuilt the monastery there, Cynsige of York (1051–60) built the tower at Beverley and further buildings were erected and lavishly decorated there by his successor, Ealdred. Laymen and laywomen built churches, too. Earl Leofric of Mercia founded Coventry Abbey in 1043 and was buried there, and he generously patronised several other monasteries including Worcester and Evesham. Queen Edith founded a nunnery at Wilton, and Earl Harold built a great church at Waltham in Essex where, it is generally thought, his remains were interred after Hastings.

Because so little of their fabric remains, it is difficult to know what these and other late Anglo-Saxon churches looked like. The prevalent style across the Channel in the eleventh century was 'Romanesque', but there is little indication that England's church builders were influenced by these trends before 1066. The majority of pre-conquest English churches probably tended to be smaller than their post-conquest replacements, simpler in form and rougher in detail. However, several dozen sites remain which still contain eleventh-century elements; they suggest that, whilst this generalised picture is probably fair, late Anglo-Saxon ecclesiastical architecture also had its sophisticated side. The huge crossing arches at Stow in Lincolnshire (c.1050) suggest a taste for the monumental. Towers both square and round were becoming increasingly widespread after 1000 as well. The best surviving examples are the square towers at

St Peter's Church, Barton-on-Humber (*c*.990), and Earl's Barton church in Northamptonshire (*c*.1020–50), both decorated with pilaster strips and blind arcading.[5] And inside the churches there would have been decoration, although its extent would depend on the wealth of the individual church and the generosity of its patrons. Walls would have been plastered, painted with biblical scenes or hung with the embroideries or tapestries for which the English were famous in the eleventh century. English sculptors would have played their part, too: crucifixes, reliquaries, chalices, patens, portable devotional scenes and individual figures and much more would have been made out of metal, ivory or wood. The two ivory figures of the Virgin and St John the Evangelist which survive from a larger crucifixion group carved in about 1000 reveal the heights attainable by the craftsmen of eleventh-century England,[6] as do the decorated or 'illuminated' manuscripts of the period produced in the workshops of England's monasteries. Book production (the writing, decoration and binding of manuscripts) had been given a huge boost by the monastic revival of the tenth century, and by 1000 the quality of English illumination was internationally renowned. The manuscripts produced during the century before the Norman Conquest are often referred to as having been executed in the 'Winchester style', although they came from monastic centres across southern England. They tended to be richly decorated with ornamental designs, often of acanthus leaves, in the borders; but figurative representations were often delicately and elegantly drawn, too. The former characteristic can best be seen in the Benedictional of St Aethelwold, produced at Winchester between 971 and 984; the latter in pages from the Tiberius Psalter (Winchester, *c*.1050), and the Old English translation of the first six books of the Old Testament, the 'Hexateuch' (Canterbury, *c*.1025–50).[7]

The one outstanding example of a late Anglo-Saxon church which consciously imitated the latest continental trends was Edward the Confessor's Westminster Abbey. Some sort of foundation already existed on the marshy and inhospitable 'Isle of Thorns' in the Thames in the first half of the tenth century, and St Dunstan's patronage may have given it greater prominence in the 960s or 970s. By the 1050s, Edward had decided to rebuild it completely, with the intention of making it his burial place. Very little of Edward's church now survives, but something of its appearance can be gleaned from the depiction of it on the Bayeux Tapestry and from the description of it in the *Vita Edwardi*.[8] It was built in the latest Romanesque style, and perhaps it was modelled in part on Archbishop Robert's abbey of Jumièges. It has also been suggested, however, that it was Westminster which provided the model for Jumièges. The Confessor's abbey was built of Reigate stone with a long nave of six double bays, and a central lantern tower overlooking the crossing. The abbey was consecrated on 28 December 1065, and its first ceremonial was the funeral of its patron about a week later. Edward did not live to see his great church functioning, but his legacy to his successors was the establishment of Westminster, with its abbey and its palace, as the heart of royal government in England.

But for all its positive attributes, central to the case made by critics of the late Anglo-Saxon Church was the position and personality of Stigand. He was probably from East Anglia and his Old Norse name suggests that he was of Scandinavian descent to some degree. After serving as a priest of Cnut, he became bishop of Elmham in 1043, bishop of Winchester in 1047 (he was succeeded at Elmham by his brother Aethelmaer) and archbishop of Canterbury in 1052 when Robert of Jumièges was expelled from England. He was also accused in the twelfth century of having had control of the revenues of several important monasteries, including St Augustine's at Canterbury, Winchester, Glastonbury, St Albans and Ely. Because he was a pluralist, and because his predecessor as archbishop was still alive when he assumed the title, Stigand's position was certainly irregular. However, he was also unlucky in having received his pallium, the symbol of his archiepiscopal office, in 1058 from Benedict X, an anti-pope whose own legitimacy was later rejected by the wider Church. He was also 'outstandingly worldly',[9] a politician first and foremost and a rich one, too, with an extensive personal landed estate. He showed no interest in the reform movement emanating from Rome, and he gave no meaningful spiritual lead to the English Church during his time as its leader. Nevertheless, he did have his better side: he was a patron of the arts and generous to the churches he controlled. He was also an efficient administrator. Even William of Malmesbury conceded that, where Stigand's personal ambitions were not involved, 'he was not lacking in judgement or inefficient'.[10] He was not a good pastor, then, but for the most recent historian of the Old English Church 'he represented a fine example of the old unreformed order of the Church, primarily a capable administrator, appreciated as such by Edward and to some extent William in his early years'.[11] Nevertheless, he was an easy target for the Norman propagandists, who were quick to identify him, most obviously on the Bayeux Tapestry, as the illegitimate archbishop who had crowned an illegitimate king.[12] Whether he actually did so is open to question. Harold must have known how irregular Stigand's position was, and how he might be tainted by association with him. John of Worcester at least is quite clear that it was Archbishop Ealdred of York who consecrated the last Anglo-Saxon king.[13]

Whatever Stigand's faults actually were, moreover, he was not typical of the English bishops of the immediate pre-conquest period. Indeed, as a group, they were reasonably impressive. Several of the foreigners received a good press from contemporaries. According to the author of the *Vita Edwardi*, Giso of Wells and Walter of Hereford were both 'men most suitably and excellently trained in their office' whilst Herman of Ramsbury was a 'famous and well-educated bishop'.[14] Archbishop Cynsige of York was venerated as a saint by the monks of Peterborough where he was buried. Leofric of Devon and Cornwall has been described as a 'conscientious and cultured bishop . . . an able administrator and a progressive force'.[15] And most outstanding of all, albeit for different reasons, were Ealdred, first bishop of Worcester (1046–62) and then archbishop of York (1062–9), and Wulfstan, Ealdred's successor at Worcester (1062–95). Ealdred, despite being a monk, enjoyed perhaps as worldly a career as Stigand. He defended the English border against the Welsh in the late 1040s, undertook royal missions to foreign courts and administered several dioceses at once in the 1050s. He wanted to hold York in plurality with Worcester after 1062 but was forbidden from doing so by the pope. However, he took care to receive his pallium from a legitimate pope, and the indications are that he was a better pastor than Stigand and took more interest in the affairs of his diocese and the standards of his diocesan clergy. His reputation was secure by 1066, and he was the obvious man to perform Duke William's coronation. As for Wulfstan, his reputation has been founded largely on the *Life* written by his chaplain Colman in about 1095 and preserved by William of Malmesbury. Wulfstan was a monk, too; but, unlike Ealdred, he was holy, ascetic, unworldly and reluctant to become a bishop. However, having accepted his appointment in 1062, he was relentlessly energetic about carrying out his duties and ministering to his flock. According to his hagiographers, he performed miracles during his lifetime, and more took place at his tomb after his death.[16] His reputation for sanctity soon spread, although he was not canonised until 1203.

Royal government and the Church

The king exercised control over the Church primarily by appointing bishops and abbots. As the ideas of the reform papacy developed through the second half of the eleventh century, such practices came increasingly to be frowned upon by the ecclesiastical authorities. However, Edward the Confessor, and Harold had he survived longer, would have seen nothing wrong with what they were doing. Other contemporary rulers did the same, and after 1066 the right to have a decisive say in such matters was jealously guarded by the Norman and Angevin kings. Edward's insistence that Robert of Jumièges should become archbishop of Canterbury in 1051, therefore, was not just a way of undermining Godwin's influence within Kent; the king was exercising his traditional prerogatives. There were good practical reasons for holding on to these powers, moreover, as the bishops in particular played a crucial part in the government and administration of the kingdom. They presided over the shire court with the earl or his deputy and they were amongst the king's *witan* who advised him on matters of policy and decisions of state. According to the *Vita Edwardi*, prior to his fall in 1052, Robert of Jumièges 'was always the most powerful confidential adviser of the king'.[17] Most obviously, Stigand was involved in many of the important events of this period: at its end, for example, he was at Edward the Confessor's bedside when the old king died, and his submission to Duke William at Wallingford in 1066 may have prompted other survivors of Harold's regime to follow his example at Berkhamsted. Some prelates might even acquire an unhealthy influence over the king: it was Robert of Jumièges who turned Edward against the Godwins in 1051, according to at least one account of the crisis.[18] Churchmen might act as emissaries for the king to foreign courts, as well. Herman of Ramsbury and Ealdred of Worcester travelled to Rome in 1050 'on the king's business' and Ealdred travelled to the imperial court in 1054 to negotiate the return of Edward 'the Exile' from Hungary. They might have military duties, too. Usually this meant no more in practice than having a responsibility to muster local troops; but individual bishops might go further. In 1049, Ealdred of Worcester fought against the Welsh, as, with fatal consequences for himself, did Bishop Leofgar of Hereford in 1056. However, it was in their capacity as great landholders that the leading churchmen were of most significance to the king. In 1066, according to Domesday Book, the Church controlled between a quarter and a third of the landed wealth of England. In this context, therefore, bishops and abbots were just like other landed magnates, and it was vital for the king that he had loyal, trustworthy men in these positions of authority. They had control over men and over other vital resources. They also paid geld, of course, a matter of no little financial interest to the king.

The make-up of the episcopate was of great importance to the king, therefore, for administrative reasons and for reasons of security. King Edward seems to have made particular efforts, indeed, to ensure that men of whom he approved were installed as bishops. During his reign there was a tendency to reduce the number of monastic bishops and to increase the number of secular (often royal) priests and foreigners presiding over English sees. In 1051–2, for example, when Edward was making a concerted attempt to assert himself against the Godwins, only four of the fifteen English bishops were monks, and three of the most important southern bishoprics, Canterbury, London and Dorchester, were held respectively by the Normans Robert of Jumièges (1051–2), William (1051–75) and Ulf (1050–2). Other foreigners, four in particular from Lorraine, were also appointed to English sees. Herman was made first bishop of Ramsbury (1045–58) and then Sherborne (1058–78). Leofric, probably an Englishman brought up in Lorraine, became bishop of Crediton in 1046 and later moved his episcopal seat to Exeter (1050–72). And Giso and

Walter were respectively bishops of Wells (1061–88) and Hereford (1061–79). Perhaps these trends should not be emphasised too strongly, and by 1066 both archbishops and most of the bishops were still English. Nevertheless, royal control over the episcopate remained a vital means of asserting royal control over the country.

Whilst the king was largely in control of the affairs of the Church, he did not have everything his own way. During the period immediately prior to 1066, papal involvement in the business of the English Church began slowly to increase. In the first half of the eleventh century, the papacy had been dominated by powerful Roman families and it had been used by them as a tool of faction. Consequently, the popes themselves had been unable to exercise any meaningful authority either within Rome or outside it. However, from the 1040s, as has been seen, this began to change. The reforming popes who took charge in Rome were determined to have their authority as leaders of the western Church acknowledged across Europe. They set about doing this in various ways, but principally by travelling widely, holding synods and pronouncing judgment on local disputes. Such policies were bound to bring them into conflict with lay rulers. This happened most obviously in Germany, but England was not untouched either. England paid an annual tribute to the papacy, 'Rome-scot' or 'Peter's Pence'. The origins of this payment are obscure, but it was already a time-honoured custom by the eleventh century. Whilst the popes were weak, the English kings could regard it as nothing more than a polite courtesy; but once they were strong it might be interpreted in Rome as a sign of English subjection to the papacy. Another potentially compromising tradition for the king dictated that, whilst the king might appoint his archbishops, no archbishop was entitled to govern his province or consecrate and preside over the bishops of that province unless he had received the symbol of his office, the woollen stole known as the pallium, from the pope himself. Thus Robert of Jumièges travelled to Rome in 1051, as did Cynsige and Ealdred of York in 1055 and 1061 respectively. Stigand was sent his pallium by Benedict X in 1058. The failure properly to comply with these formalities could have personal repercussions for the authority of the individual concerned, as Stigand found to his cost: Giso of Wells and Walter of Hereford travelled to Rome in 1061 to be consecrated by the pope because of Stigand's incapacity. There could also be political consequences for the king or even, as Harold discovered, for a claimant to the throne. English bishops and abbots might leave the kingdom for other reasons, too. For example, several English prelates attended Pope Leo IX's councils at Rheims in 1049 and at Rome and Vercelli in 1050; here they would have been exposed to the progressive ideas of one of the great reforming popes. And there are other signs that reforming ideas were gaining ground in England before 1066. Two of the Lotharingian bishops imported by

Edward, Herman of Ramsbury and Leofric of Devon and Cornwall, began the practice, later accelerated by William I and Lanfranc, of bishops establishing permanent diocesan centres, and their accompanying cathedrals, in major towns, Leofric in Exeter (from Crediton, with papal approval) and Herman in Sherborne.

The popes interfered in the affairs of the English Church in other ways which impinged upon the authority of the king more directly. When Robert of Jumièges moved from the see of London to become archbishop of Canterbury in 1051, Edward nominated as his successor his own goldsmith, Abbot Spearhafoc of Abingdon. On his return from Rome, however, perhaps because rumours had reached Leo IX that Spearhafoc had obtained his position through simony, Archbishop Robert refused to consecrate the royal nominee. In the short term the king was not disadvantaged significantly and the royal priest William, a Norman, was consecrated instead. But such acts of assertiveness by an archbishop acting under papal influence were significant indicators of the extent to which papal authority was beginning to spread across Europe. It was exercised again in 1061. Archbishop Cynsige of York died in that year and Ealdred, already bishop of Worcester, was chosen as his successor and travelled to Rome for his pallium. However, Nicholas II was not only unwilling to give the pallium to Ealdred; he went as far as to depose him as a bishop entirely because he had moved from one bishopric to another without papal consent. It was not until he had been attacked by robbers and fled back to Rome to acknowledge his offence that Ealdred was given his pallium; and even then only on the strict understanding that he surrendered his claims to the bishopric of Worcester. The king's absolute freedom to choose his own bishops, therefore, and their own freedom to hold more than one see at a time was beginning to be whittled away by a foreign power. By 1066, papal influence in England was still limited and exercised only occasionally; no major conflict arose under Edward the Confessor or Harold and there was no fundamental clash between king and pope. But it was perhaps only a matter of time before the tension inherent in their rival claims to authority over the English Church became unbearable.

A backward Church in need of reform?

The pre-conquest English Church had its deficiencies and shortcomings. Royal control of it was intensive, and its bishops and abbots were often distinguished from members of the lay aristocracy only by their appearance. Examples of simony, pluralism and clerical marriage at the highest level can be cited. Local priests were often poorly-educated family men. Edward the Confessor and Stigand showed no interest in continental reforming trends, and made no effort either to root out abuses in or otherwise modernise the English Church. However, in the decades before 1066 there was nothing unusual about any of this by wider European standards. Across continental Europe, lay rulers appointed bishops and abbots, and the latter played essential roles in central and local government. Abuses of the sort present in England were probably just as, if not more, prevalent elsewhere. On the credit side, the variety of personalities and the range of backgrounds and abilities within the English episcopate during these years are striking; and the Church as a whole appears to have been well-organised and efficiently administered. And whilst the late Anglo-Saxon Church produced no figure equivalent to a Dunstan or an Anselm, someone who might have tried systematically to introduce new ideas and to reinvigorate English religious life, the signs are that the principles and practices of the reform papacy were gradually beginning to seep into the kingdom by 1066, and that they were not simply another piece of Norman luggage carried across the Channel to Hastings. In Golding's words, 'William [the Conqueror] may have accelerated the pace of change, but he did not alter its direction'.[19] Serious reform of the English Church may have been inevitable by 1066, and it is fascinating to speculate about how it would have developed under a vigorous and apparently pious king like Harold. Whatever the nature of that change, moreover, and most significantly here, the importance of the Church in the government of the kingdom was to remain at least as great after 1066 as it had been before.

Notes

1 *NC*, p. 116.
2 Barlow, *The English Church, 1000–1066*, p. 27.
3 *NC*, p. 116.
4 Loyn, *The English Church*, p. 57.
5 *The Golden Age of Anglo-Saxon Art, 966–1066*, p. 141, figures 4–5.
6 Ibid., pp. 118–19, and colour plate XXVII.
7 Brown, *Anglo-Saxon Manuscripts*, plates 54, 72, 76.
8 *NC*, pp. 89–90; *EHD II*, pp. 268–9 (Plates XXX–XXXI).
9 Barlow, *The English Church, 1000–1066*, p. 78.
10 *WMB*, p. 25.
11 Loyn, *The English Church*, pp. 60–1.
12 *EHD II*, p. 271 (Plate XXXIII).
13 *NC*, p. 69.
14 *V.Ed.*, pp. 35, 47.
15 Barlow, *The English Church, 1000–1066*, p. 84.
16 See, for example, *WMB*, pp. 187–96.
17 *NC*, p. 83.
18 *NC*, p. 84.
19 Golding, *Conquest and Colonisation*, p. 146.

Part II

Anglo-Norman England, 1066–1154

5

The Reigns, 1066–1154

William I 'the Conqueror', 1066–1087

1066–1068

After his coronation King William remained in England until March 1067. During these weeks, according to William of Poitiers, 'he came to divers parts of the kingdom arranging everything to his convenience and that of the inhabitants. Wherever he went all laid down their arms. There was no resistance, but everywhere men submitted to him or sought his peace.'[1] In fact, England was now a kingdom under military occupation by a foreign ruler. Castles and garrisons were the order of the day.

On leaving England in March 1067, William took with him Archbishop Stigand, Edgar *aetheling*, and Earls Edwin, Morcar and Waltheof. These men had been allowed to keep their lands, but they were the obvious focal points for English resistance. They were also spoils of victory, and William displayed them along with his other looted treasures when he processed solemnly and victoriously through Rouen and Fécamp on his return to his duchy. Whilst the king was away from England, his half-brother, Bishop Odo of Bayeux, was left in charge at Dover, and another of his closest followers, William FitzOsbern, oversaw affairs from Winchester. William of Poitiers' view was that Odo and FitzOsbern 'laudably performed their respective stewardships in the kingdom . . . But neither fear nor favour could so subdue the English as to prefer peace and tranquillity to rebellions and disorders.' Orderic Vitalis, by contrast, blamed the growing English discontent of 1067 on Odo's and William's shoulders, and on other oppressive lords who ignored royal orders.[2]

In 1067, Count Eustace of Boulogne, William's former ally (and Edward the Confessor's brother-in-law), attacked but was seen off by the garrison at Dover. Perhaps he was dissatisfied at the amount of land he had been given by the new king. More serious in the longer term was the English habit, emphasised by William of Poitiers, of sending envoys to the Danes 'or to anyone else from whom they could hope for help'.[3] It is impossible to know how much truth there was in these allegations, but William returned to England in December 1067 'to confront turmoil'.[4] One challenge to Norman authority was launched by the mysterious figure known as Eadric 'the Wild', who attacked Hereford with Welsh support. But most serious was the opposition William was forced to confront in Exeter, where Harold's mother, Gytha, was based. William marched into Devon at the head of a large force and, according to the *Anglo-Saxon Chronicle*, laid siege to Exeter for eighteen days 'and there a large part of his army perished'. According to Orderic, after the town's surrender the king was generous to those who had opposed him. Having accepted their submission, however, he did begin the construction of a castle within the town walls. The king's relatively lenient approach may have been dictated by a need to secure support in the south-west; after leaving Exeter he travelled into Cornwall to show his strength and then returned to Winchester for Easter. It must have been soon after this that William summoned his wife Matilda from Normandy. She was crowned queen in May 1068.[5]

Whilst William had been besieging Exeter, an invasion fleet led by three of King Harold's sons had been launched from Ireland and had landed in south-west England. It is conceivable that this invasion was supposed to reinforce the rebellion at Exeter, but there is no proof of this. In any event, part of this force went to Bristol, where it was seen off, and it was defeated again by another survivor of the old regime, Eadnoth, who was killed in the process. Much more serious in 1068 was the revolt of Edwin and Morcar. According to Orderic, Edwin rebelled because the marriage which had been arranged between him and William's daughter had never taken place, and he states that the brothers had much support for their stand, especially from the Welsh.[6] In reality, Edwin was probably more aggrieved by increasing Norman influence within his earldom, especially in Herefordshire where William FitzOsbern had recently been sent. To complicate matters further, there was upheaval in the north of England at the same time, where some of the leading men, including the new earl Gospatric, rose up against their new king. To avert the possibility of the earls' supporters joining up with the northern rebels, William marched through Mercia, first to Warwick where he built a castle, whereupon Edwin and Morcar surrendered; then to Nottingham where the construction of another castle began. Finally in the north, he went to York, where, again, he built a castle to set the seal on his authority. Then, on his way back south, he set in train the construction of yet more castles at Lincoln, Huntingdon and Cambridge. Loyal men were placed in charge of all these new fortifications, Robert FitzRichard in York, William Peverel at Nottingham and Henry, son of Roger of Beaumont, at Warwick. Late in 1068, the king returned to Normandy.

1069-1070

'In the period 1069-70 William's rule in England faced its greatest crisis.'[7] In 1069 Harold's sons tried their luck again. This time they landed at Exeter and ravaged much of Devon; they were joined by supporters from Devon and Cornwall but Exeter, the town which had defied William only a year before, remained loyal to the new regime. Meanwhile, northern England continued to provide William with his biggest problems. His first attempts to deal with the north had led to the appointment by him as earl of Northumbria of Copsi, a former associate of Earl Tostig. This was an imprudent step and demonstrated William's ignorance of northern politics. Copsi was murdered by his local rival Oswulf of Bamburgh as soon as he arrived in the north to take up his post early in 1068, and was succeeded by Gospatric, another survivor of the old regime. Gospatric proved just as unwise an appointment as Copsi; he rebelled in 1068 and fled to Scotland. To make matters worse still, under King Malcolm's protection at the Scottish court was Edgar *aetheling*, who had fled there after the failure of the revolt of Edwin and Morcar. Then, according to Orderic, Edgar, Earl Gospatric and other rebels joined forces late in 1068 whilst William was still abroad. It was during this rising, at the end of January 1069, that the latest earl of Northumbria, Robert de Commines, was slaughtered in Durham along with his knights. The rebels then travelled south to York, where the castellan, Robert FitzRichard, was killed. The new sheriff of Yorkshire, William Malet, appointed by William in the previous year, was besieged in his new castle at York. The king responded swiftly: he returned to England early in 1069, travelled north, relieved the York garrison, built a second castle there and left William FitzOsbern in charge.[8] At the same time, another potential threat to Norman rule emerged even further north, in the shape of Sweyn Estrithson, king of Denmark. He maintained a claim to the English throne as the son of Cnut's sister and the cousin of Harthacnut, and by mid-1069 a large invasion from Denmark was imminent. When it arrived it was led by Sweyn's brother, Osbeorn, and three of his sons, and it is said to have consisted of a fleet of between 240 and 300 ships. On landing on the banks of the Humber the Danes joined forces with the northern rebels, returned to York and captured it in September. According to the *Anglo-Saxon Chronicle* they killed 'many hundreds of Frenchmen'.[9] However, the rebels chose not to press home their initial success; instead they dispersed and the Danes retreated back beyond the Humber. Having heard of the invasion whilst hunting in the Forest of Dean, the king moved north and began to encircle them. By Christmas 1069 they were confined, short of supplies, on the banks of the Humber estuary. They submitted to William and agreed to leave England in the spring of 1070.

Therefore, by the start of 1070 William had dealt with the immediate threat posed by the Danes. However, he had not dealt with northern England as a whole. So, having undertaken three expeditions north in the space of eighteen months, he decided to teach his opponents there a decisive lesson. In the process began one of the most notorious episodes of William's reign, the so-called 'Harrying of the North'. According to the *Anglo-Saxon Chronicle*, the king went north 'with all his army that he could collect, and utterly ravaged and laid waste that shire'. Orderic's account is more graphic: according to him, William 'continued to comb forests and remote mountain places, stopping at nothing to hunt out the enemy hidden there. His camps were spread over an area of 100 miles. He cut down many in his vengeance; destroyed the lairs of others; harried the land and burned homes to ashes.' Orderic even becomes critical of William at this point:

> Nowhere else had William shown such cruelty. Shamefully he succumbed to this vice, for he made no effort to restrain his fury and punished the innocent with the guilty. In his anger he commanded that all crops and herds, chattels and food of every kind should be brought together and burned to ashes with consuming fire, so that the whole region north of the Humber might be stripped of all means of sustenance. In consequence [he concludes], so serious a scarcity was felt in England, and so terrible a famine fell upon the humble and defence-less populace, that more than 100,000 Christian folk of both sexes, young and old alike, perished of hunger.[10]

Orderic's assessment of the number of people who died as a result of William's conduct in the north may be exaggerated; if true it would mean that something approaching 5 per cent of England's population died in the winter of 1069–70. It is a pardonable overestimate, however, and reflects the scale of William's terror tactics. If the king's plan had been to ensure that the North could not support rebellion again, he was successful. But his methods were also brutal and destructive and north-ern England did not recover for generations. In 1086, Domesday Book bluntly designated a third of Yorkshire as 'waste'.

But even the Harrying of the North did not put an end to rebellion everywhere. In January or February 1070 William travelled to the west to deal with a rising on the Welsh border, new castles were constructed at Chester and Stafford and arrangements were made for the security and government of the Welsh borders. Roger of Montgomery became earl of Shrewsbury, Hugh of Avranches became earl of Chester and, in 1071, on the death of William FitzOsbern, his son Roger became earl of Hereford. At Easter 1070, William held court at Winchester in great style and was re-crowned by visiting papal legates. Archbishop Stigand of Canterbury was now also removed from office and a wide-ranging reform of the structure of the English Church was begun.

1070–1072

In 1070, King Sweyn of Denmark finally arrived in England and joined up with those of his countrymen who had never left England as they had agreed to do at the start of the year. According to the *Anglo-Saxon Chronicle* there was a genuine expectation at the time that Sweyn was going to conquer the country.[11] He sent part of his army to Ely where its forces combined with some remaining English resistance under the leadership of a figure of later legend, Hereward. Hereward was probably a Lincolnshire thegn who lost lands in the aftermath of the conquest, and he set up his rebel base in the Fens. However, after he and his new Scandinavian allies mounted an unsuccessful attack on Peterborough, the Danes made peace with William and finally returned home with their loot. Hereward was then joined by Morcar, whose brother Earl Edwin was killed at the same time, probably recruiting support for the rebels in the north. The king besieged the rebels on the Isle of Ely, and when they finally surrendered, Morcar was imprisoned for life. Hereward by contrast was given back his lands by the king.

William set the seal on this phase of the conquest by marching north to Scotland in 1072. In 1070 King Malcolm had campaigned in Cumberland and Northumbria. Then, in 1071, he had married Margaret, the sister of Edgar *aetheling*. This formal link between the royal house of Scotland and the old ruling house of Wessex was potentially threatening to William. So his intention in marching north the following year was to intimidate Malcolm and warn him about further meddling in the affairs of northern England. The two kings reached an agreement in 1072, known as the Peace of Abernethy: according to the *Anglo-Saxon Chronicle*, Malcolm became William's vassal and expelled Edgar from his court.[12] On his return south, William also appointed a new earl of Northumbria. Gospatric, who had made his peace with the king after the revolt of 1069, was dismissed and replaced by Waltheof, the earl of Northamptonshire and Huntingdonshire, who had been another of the northern rebels in 1069. Waltheof's submission to the king after the revolt had been followed by his marriage to the king's niece, Judith, in 1070.

1072–1075

After his Scottish campaign of 1072, William returned to France and spent the early part of 1073 subduing the county of Maine. He then returned for a short time to England, but the main focus of his attention, now that England seemed relatively stable, was Normandy, where he spent the whole of 1074. England was left under the control of some of William's more important barons, amongst whom Richard FitzGilbert and William de Warenne were the most prominent. During this period Edgar *aetheling* finally submitted to William.

William spent most of 1075 in Normandy, too, where he heard news of a major revolt against his authority in England. There were three main conspirators, who also appealed for help from the Danes: Earl Ralph de Gael of Norfolk, Earl Roger of Hereford (the son of William FitzOsbern, who had died in 1071), and, to an extent which is less clear, Earl Waltheof of Northumbria. The plot may have been hatched at a wedding feast celebrating the marriage of Earl Ralph to Earl Roger's sister, Emma. Why they chose to rebel is quite obscure. Earl Roger was probably unhappy that he had not assumed all of his father's authority on the latter's death, and he complained that the king had wrongfully sent royal sheriffs to hear pleas on his lands. William, who was in Normandy when the revolt broke out, left it to be dealt with by his deputies. William de Warenne and Odo of Bayeux amongst others forced Ralph to flee abroad; his lands were forfeited and he continued the fight from his lands in Brittany. Earl Roger, meanwhile, surrendered under pressure from an army led by English clerics, Bishop Wulfstan of Worcester and Abbot Aethelwig of Evesham. His lands were taken from him and he was imprisoned for life. When the Danes finally arrived, with a fleet of two hundred ships, the revolt was effectively over; they sacked York Minster and retired to Flanders. William returned to England in autumn 1075, leaving Normandy in his wife's hands. He was in time for the mopping up of the rebellion, and at Christmas 1075 he wore his crown and arranged the burial of Edith, the wife of Edward the Confessor, in Westminster Abbey. Meanwhile, Earl Waltheof, who had travelled to Normandy and begged for mercy in front of William himself, was arrested and, in May 1076, beheaded.

1076–1081

William probably returned to Normandy in the summer of 1076, where his main preoccupation was the problems being caused on the western borders of Normandy by the fugitive Earl Ralph. William led an army to the castle of Dol where Ralph was holed up in September 1076. He laid siege to the castle, but in November he was taken by surprise by the French king, Philip I, and decisively defeated in battle. This was a rare defeat for the victor of Hastings and a blow to his reputation for invincibility. From this point on, it was affairs in Normandy, and his deteriorating relationship with members of his family, that dominated William's concerns.

According to Orderic Vitalis, it was a trivial quarrel between William's three sons, Robert, William and Henry, which led to the eldest, Robert, making war on his father.[13] Robert was in his mid-twenties and keen to be given lands and power of his own; but his father was not prepared to set him up as an independent ruler. In contrast, William's enemies out-side Normandy were happy to lend Robert and his young, violent com-panions a sympathetic ear. By the winter of 1078–9, Robert had occupied the castle of Gerberoi, south-east of Normandy, which he had been given by King Philip, from where he started to raid across the Norman frontier. In January 1079, William besieged the castle until the garrison emerged and battle ensued. Father fought against son, and Robert injured William in the hand. The king's second son, William, who fought with his father, was also wounded. Peace was not made until Easter 1080 when, at a great assembly at Rouen, Robert was confirmed as the heir to Normandy.

In the summer of 1080, William returned to England for the first time in four years. Problems in Scotland and Wales preoccupied him when he did. King Malcolm of Scotland had invaded northern England in 1079, and in May 1080 Bishop Walcher of Durham, whom William had allowed to purchase the earldom of Northumbria after the execution of Waltheof, was murdered. In summer 1080, Bishop Odo travelled north and devast-ated Northumbria and in the autumn Robert followed him to try to deal with Malcolm. After locating him, Robert obtained Malcolm's homage and promises of future good behaviour. On his return from the north, Robert built the so-called 'New Castle' at what is now Newcastle upon Tyne, and the earldom of Northumbria came into the possession of Robert de Mowbray.

In 1081, William travelled to Wales for the only known time. He went further than Norman influence had hitherto penetrated, to St David's in the far south-west. The occasion for this expedition was probably the death of King Caradog ap Gruffudd, the ruler of Glamorgan, in 1081 and William's desire to assert his authority over the new power in Wales, Rhys ap Tewdwr, king of Deheubarth. Later in 1081, William returned to Normandy to deal with an attack on southern Maine by the count of Anjou in alliance with the count of Brittany. An uneasy settlement was reached between the great princes.

1082–1087

The first two years of this phase of the reign are very obscure. One of the most significant events was the fall of Bishop Odo of Bayeux, William's half-brother, early in 1083. Writers of the early twelfth century alleged that Odo had hatched a plan to buy the papacy for himself. Pope Gregory VII was certainly having difficulties with Emperor Henry IV in the first half of the 1080s, but the story is still bizarre. In any event, William accused Odo of trying to take knights out of the country for his private purposes when they were needed to defend the realm. An argument ensued, and the result was Odo's seizure and imprisonment at Rouen. William and Matilda were back in Normandy by July 1083, and Matilda died there in November. William's son Robert was exiled again in 1084, although it is unclear whether anything specific happened to cause this.

Also in 1084, William had to deal with another revolt in Maine and, more importantly, with the threat of a fresh Danish invasion led by King Cnut IV and his father-in-law, Count Robert of Flanders. William returned to England in 1085 with 'a larger force of mounted men and infantry from France and Brittany than had ever come to this country'.[14] The king and his forces remained on standby during the latter part of 1085 and the first half of 1086 until news was received that Cnut had been murdered. During this period, as William's mercenary troops ravaged the coastline and lived billeted on the kingdom, the *Anglo-Saxon Chronicle* noted the sufferings and hardship inflicted on the English people.[15] William was certainly paying particular attention to what his kingdom could produce at this point, because it was at Gloucester at Christmas 1085 that he gave orders for a survey of England's resources to be carried out. The results of this survey, which was completed at the latest by autumn 1086, were collected together in what has been known since the twelfth century as Domesday Book. However, before that, on 1 August 1086, 'all the people occupying land who were of any account over all England, no matter whose men they were' waited on the king at Salisbury and swore oaths of loyalty to him.[16]

William returned to Normandy in autumn 1086 to deal with further threats from his enemies, in particular King Philip, who had used William's absence in England to make raids across the Norman border. In July 1087, the king and his troops headed for the town of Mantes in the French Vexin, which had been the base for the raids. During the sack of the town William was taken ill and carried back to Rouen where he made his bequests. There is no definitive account of what happened, but most historians rely on the substance of the description of the scene at the king's death-bed given by Orderic Vitalis.[17] William made gifts to various religious houses and agreed to the release of all his prisoners, except his half-brother, Odo, an act of revenge from which he was dissuaded. As for the succession, William reluctantly confirmed that his son Robert would succeed to Normandy. According to Orderic, the king then bequeathed England to God, and expressed the hope that his second son, William, would flourish there. The understanding was clearly that he would be the next king. The third son, Henry, was given £5,000 but no land. William I died at Rouen on 9 September 1087.

William II 'Rufus', 1087–1100

1087–1088

Rufus was about 27 at the time of his father's death. He crossed to England after hearing his father's bequest, gave an explanatory letter from his father to Lanfranc, the archbishop of Canterbury, and was consecrated at Westminster on 26 September 1087.

With Robert as the new duke and William as the new king, Normandy and England were now in separate hands, and by the beginning of 1088, Rufus faced a nationwide coalition of leading magnates determined to fight for Robert's claim to the English throne. Of the ten greatest baronial landholders in Domesday Book, six were on the rebels' side. They were led by Odo of Bayeux, who had been released from prison on the Conqueror's death. The main centres of revolt were in the south-east, particularly in Kent, Odo's stronghold, and in the south-west, although leading northern barons such as the bishop of Durham and Robert de Mowbray were involved, too. Rufus dealt vigorously with his uncle, who held out first at Rochester and then at Pevensey before he was banished and disinherited. With the failure of the south-eastern rising, that in the south-west soon collapsed.

1089–1095

As soon as he was supreme in England, Rufus set about reuniting Normandy and England under his sole leadership. His first expedition to Normandy after becoming king took place in February 1091 and led to a truce with his brother, whereby each agreed to become the heir of the other if either died childless. In reality, Rufus now had the upper hand over Robert. Both brothers then returned to England in August to deal yet again with King Malcolm of Scotland who had invaded Northumbria in May. A settlement was reached in September as a result of which Malcolm did homage to the English king and surrendered to him his son Duncan as a hostage. Rufus had to return to the north again in 1092 to deal with disruption in Cumbria, an area ruled hitherto by a lord dependent on the King of Scotland, and during this campaign he began the construction of a castle at Carlisle. Also, according to the *Anglo-Saxon Chronicle*, he sent from the south 'many peasant people back there with their wives and cattle to live there to cultivate the land'.[18]

In 1093, the king fell ill and his death was widely expected. In fear of his soul, Rufus made various promises about his future conduct and he also agreed to appoint Anselm to the archbishopric of Canterbury, which had been vacant since the death of Lanfranc in 1089.[19] Anselm, abbot of Le Bec, was a renowned philosopher and scholar with a reputation for holiness. He was reluctant to take the office, but he was eventually consecrated in December 1093. Rufus recovered from his illness only to find himself confronted once more by problems from Scotland. King Malcolm complained that the king had broken the terms of the treaty of 1091; so when William snubbed Malcolm by summoning him to his court and then refusing to see him, an offended King of Scotland returned north and began raiding once more in northern England. Then, on 13 November 1093, Malcolm was ambushed near Alnwick by Robert de

Mowbray, earl of Northumbria, and killed, together with Edward, his son and heir. His wife, Margaret, the sister of Edgar *aetheling*, died very shortly afterwards. This led to chaos in the Scottish kingdom. The throne was seized by Malcolm's brother, Donald Ban, whilst Malcolm's son, Duncan, who had been at the English court since 1091, tried his luck with English support. He drove out his uncle and ruled for a time as Duncan II, but he was killed in 1094 and Donald Ban resumed the kingship.

Also at the end of 1093, Rufus's relationship with his brother Robert fell apart once again. The English king crossed to Normandy in March 1094 and soon afterwards summoned the English *fyrd* to assemble, ready to come and assist him abroad. Once it had gathered, however, the king's chief minister, Ranulf Flambard, took from each of the men the ten shillings they had been given by their districts for their maintenance and sent them home. The money was better spent on experienced mercenaries. The campaign dragged on inconclusively until the end of the year when Rufus was forced to return home because of the second major rebellion of his reign. The leader of this conspiracy was Robert de Mowbray, earl of Northumbria. Why he rebelled is unclear; he was certainly very powerful, with lands in southern England as well as the north, and it is possible that he was aggrieved about the way the king had denied his claims to certain lands and castles within his earldom. In any event, the earl managed to draw other leading nobles into his revolt, including the earl of Shrewsbury and the count of Eu. Even so, Rufus marched north and dealt masterfully with the situation. He besieged Newcastle, captured and imprisoned Robert de Mowbray and extracted a large payment from the earl of Shrewsbury to enable the latter to regain the king's favour. Rufus then summoned all his tenants-in-chief to appear at his court at Christmas. The court was to be held at Windsor, significantly the same place where Earl Robert was imprisoned.

1095–1100

Pope Urban II's speech at Clermont in November 1095 changed the fortunes of England and Normandy. Rufus never showed any signs of wanting to go to the Holy Land, but his brother Robert was a leading participant on the First Crusade. This meant leaving his duchy behind and so a deal between the two brothers was essential. During the summer of 1096, Rufus agreed to lend Robert £6,666 and take Normandy as a pledge for repayment. The money was raised by harsh taxation in England, and in September 1096 Rufus crossed to Normandy with it and Robert departed for Jerusalem.

The suppression of a Welsh revolt in 1097 aside, Rufus spent much of the rest of his reign defending Normandy from external attack. King Philip of France's heir, Louis, was flexing his muscles in the Vexin, on the border between Normandy and the French royal lands, and the

DEBATE 3
Was William Rufus murdered?

William Rufus was killed by an arrow while hunting in the New Forest on 2 August 1100. Contemporaries noted that these violent events were presaged by supernatural ones, and historians have been intrigued by the circumstances of the king's death. It has even been suggested that Rufus was the victim of a ritual killing by devotees of a pagan fertility cult.[1] Such speculation is wild; however, the idea that the king was the victim of a murderous conspiracy is not completely fanciful. Behind it, perhaps, was the king's younger brother, Henry, or some of his supporters. The course of events immediately after Rufus's death could certainly give rise to suspicion. The man usually thought to have shot the fatal arrow, Walter Tirel, lord of Poix, immediately fled to his lands in France; and Henry, who was in the royal hunting party when the king died, left it in order to secure the royal treasury at Winchester and claim the throne for himself. Conspiracy theorists have also pointed to the imminence of Robert Curthose's return from crusade in the summer of 1100 and the need for Henry to act quickly if he was to stake any claim to the throne. Also, it has been suggested that, during his reign, Henry I showed particular favour to certain families, including the Clares and the Giffords who were related by marriage to Walter Tirel. However, Hollister did most to discredit notions of a plot. Hunting accidents were far from uncommon, and it was only prudent for a potential successor to act quickly on learning of his predecessor's death. Hollister also showed that the Clares and the Giffords were shown no more favour by Henry I than other high-ranking, prestigious families.[2] One contemporary, moreover, claimed to have heard Walter Tirel swear repeatedly that he had not been near the king when he was shot.[3] Rufus's latest biographer follows Hollister in concluding that the king's death was an accident.[4] However, in Mason's view, Rufus's ambitions in Normandy and Aquitaine were enough to worry the king of France and the ruler of Anjou; they had as much to gain from his death as Henry and his supporters. According to Mason, 'there are grounds for suspicion that William Rufus died in consequence of a French-inspired plot, engineered through the double agent Walter Tirel'.[5] The idea that Rufus was assassinated refuses to go away.

1 M. Murray, *The God of the Witches*, 2nd edn (1952).
2 C.W. Hollister, 'The Strange Death of William Rufus', *Speculum*, XLVIII (1973), pp. 637–53.
3 Suger, *Deeds of Louis the Fat*, trans. Richard C. Cusimano and John Moorhead (Washington, 1992), p. 28.
4 Barlow, *William Rufus*, ch. 8.
5 Mason, 'William Rufus and the Historians', pp. 17–20.

count of Anjou was a threat in Maine, too. During the winter of 1097–8, the king managed to secure some degree of control over Maine and he held his own against Louis; and 'by 1099 Rufus had completely restored the territorial position which his father had left. That was no trivial achievement.'[20] He had also transformed the situation in Scotland, albeit at a distance. In October 1097, on the king's orders, Edgar *aetheling* had travelled north, deposed Donald Ban, who had taken the throne after the death of his brother Malcolm III in 1093, and replaced him with Edgar, Malcolm's eldest surviving son and the *aetheling*'s nephew. In the spring of 1099, Rufus returned to England, perhaps to attend the opening of the great hall he had built at Westminster. He then embarked upon a light-ning expedition to Maine whence he returned to indulge in some hunt-ing in the New Forest. Orderic Vitalis and William of Malmesbury even report that William was negotiating with Duke William IX of Aquitaine, who wanted to go on crusade: an arrangement similar to that entered into between William and Robert over Normandy may have been envis-aged.[21] Before any such plan could take effect, on 2 August 1100 whilst out hunting, Rufus was killed by an arrow shot by Walter Tirel, lord of Poix, and buried at Winchester. Whether accident or assassination (and almost certainly the former), the main beneficiary of Rufus's death was his younger brother, Henry, who had been on the hunting expedition when the king had fallen.

Henry I, 1100–1135

1100–1101

Immediately after Rufus's death Henry rushed to Winchester and secured the royal treasury. Then, on 5 August 1100, he was crowned king at Westminster by the bishop of London (Anselm, archbishop of Canterbury, was still in exile). After another month, Robert of Normandy arrived back in his duchy from crusade. He was rich and a hero, and Normandy sub-mitted to him without a problem. Kingdom and duchy were in separate hands once more.

   In an attempt to gain the support he needed at the start of his reign, Henry issued a 'charter of liberties' at his coronation in which he prom-ised to abandon the unjust practices of William II.[22] And to further distance himself from Rufus's regime, he imprisoned Ranulf Flambard in the Tower. He also wrote a submissive letter begging Anselm to return from exile (he came back in September), and in November he married Edith, the daughter of Malcolm, King of Scotland and Queen Margaret. Edith was also the niece of Edgar *aetheling* and, therefore, the representa-tive of the Old English royal line. On her consecration, she adopted the name Matilda.

In the summer of 1101, Duke Robert made his move against England. Ranulf Flambard had fled to his side after escaping from captivity, and the duke also had influential support within England from some of the country's most powerful magnates: the earls of Surrey and Buckingham and the three Montgomery brothers, Robert of Bellême ('the single most powerful Norman after the royal family'[23]), Arnulf and Roger. For his part, Henry had recruited the support of the count of Flanders, Robert, who promised to supply the king with 1,000 knights in return for an annual pension of £500; he also had the backing of the English Church and could summon the English *fyrd*.

Robert landed unexpectedly at Portsmouth late in July 1101, and eventually the two armies confronted each other at Alton near Winchester. No battle was fought and settlement terms were embodied in the so-called 'Treaty of Alton'. Robert renounced his claim to the English throne, whilst Henry surrendered his claims to Normandy and agreed to pay his brother £2,000 a year. Each agreed to be the other's heir in default of other issue, to forgive all their enemies and allow them to keep their lands.

1102–1106

Henry did not stick to the terms of the treaty. In 1102 he deprived Robert of Bellême of his vast English estates and drove him and his brothers into exile. He also had not abandoned his ambition to rule both England and Normandy, and once his hold over his new kingdom was secure, the conquest of the duchy became his primary objective.

From 1103, Henry set about acquiring allies. The counts of Brittany, Flanders, Anjou and Maine were all bought off with money payments or advantageous marriages. Then, after a brief trip to Normandy in 1104, Henry invaded the duchy for the first time in the following year. Calling on his vassals and allies to support him, he secured control of the western part of the duchy before returning to England. In June 1106, he invaded for the second time and was joined by the counts of Maine and Brittany. In September Henry began the siege of the castle of Tinchebrai, which was held by one of Duke Robert's most important supporters, his cousin, William of Mortain (William was the son of Robert of Mortain, the Conqueror's half-brother). Robert came to relieve the castle, and after negotiations failed, battle was joined. Bucking the contemporary trend, the victory was won by Henry with an army made up largely of footsoldiers; Robert's cavalry, lances couched in crusading style, made little impression. The duke was captured and, like William of Mortain, imprisoned for the rest of his life (he died in 1134). His young son William 'Clito', born in October 1102, was also seized during the rout and given in wardship to the count of Maine.

1106–1124

After Tinchebrai, Henry was supreme in England and Normandy. However, he soon faced a new set of adversaries, all more powerful and aggressive than their predecessors. King Philip of France died in 1108 and was succeeded by his son Louis VI; in 1109, Count Fulk IV of Anjou died and was succeeded by his son, Fulk V; and in 1111 Count Robert of Flanders died and was succeeded by his son, Baldwin VII. But the most prominent 'spectre at the feast' was William 'Clito'. He was determined to pursue his own claims to England and Normandy, but he was also a useful tool for Henry's other enemies: 'It was very easy for them to throw a virtuous cloak over their rebellion by claiming to be supporting the rightful claims of William Clito.'[24]

In defence of Normandy, Henry fought three major wars between 1106 and 1135.

1109–1113

Henry achieved some limited success allied with the counts of Brittany, Flanders and Blois against Louis VI, the count of Anjou and other disgruntled Normans, including the ever troublesome Robert of Bellême. Robert was arrested and imprisoned for life by Henry in 1112. A truce was made by Henry with Louis VI and Count Fulk of Anjou in 1113.

1116–1119

Henry, supported by the counts of Blois and Brittany, fought against Louis VI and the counts of Anjou and Flanders. Henry, also facing rebellion in Normandy, was defeated by Count Fulk of Anjou at Alençon in 1118. Henry's hold on his French lands had been seriously weakened. However, Fulk wanted to go on crusade and needed peace before he could leave; so a marriage was arranged between Henry's son, William, and Fulk's daughter, whose dowry was to be the county of Maine. Henry's position was further strengthened in 1119 when he decisively defeated Louis VI at the battle of Brémule.

Then, on 25 November 1120, Henry's long-term plans were dealt a disastrous blow. The king's only legitimate son, William, was drowned with his companions in the so-called 'Wreck of the White Ship' during a crossing from Normandy to England. Henry's daughter, Matilda, was now his nearest heir, but the claims of William Clito to the Anglo-Norman succession were now bound to gather strength. In an attempt to produce another son, Henry married Adeliza of Louvain early in 1121 (his first wife, Matilda of Scotland, had died in 1118). Henry and Adeliza had no children and the question of the succession remained unresolved.

1123–1124

After marching to the north of England in 1122 and beginning the construction of the keep at Carlisle castle (a move which reasserted royal authority in Cumberland), Henry took on Louis again. He was supported this time by Theobald, count of Blois, and his brother, Stephen, Godfrey, duke of Lorraine and the emperor, Henry V, who had been married to Henry's daughter, Matilda, since 1114. Against them on Louis' side were some Norman rebels, Fulk of Anjou (who wanted to recover Maine after the death of William, the king's son, in 1120) and William Clito. The Norman rebels and their French supporters were decisively defeated by Henry's troops at the battle of Bourgthéroulde in 1124.

1125–1135

In 1125, after the death of her husband, Emperor Henry V, Matilda was recalled by her father from Germany. Then at his Christmas court of 1126–7 Henry made his barons, Stephen of Blois amongst them, swear to accept his daughter as his heir. At the same time, the French king married William Clito to his wife's half-sister and granted him the Vexin. Then, after the murder of Charles, count of Flanders in March 1127, Louis was able to force William on to the barons of Flanders as their new count. This was a direct threat to Henry, who therefore began to look for a powerful new husband for his daughter who would support her claim to the throne on his death. At the end of 1127, therefore, Matilda was betrothed to Geoffrey, heir to the county of Anjou, with Geoffrey agreeing to succeed Henry as king and duke if the latter failed to have a son. In June 1128, Matilda and Geoffrey were married. Then, fortuitously for them and the king, William Clito was killed in Flanders in July.

Matilda and Geoffrey produced a son, Henry, in March 1133. A second son, Geoffrey, was born in 1134. At this point, however, Matilda and Geoffrey fell out with the king. Geoffrey demanded control of some Norman castles and the homage of the Norman barons; and his wife wanted a secure foothold in the duchy before her father died. Henry refused their requests and, in response, Geoffrey invaded Normandy. With this dispute still unresolved, Henry died on 1 December 1135, aged about 67. It is possible that, as death approached, he had released his magnates from the oaths they had sworn to his daughter and her husband.

Stephen, 1135–1154

1135–1141

Stephen was the son of Stephen, count of Blois and Adela, daughter of William I. He had spent most of his youth in England, and had been richly patronised by Henry I; by 1135 he was count of Mortain and the holder of extensive estates in east and north-west England. He had also married, in 1125, Matilda, the heiress to the rich and strategically-vital county of Boulogne. He was one of the greatest men in the Anglo-Norman realm, and he may have been awaiting King Henry's death with anticipation for some time. Certainly, the prospect of a Norman–Angevin alliance reinforced by the wealth of England threatened the security of Stephen's home county of Blois, and he would almost certainly have discussed the possibility of making a bid for the throne with his elder brother, Count Theobald, before 1135.

On Henry I's death, Stephen, in Boulogne, was better-placed than Matilda, who was fighting in Normandy, to make a bid for the throne. He landed in England early in December 1135. On arriving in London soon afterwards, Stephen was acclaimed king by the citizens there. He also had the influential support of his brother, Henry of Blois, bishop of Winchester. Henry was instrumental in persuading Archbishop William of Canterbury to consecrate Stephen at Canterbury on 22 December. He also secured the support of Henry I's chief minister, Roger, bishop of Salisbury and his powerful family. Stephen was accepted as duke by the barons of Normandy, too, although he was not their first choice. Initially on Henry I's death, they had sought assistance against Geoffrey and Matilda from Stephen's brother, Theobald. However, on hearing that Stephen had become king in England, the Anglo-Norman baronage switched their allegiance to him and Theobald returned home.

Late in 1135, King David I of Scotland invaded northern England and occupied Cumberland and Northumberland in support of the claims of his niece, the Empress Matilda, to the English crown. In the early weeks of 1136 Stephen marched north and a truce was arranged at Durham. Then, at his Oxford court at Easter 1136, Stephen was attended by three archbishops and sixteen bishops from England, Wales and Normandy, five earls and more than two dozen other significant barons. Many more men of influence and standing would have been present, too. But although he had been accepted as king by those who mattered, long-term stability was elusive. There was a serious rising in the Welsh marches in mid-1136, and fighting continued in Normandy for much of the year. Stephen left his deputies to deal with the deteriorating situation in Wales and did not visit Normandy in person until March 1137. Once there, he stayed for nine months during which he secured the recognition of King Louis VI of France and agreed a three-year truce with Geoffrey of Anjou. However, Stephen had failed to deal the Angevin cause a decisive blow.

Early in 1138, David of Scotland invaded again, and whilst Stephen pushed him back with a march north in February, he could not stay long and David attacked once more in April. Then, in May 1138, Robert, earl of Gloucester, one of England's most powerful barons, declared his support for Matilda's claim to the throne. He was one of the illegitimate sons of Henry I and Matilda's half-brother. His English lands lay mainly in the west. By the summer of 1138 there were risings against Stephen in all parts of his lands, and on this occasion he and his deputies were up to the task. The rebels were defeated in the Welsh marches, and in Normandy Robert of Gloucester and Geoffrey of Anjou were kept at bay. Then in England, near Northallerton in Yorkshire, on 22 August 1138 English forces under the authority of Thurstan, archbishop of York, defeated the Scots at the battle of the Standard. A more permanent peace was achieved in April 1139 when King David's son, Henry, was made earl of Northumbria. Stephen's reaction to the several threats of 1138 has been described as 'a military achievement of the first rank, and [it] outmatched the campaigns of all of Stephen's predecessors since the Conqueror's great wars of the 1070s'.[25]

The year 1139 was a central one in Stephen's reign. The family of Roger, bishop of Salisbury controlled the main departments of English government. Roger himself had been the chief minister of Henry I and still oversaw the royal administration, and his son, also called Roger, was chancellor; two of his nephews, Nigel and Alexander, were respectively bishop of Ely and royal treasurer, and bishop of Lincoln. They were immensely powerful in terms of land, too, and controlled many castles across central England. In the summer of 1139 rumours were circulating that they were about to declare their support for Matilda's claim to the throne, and they were summoned to court at Oxford and ordered to surrender their castles. When a fight broke out at court involving their followers, the two Rogers and Bishop Alexander were arrested whilst Bishop Nigel escaped. Roger and his family were the victims of a court conspiracy led by the Beaumont family, Stephen's closest supporters at the time. Then, on 30 September 1139, Matilda and Robert of Gloucester landed on the south coast near Arundel and civil war began. Robert made straight for Bristol and his west-country heartland, leaving Matilda at Arundel. There she soon found herself surrounded by Stephen's army, but he allowed her to go free and join up with Robert at Bristol. During 1140, support for the Empress became more widespread and public, but no military advantage was gained by either side.

Some time before Christmas 1140, the castle of Lincoln was seized by Ranulf, earl of Chester and his half-brother, William de Roumare. Ranulf's centres of power lay in northern England and the north midlands, and his actions at Lincoln may have been a protest against Stephen's generous treatment of Henry, earl of Northumbria, in 1139, as well as an attempt to make good his long-held claim to the castle. Stephen marched to the castle and reached a settlement, presumably feeling that the earl was too important a man to alienate. But he was too generous, granting Ranulf control over the castle as well as what has been described as 'a great corridor of influence from Cheshire across the north midlands and into southern Lincolnshire'. At his Christmas court, it has been suggested, Stephen probably encountered a storm of protest from other magnates about his reckless prodigality.[26] Thinking better of what he had done, the king returned to Lincoln in January 1141 and laid siege to the castle. Ranulf managed to escape and looked for support to his father-in-law, Robert of Gloucester. Ranulf and Robert led a large army to Lincoln at the beginning of February. On the morning of the 2nd, battle was joined. All contemporary accounts of the battle stress the king's personal bravery and impressive martial skill, but his forces were outnumbered and after a brief and bitter struggle he was felled by a rock thrown at his helmet and captured. Defeat at Lincoln was a humiliating disaster for Stephen. Suddenly, it seemed inevitable that Matilda would become queen.

'Until the defeat [at Lincoln, Stephen] remained in control of the bulk of his kingdom and his court while the number of Angevin adherents remained small . . . After Lincoln, Stephen's chances of victory evaporated for good and the balance of support tipped away from him – first towards neutralism and then towards the Angevin cause.'[27] However, immediately after Lincoln supporters did not flock to the Empress's banner. Vital to any chance she had of taking the crown was control of Winchester and London, the homes of the royal treasury and the royal administration respectively. Her progress was slow. She eventually entered London in the summer after the Keeper of the Tower, Geoffrey de Mandeville, was bought off with an earldom. But she soon offended the influential Londoners by refusing to confirm their commercial privileges and by making extortionate financial demands of her own. They sent messages to Stephen's supporters, led by his queen, also called Matilda, in Kent, and on 24 June the citizens drove the Empress and her supporters out of the city.

Bishop Henry of Winchester, who had gone over to the Empress after Lincoln but soon returned to his brother's side, was attacked at Winchester by Matilda in August 1141. Her forces in turn were hemmed in by the queen's, and a double siege ensued from which the Empress and her uncle, King David of Scotland, just managed to escape. Many of her followers were seized, including Earl Robert of Gloucester. A deal was then struck by the two sides whereby, on 1 November 1141, the king was freed in return for Robert's release.

1142–1148

This is the period when the so-called 'Anarchy' was at its height and when civil war afflicted parts of England. It is a period of confusing detail and few decisive moments; no battles, but much siege warfare based around the castles of each side's supporters. Individuals used the political vacuum to pursue their private disputes, and such conduct only made the war more difficult to end. Certainly Stephen prosecuted his campaigns with great vigour. However, despite this and the deaths of some of Matilda's most influential supporters (most notably Robert of Gloucester in October 1147), and the Empress's departure from England in the spring of 1148, the king lacked the resources and the support required to inflict a final, telling blow and England remained divided. Indeed, by this time the tide of events was beginning to turn against Stephen. He was increasingly confined within a restricted area of southern and eastern England. And across the Channel, large parts of Normandy had submitted to Geoffrey of Anjou after Lincoln and in 1143–4 he had finally overrun the rest of the duchy. He was now duke of Normandy as well as count of Anjou.

1148–1154

Although he never came to England himself, Count Geoffrey did allow his son Henry to travel there in 1142, 1147 and 1149. But by the time he arrived for the fourth time in 1153, the situation had been transformed. Henry had become duke of Normandy in 1149 and count of Anjou on his father's death in 1151. In the following year, he had also become duke of Aquitaine by marrying Eleanor, countess of Aquitaine. This marriage took place only six weeks after Eleanor had been divorced by Louis VII. All of a sudden, Henry was in control of most of France.

Henry's marriage to Eleanor had angered King Louis, who organised a coalition from both sides of the Channel, the members of which were all threatened in some way by recent events. Louis soon withdrew ill from the fray, but Henry was as bold as he was fortunate, and in January 1153 he landed in England to resurrect the Angevin claim to the throne. The two sides manoeuvred inconclusively for much of the year, but the stuffing was finally knocked out of the royalist cause when Stephen's son Eustace died in August 1153. This finally ruined the king's plans for the succession (the English bishops had already refused to confirm Eustace as heir to the kingdom in 1152) and almost certainly added to his personal woes after the death of his wife in May 1152. Thus, although he had another son, William, there was little enthusiasm on the part of Stephen or his supporters to carry on the struggle. In fact, there was no willingness on the part of the English barons to carry on fighting for either side. So, by the Treaty of Winchester of November 1153, both sides agreed to lay down their arms, and Stephen recognised Henry as his heir in return for lifelong possession of the throne. Stephen's son William was allowed to keep his family lands in England and Normandy but had to abandon his claim to the throne.[28] Henry then returned to Normandy, but he did not have to wait long to become king. Stephen died on 25 October 1154 and Henry was consecrated at Westminster on 19 December.

DEBATE 4
Was there 'Anarchy' in Stephen's reign?

During Stephen's reign, the *Anglo-Saxon Chronicle* claimed, 'there was nothing but disturbance and wickedness and robbery, for forthwith the powerful men who were traitors rose against him'.[1] On the basis of comments like
this, in the late nineteenth century the civil war of Stephen's reign was
labelled 'the Anarchy'; and for most of the twentieth century, the label
stuck. The standard view was that Stephen was weak and unable to control
his barons. They for their part were innately violent and unscrupulous; they
took advantage of the absence of strong central authority to pursue their
selfish interests. However, over the last thirty years, this consensus has been
challenged.[2] For one thing, the troubles of 1139–53 were intermittent and
they never involved the whole kingdom to the same extent; indeed, many
parts of England remained untouched by military activity throughout the
reign. Moreover, at no stage did England simply fall apart. The social and
political order remained intact and the opposing sides in the conflict fought
with clear objectives. Within his restricted sphere of direct control, Stephen
carried out his normal kingly responsibilities, and both David of Scotland
and Robert of Gloucester were praised by contemporaries for keeping order
within theirs. Certainly, individual barons were violent, but it is now possible to argue that they acted in order to establish local stability, not in order
to gain independence from the king or prey upon the defenceless. Whilst
important, such views should not be pressed too far. Stephen's England was
a much more violent place than the England of Henry I and Henry II. In
those parts of the country most directly affected by the civil war, towns
were sacked, armies plundered and many innocent (mostly peasant) lives
were ruined. And although they should not be damned as a class, some
barons were indeed thugs who exploited Stephen's difficulties to gain land
and inflict pain. Stephen's best recent biographer, David Crouch, claims
that 'Stephen's misfortune was to be the successor of Henry I and the
predecessor of Henry II, both the darlings of the school of Anglo-American
constitutionalist and administrative historians who dominated the writing
of history between the 1870s and the 1970s.'[3] But whilst there is much to
be said for this view, Stephen was still an inadequate king. He failed to
hold his inheritance together, and the kingdom he left to Henry II was
impoverished and traumatised.

1 *EHD II*, p. 209.
2 A recent stimulating, if perhaps over-sympathetic, account of Stephen's reign
  is Stringer, *The Reign of Stephen*.
3 Crouch, *The Reign of King Stephen*, p. 342.

Notes

1 *NC*, p. 39.
2 *NC*, p. 41; *OV* ii, p. 203.
3 *NC*, p. 41.
4 Bates, *William the Conqueror*, p. 100.
5 *NC*, pp. 73, 100–1.
6 *NC*, p. 101.
7 Bates, *William the Conqueror*, p. 103.
8 *NC*, p. 102.
9 *NC*, p. 74.
10 *NC*, pp. 74, 103.
11 *NC*, p. 74.
12 *NC*, pp. 75–6.
13 *OV* ii, pp. 356–61.
14 *NC*, pp. 77–8.
15 *NC*, p. 78.
16 Ibid.
17 *EHD II*, pp. 305–14.
18 *EHD II*, p. 177.
19 Ibid.
20 Barlow, *Feudal Kingdom*, p. 135.
21 *OV* v, p. 280; *EHD II*, p. 318.
22 *EHD II*, pp. 432–4.
23 Crouch, *The Normans*, p. 174.
24 Ibid., p. 185.
25 Ibid., p. 256.
26 Crouch, *The Reign of King Stephen*, p. 139.
27 Ibid., p. 135.
28 *EHD II*, pp. 436–9.

6

Ruling the Kingdom, 1066–1154

The Norman kings inherited a sophisticated and powerful system of royal administration from their Anglo-Saxon predecessors. Not surprisingly, therefore, they left much of it intact. Royal rule was as energetically personal a business after 1066 as it had been before. The king's relations with his lay and ecclesiastical nobility remained fundamental in determining the course of political events. The basic structure of government stayed largely the same, too: the royal household was still at the heart of affairs and, in the localities, sheriffs in their shires and reeves in their hundreds continued to bear their Old English responsibilities. There were changes to this system after 1066, however. Modification and experimentation were necessary for various reasons. For at least several decades after Hastings, the Norman kings remained unwelcome military occupiers of a foreign and unfamiliar land. Conquest, pacification and assimilation were slow, difficult and often painful processes. Moreover, for the first time since Cnut's reign, the king of England had more to think about than England alone: for most of the first century after 1066, he was Duke of Normandy, too, and this meant that he had to divide his time between his two different principalities. The defence of their cross-Channel lands against internal opponents and external enemies was therefore the central preoccupation of William I, his sons and Stephen; and in order to defend them effectively they needed money. Indeed, it was the king's need for cash with which to fight his wars which resulted in the most profound changes to the system of English royal government after 1066. Or, in the famous words of a great medieval historian, 'The whole history of the development of Anglo-Norman administration is intelligible only in terms of the scale and pressing needs of war finance.'[1]

King and nobility

After 1066 there was little change to the theoretical authority of the English king. Only he could make laws which applied to the whole of his kingdom. Only he could raise money on a national scale to fight wars. Certain types of legal case ('royal pleas') could only be heard by the king or his judges. He was also set apart by special ceremonies and symbols. Central to the coronation ceremony (more important indeed than the placing of the crown on the king's head) was his anointing with holy oil on his chest and arms, and chrism on his head. This established the sacred nature of his office and divine approval for his rule. Next, the king was girded with a sword with which to defend the Church and protect the weak, and then he was crowned and invested with ring, sceptre and rod. This image of the king enthroned in majesty was imprinted on one side of his seal; on the other he rode his warhorse, sword in hand. It was at the coronation, too, that the king made certain solemn promises: to protect the Church, to act justly towards his people and to abolish bad laws and maintain good ones. Henry I and Stephen embodied these promises in written charters; William I and William II may have done something similar.[2]

Periodically, these or similar rituals (except the anointing, which only happened once) were repeated. Usually known as 'crown-wearings', the king used these special occasions to display himself in an atmosphere of public splendour. Edward the Confessor may have begun to celebrate in this way, but the *Anglo-Saxon Chronicle* records that William I wore his crown three times a year, at Easter at Winchester, at Whitsun at Westminster and at Christmas at Gloucester; and William of Malmesbury makes it clear that feasting was an important part of the ritual. According to him, 'the dinners in which [William I] took part on the major festivals were costly and splendid . . . all great men of whatever walk of life were summoned to them by royal edict so that envoys from other nations might admire the large and brilliant company and the splendid luxury of the feast.'[3] On these occasions, all the great men of the realm would gather with the king, and the so-called *Laudes Regiae* were sung, as they had been at the coronation. These asked for 'peace, safety and victory for the king of the English, crowned by God'. Such rituals emphasised the uniqueness of the king's position, stressed the divine favour he enjoyed and 'were of immense importance in securing service and stilling revolt'.[4]

The personality of the king remained crucial in determining how effectively he could put his theoretical powers into practice. Ideally, contemporaries thought, the king should be pious, generous, just and a strong warrior. In post-conquest England particularly, where the king was in effect the commander of an occupying army, it was essential that he was determined, ruthless and domineering. To be sure, William I and his sons were all capable politicians; but they were soldiers above all else, prepared to be brutal and violent when necessary. Contemporaries tended not to like them, but, after William I had made it clear between 1066 and 1072 that he was in England for the long haul, they quickly if grudgingly came to respect his authority and fear his wrath. And while William II and Henry I were both tested at the start of their reigns, they soon stamped their authority on the kingdom. For the *Anglo-Saxon Chronicle*, William I 'was a very wise man, and very powerful . . . and stronger than any predecessor of his had been. He was gentle to the good men who loved God, and stern beyond all measure to those people who resisted his will.' William II, by contrast, 'was very strong and fierce to his country and his men and to his neighbours, and very terrible . . . he was always harassing this nation with military service and excessive taxes, for in his days all justice was in abeyance'. However, contemporaries could not deny that he was generous. According to William of Malmesbury, Rufus 'earned the love of hired soldiers for he was lavish in his gifts to them'. In other words, Rufus taxed his subjects so that he could pay mercenaries. This was pragmatic military leadership, not loose prodigality. And as for Henry I, 'He was a good man', the *Anglo-Saxon Chronicle* said, 'and people were in great awe of him. No one dared injure another in his time. He made peace for man and beast.'[5]

Whilst there were differences between them, therefore, the Conqueror and his sons were all forceful, intimidating and resolved to get their will done. Opponents were dealt with decisively, even if they were members of the family: witness the fates of Odo of Bayeux in 1082 and 1088 and Robert of Normandy after 1106. And the brutality of William I's treatment of northern England in 1069–70 quickly became legendary. Stephen, on the other hand, was cast in a different mould. He was widely recognised as a brave soldier and as an affable, good-natured man. He could act decisively and assertively, as his prompt seizure of power on the death of Henry I showed; but William of Malmesbury summed up the ambivalence with which contemporaries viewed him: 'He was a man of energy but little judgement, active in war, of extraordinary spirit in undertaking any difficult task, lenient to his enemies and easily appeased, courteous to all: though you admired his kindness in promising, still you felt his words lacked truth and his promises fulfilment.'[6] Of course, none of these assessments is objective or conclusive, but they reflect more or less contemporary perceptions of these kings which were just as important as the reality. The image they conveyed to their subjects, which was ultimately based on the actions they took, was central to the effective exercise of their authority.

As were the king's relations with his nobility. High politics during this period was the preserve of no more than about 200 rich, landed laymen in addition to the king and his leading churchmen. And the test for the

Norman kings remained the same as it had been for their Anglo-Saxon predecessors: could they dominate their nobles without losing their support? One way of doing this was through the exercise of military discipline and the harsh suppression of opposition. Another was through the distribution of patronage. William I and his sons had at their disposal more territorial resources than any previous kings. They benefited hugely from the way the lands of the Godwin family had been united with the royal demesne when Harold had become king, and the Conqueror's demesne was probably twice the size of the Confessor's. What is more, many of those estates were in areas hitherto untouched by direct royal influence. They also benefited from the fundamental change to the English political landscape that had come about after 1066 as a result of the death and expropriation of the Old English aristocracy. A large proportion of the Anglo-Saxon nobility perished at Hastings and whilst some survived they did not last. Earls Edwin, Morcar and Waltheof were all destroyed by rebellion, whilst other magnates and thegns were simply dispossessed. By 1086, Domesday Book recorded the names of only four English land-holders of any note. The lands of their compatriots had come into the king's hands and been used by him to create a new French aristocracy. At the top of the tree were men like Odo of Bayeux (until his fall in 1082) and Robert of Mortain, William I's half-brothers, and the king's long-term associates, Geoffrey, bishop of Coutances, Roger of Montgomery, William FitzOsbern and William de Warenne. Henry I acted in similar fashion, raising up his illegitimate son Robert to the earldom of Gloucester; whilst his nephew Stephen had acquired the county of Boulogne through marriage and become the richest landholder in south-eastern England by 1135. They profited from loyal service to the king, receiving lands across the conquered territories and becoming fabulously rich as a result. Below men like this were other beneficiaries who received smaller amounts of land from the king, and also a much larger number of men ('sub-tenants') who received land from one of the greater lords in return for a promise of service and loyalty to him. In this way, new structures of power based on landholding were set up across England which linked the king with his tenants and the latter with theirs in a direct and unprecedented way. As will be seen below, moreover, the king's position after 1066 as the ultimate feudal lord meant that he had more than just land to give away. This gave him even more power, but also increased the potential for discord and division.

Another way of keeping members of this new nobility loyal was by including them within the process of decision-making. The king was obliged to listen to and heed the advice of his great men. According to the *Anglo-Saxon Chronicle*, for example, the Domesday survey was commissioned by William I after he had had 'deep speech' with his advisers at Gloucester at Christmas 1085, and its findings may have been confirmed at Salisbury the following year when 'his counsellors came to him' along with all the landholders 'who were of any account over all England' and swore allegiance to the king. More regularly, the Conqueror would have used his crown-wearings to meet his leading men and to discuss the business of the realm.[7] Henry I was doing something similar in 1127 when he ensured that all his great men swore publicly to uphold the claim of his daughter Matilda to the English crown. The danger for the king was that he would draw his advice from too shallow a well, and that he would be accused of favouritism towards some men at the expense of others. Stephen fell into this trap in the early years of his reign when he was influenced heavily by the twin Beaumont brothers, Waleran and Robert. They and their supporters were probably responsible for the whispering campaign at court which led to the downfall of Bishop Roger of Salisbury and his relatives in 1139.

Cross-Channel government

Circumstances were different for the Norman kings after 1066, then, even if the essentials of the job description remained the same. Another novelty arose from the fact that, for most of this period, apart from intervals between 1087–95, 1100–6 and during much of the 1140s and until 1154, the king of England was also the duke of Normandy. This gave him more land to rule, but matters were complicated further because the Norman duke was also the vassal of the king of France and in theory subordinate to him. Until the last quarter of the twelfth century, the French kings were not as strong as their English rivals, and they found it difficult to enforce their rights or impose their notional authority over them. Nevertheless, as Louis VI showed by his support for William Clito, they could still involve themselves in English and Norman affairs in ways which imposed new, mostly financial strains on England after 1066. Secondly, the king now had to deal with an aristocracy which had lands on both sides of the Channel, and that aristocracy wanted to feel that its possessions were safe and secure under a single ruler. The fear of having different lords for their English and Norman lands was a real one, and Orderic Vitalis expressed the concerns felt by the Anglo-Norman baronage in 1087 on the death of William I. It is a concocted speech, but it almost certainly reflected contemporary attitudes:

> What are we to do? Now that our lord is dead, two young men have succeeded and precipitately divided the lordship of England and Normandy. How can we properly serve two lords who are so different and so distant from each other? If we serve Robert . . . worthily, we will offend his brother, William, and we will be stripped by him of our great revenues and large estates in England. On the other hand, if we obey King William fittingly, Duke Robert will deprive us of all our inherited lands in Normandy.[8]

Odo of Bayeux and Robert of Bellême fell from power in 1088 and 1102 respectively because they had supported the claims of Robert of Normandy to hold the kingdom and the duchy together. In 1135, on the death of Henry I, the Norman nobles initially offered the duchy to Theobald, count of Blois, but when they heard that his brother Stephen had already secured England, they abandoned Theobald without delay. According to Orderic, they wanted 'to serve one lord, on account of the great estates that the barons possessed in each region'.[9] It was in the interests of the cross-Channel aristocracy that England and Normandy be ruled by a single man, preferably 'the weakest and least burdensome' of the rival claimants.[10]

Given his responsibilities in Normandy, ways had to be found to keep England well-governed, stable and productive whilst the king was in his duchy. When he was absent, therefore, control of England was delegated to others who acted on the king's behalf. William I, after 1072, spent approximately three-quarters of the rest of his reign abroad, and he was content largely to give responsibility to members of his family or his closest supporters. Thus when he returned to Normandy in 1067, England was left under the control of his half-brother Odo of Bayeux and his friend William FitzOsbern. Archbishop Lanfranc regularly acted as regent later in the reign. Under William II there was less need for a regent because the king made no long visits to Normandy until 1096. However, Ranulf Flambard controlled the day-to-day operations of English government during the last years of the reign whilst the king was abroad, and Orderic Vitalis described him as the 'chief manager of the king's wealth and justice'.[11] He authorised writs, raised money and acted as a judge. Once England and Normandy had been permanently reunited in the hands of Henry I in 1106, problems of cross-Channel government arose again. On one estimate, Henry I spent nearly two-thirds of his reign in Normandy between 1106 and 1135. Until her death in 1118, Henry usually left England in the care of his wife, Matilda, and between 1118 and 1119 his son William took her place.

The king's absences did not just lead to the appointment of regents. As the kings were stretched between the different parts of their cross-Channel realm, and as the demands on England's resources grew, English government became too complex for one individual and his associates to manage. Below the level of the regent, therefore, and by the early 1100s, there had emerged what Hollister has referred to as 'a clearly identifiable body of viceregal administrators' headed by the king's chief minister Roger, bishop of Salisbury. Roger had no formal title within government and his main seat of power was the royal Exchequer. He was an all-round administrator and judge; he had overall responsibility for finance and justice, and so was accustomed to sitting in the royal courts as well as the Exchequer. His career, and that of Ranulf Flambard before him, foreshadowed those of the Angevins' 'chief justiciars'. Overall, indeed, royal government was gradually becoming more profession- alised by 1135, and Roger and his relatives (including his nephew, the treasurer Nigel, who became bishop of Ely in 1133) dominated it for most of Henry's reign and the first years of Stephen's. Below them, too, had emerged a group of dedicated royal servants, some of them, according to Orderic, 'of base stock' and raised 'from the dust' by Henry I.[12] They owed their fortunes to Henry and were conspicuously loyal as sheriffs and judges as a result. As will become clear, therefore, the Norman kings' absenteeism 'solidified rather than sapped royal government since it engendered structures both to maintain peace and extract money in the king's absence'.[13]

The royal household

Every lord had his own household. It contained his family members, friends, followers, armed men, officials, chaplains and servants. The king's household, the *familia regis*, was larger than any other household, and, as it had been under Edward the Confessor and Harold, it was the beating heart of royal authority and central government in England after 1066. Either directly or at a distance the royal household controlled every aspect of governance. It had no fixed form and there were no clear lines separating one part of the household from another; individuals could perform more than one role within it and there was considerable overlap between the different functions outlined here.

The domestic function

On the most basic level, the household was responsible for meeting the daily needs of the king and of those members of his immediate family who were with him at any particular time. Like their Anglo-Saxon prede- cessors, English kings after 1066 were constantly on the move between their estates in England. After 1066, additionally, they had to cross the Channel regularly to visit their continental lands. Wherever the king went, his domestic household, his *domus*, travelled with him. The multi- plicity of functions carried out by the *domus* and its sheer size are revealed by the so-called *Constitutio Domus Regis*, written at the end of Henry I's reign.[14] It lists well over a hundred members of the royal staff and groups them into various departments: the chapel, pantry, larder, buttery and more. Each officer and servant received a daily allowance in a mixture of cash, food, drink and candles. The job of feeding and clothing the king, his wife and their children required a sophisticated level of planning and organisation. The master butler, the larderer and the stewards made sure that there were enough provisions for the king, and that the places where he stayed were prepared in advance for his arrival; the roles of the washerwomen and bathmen are obvious enough. The *domus* had other functions, too. It contained the king's hunting establishment, his hunts-men, dog-handlers and horn-blowers. It also contained the king's chapel, headed by the chancellor and manned by his priests. They took care of the king's spiritual needs, saying mass, hearing confession and keeping his relics.

The administrative function

The staff of the royal chapel also met the king's secretarial needs. At the start of this period, as had been the case under the Anglo-Saxon kings, a large proportion of royal documents, principally charters and writs, were drafted by the royal priests supervised by the chancellor. Under William I, Regenbald, referred to as 'chancellor' towards the end of Edward the Confessor's reign, kept his place for a while, but by the end of 1067 one Herfast was holding the post. He was succeeded by Osmund, who in turn was replaced by Maurice and then Gerard. All of these men were rewarded for their services with bishoprics. Gerard did particularly well. Having continued to serve William II as chancellor, he became bishop of Hereford in about 1096 and was made archbishop of York by Henry I in 1101. Henry I's chancellors were Roger, Waldric, Ranulf and Geoffrey. Only one of these, Ranulf, did not become a bishop, and Roger did best of all, as has been seen. As well as becoming bishop of Salisbury in 1107 (after which he stepped down as chancellor), he was in overall charge of the royal administration by 1110. The chancellor had his subordinates within the chancery, as the *Constitutio* makes clear, most important amongst whom was the master of the writing office. He had the custody of the king's great seal, an impression of which was attached to every document issued in the king's name. The most important of the holders of this office during this period was Ranulf Flambard, who served under Chancellor Maurice during William I's reign and went on to dominate royal government under William II and become bishop of Durham in 1099.

The military function

Constantly in attendance upon the king would have been his household knights, his military *familia*. These men were central to the military organisation of the kingdom and formed 'something between a royal bodyguard . . . and a small standing army'.[15] Some of these were great men of the realm in their own right, who attended the court from time to time. William FitzOsbern served in the military household of William I and was made earl of Hereford in 1067, for example; and Henry I's illegitimate son, Robert, served in his father's *familia* and was made an earl in 1122. However, at the heart of the military *familia* were the knights of more lowly status, perhaps penniless younger sons of minor landed families, who were paid wages by the king and provided with food and shelter at his court. These men were well-trained professional soldiers who provided the core of the royal army in wartime (in 1084–6, 1089–90, 1105–6, 1118–19 and 1124, for example), and garrisoned castles. Their chances in life depended on the rewards they might receive from the king in return for the service they performed, and they were aware of the consequences of failing him. Orderic Vitalis described the anxieties of one of Henry I's knights on the eve of battle in 1124: if we fail to do our duty, he said, 'how shall we ever dare to enter the king's presence? We shall forfeit both our wages and our honour, and . . . shall never again be entitled to eat the king's bread.'[16] The number of knights in attendance at court at any one time would fluctuate, depending on whether the king was on campaign or not, but Orderic's story clearly suggests that it was always large enough to constitute a significant drain on his resources.

The financial function

The king's clothes and bathing equipment were kept in his chamber. The officials of the chamber were also responsible for the safe-keeping of the king's valuables, his robes, plate and jewels. In addition, 'The chamber was the financial office of the itinerant household and, as such, the government's chief spending department.'[17] By the reign of Henry I, it was presided over by the treasurer (Nigel, nephew of Bishop Roger of Salisbury) and the chamberlains, and wherever the king went he would be accompanied by them and followed by carts loaded with barrels and sacks full of silver pennies. In England, most of this money was supplied to the household from the principal royal treasury at Winchester and later London. The king also kept smaller reserves of cash at some of his castles, so that he could draw on them during his travels. Such castle treasuries could be found at Gloucester, Colchester, Salisbury, Oxford and Guildford. Other sums might simply be paid into the chamber as and when they were received, from suitors and petitioners who met the king *en route*. Not all of these sums would have been accounted for at the Exchequer, so it is difficult to get an accurate idea of how much money the king had at any one time.

The judicial function

In its most formal and public capacity, the household formed the king's court or *curia regis*. This was where the king listened to his counsellors, received important visitors, made important announcements and dispensed justice to his tenants and the rest of his subjects. Regularly, when the court was augmented by the presence of great lay and ecclesiastical magnates, the contemporary chronicles refer to a royal council being held. Often these meetings were used for settling some singularly important business: at Gloucester in 1085 William I, after having had 'deep speech' with his counsellors, decided to undertake the Domesday survey; at the council of London in 1107, Henry I brought an end to his quarrel with Archbishop Anselm on the question of royal investiture. Henry, indeed, made a point of taking 'counsel' from his nobles: he probably valued their advice but, as has been seen, this was also a way of keeping his leading subjects in the political loop.

Local government

One obvious change to the English political landscape after 1066 was in the status and role of the earls. Nobody succeeded Harold as earl of Wessex, but during the early years of his reign William I allowed several of the Anglo-Saxon earldoms to survive. However, by the early 1070s, the king had decided to get tough with his new subjects, and for the rest of the reign there were no more than seven earls at any one time. Several earldoms were created during the reigns of William II and Henry I, but others lapsed and there were still only seven by 1135. Gone were the great earldoms of Wessex, Mercia and Northumbria, and as well as stabilising the number of earldoms the Norman kings reduced the number of counties under an individual earl's authority. They had no intention of being dominated by their leading subjects as Edward the Confessor had been. More immediately, William's appointments reflected the new realities of Norman England. His earls were military governors with authority over more compact areas which were dangerous and vulnerable, particularly the so-called 'marches' on the borders of Wales. Thus Roger of Montgomery and Hugh of Avranches had become respectively earls of Shrewsbury and Chester by the early 1070s. Both of these areas were exposed to the threat of Welsh attacks. Odo of Bayeux, William's half-brother, became earl of Kent, a strategically-vital area which guarded the route to the English Channel and Normandy.

Military pragmatism lay behind the creation of the marcher earldoms, just as it was responsible for the emergence of another novel administrative unit, the rapes of Sussex. After 1066 Sussex was a frontier zone as well as the link between England and France. The strategic importance of the county, therefore, cannot be overstated. The Domesday survey shows that, by 1086, Sussex was divided into five separate parts or 'rapes', namely Hastings, Pevensey, Lewes, Bramber and Arundel. Each was a strip of land running from the northern border of the shire to the south coast, and it has been suggested that this shape was adopted to allow the king ease of access from London to the sea and, thence, to Normandy. The rapes were all organised along similar lines. Each was under the control of one of William's leading vassals. Hastings was held by Robert, count of Eu, Pevensey by Robert, count of Mortain, Bramber by William de Braose, Arundel by Roger of Montgomery and Lewes by William de Warenne. Each of these men was a member of the king's inner circle, and had close personal ties to the royal family. Each rape also had a major castle, which was sited near the coast. The Normans' treatment of Sussex was unique, and had no parallels in England or on the continent.

By 1135, the need for military governors had diminished as England and its neighbours had come slowly to accept the reality of Norman rule. Earls were still important, but the title was becoming increasingly honorific. Stephen tried to reverse this trend in the early years of his reign. He created more earldoms than his predecessors (twelve between 1138 and 1140), to the extent that some historians have discerned a royal policy intended, eventually, to create an earl for every shire. By 1141, there were twenty English earldoms in all. What is more, Stephen granted many of these earls real power in the localities as well as titles, so that they acquired overall responsibility for peace-keeping and the exercise of royal authority. Thus Waleran of Meulan, one of the Beaumont twins, was made earl of Worcester to counter-balance the power of Earl Robert of Gloucester in the west country. Appointments such as this, it has been suggested, amounted to a policy of deliberate decentralisation which reflected Stephen's inability to control England in the traditional ways by the late 1130s. In a sense it was certainly something of a return to the Anglo-Saxon system, although the earldoms remained small compared with those of pre-conquest England. Stephen's experiment did not last beyond his capture at Lincoln in 1141. Autonomous earls were a threat to royal authority, not least because their extensive powers allowed them to collect and keep money which would previously have gone to the king; and, in those areas where he was able to exercise effective authority, Stephen attempted to rely for the rest of his reign on what Crouch has called 'regional military governors' who were more closely tied to the king, men such as William of Ypres in Kent and Richard de Lucy in Essex and Middlesex. This was, according to Crouch, 'a step back towards centralisation and away from regionalism'.[18]

Below the earls the Normans introduced new categories of official into the system of local government. Most important amongst these were those men who had custody of royal castles ('castellans') and those who supervised the royal Forest. There was nothing particularly systematic about the appointment of castellans, but they had to be loyal and dependable. Sometimes the sheriff did the job, sometimes the local lord. At other times, men were specifically appointed to these posts. Colchester Castle was placed in the custody of Eudo the steward in 1101, for example. As for officials of the Forest, Judith Green has identified a number of these from the pipe roll for 1129–30: William FitzWalter, constable of

Windsor Castle, had custody of the Forests of Berkshire and the New Forest was in the custody of Waleran, son of William.[19]

Where the sheriff did not carry out these new responsibilities himself, some realignment of jurisdictions was probably necessary in individual cases. However, the sheriff retained his place as by far the most important royal officer in the localities. In theory, the sheriff was still the earl's deputy, and in the areas where an earl retained meaningful authority, on the frontiers in the years after Hastings, and across England during Stephen's early years as king, his authority over the sheriff was maintained. At other times, and as the number of earls and the size of earldoms shrank, the sheriffs' authority increased: 'indeed, their power was never greater than between 1066 and 1100'.[20] The sheriff was responsible for making the annual payment (the 'farm') which each county owed to the king, and he presided over the shire court. He also collected taxes, raised armies, repaired royal castles, transported treasure and more. Essentially, the sheriff was the principal link between the king and the localities: to the former, his job was to collect money and carry out orders sent in the form of royal writs; to the latter, he was the personification of royal authority. Several English sheriffs retained their posts after 1066, such as Tofi of Somerset and Edmund of Hertfordshire, but they were all eventually replaced. The king needed loyal and trustworthy men in posts of such political importance and sensitivity. Many of the Conqueror's sheriffs were substantial barons: Geoffrey de Mandeville, for example, who held lands worth £800 a year, was also sheriff of Middlesex. All the kings of this period appointed members of their household as sheriffs. Others, according to Orderic Vitalis, were raised by Henry I 'from the dust' to positions within the royal administration.[21] Several of the men he names, Geoffrey de Clinton, Rayner of Bath and Hugh of Buckland, for example, became sheriffs. Geoffrey was sheriff of Warwickshire and Rayner of Lincolnshire; Hugh, meanwhile, was sheriff of no fewer than eight separate counties.

Being a sheriff was attractive because it gave a man great status and influence within a local community. But the job could also make a man rich or, in the case of a Geoffrey de Mandeville, richer. It was accepted that during the course of a year the sheriff would collect much more money from the people of his shire than he owed the king by way of his farm. The sheriff could keep the surplus for himself. Not surprisingly, therefore, men were willing to pay for the privilege of becoming a sheriff: in 1130, for example, Robert d'Oilly, sheriff of Oxfordshire, owed the king £266 'for having the county'. Payment for such offices was another lucrative source of income for the king. However, it was also a source of danger as powerful sheriffs could get ideas above their station and become 'over-mighty subjects'. Henry I was certainly aware of this danger. In a writ of about 1108 he criticised those sheriffs who summoned the shire

DEBATE 5
How advanced was Anglo-Norman government?

Historians have always tended to admire William I and his sons. They may not have been attractive personalities, but they possessed the ruthless, decisive qualities required of strong, masterful kings. Henry I, in addition, has been seen, particularly in the pioneering work of Warren Hollister, as an imaginative administrator whose policies and innovative reforms hastened England's progress towards 'modern' centralised government. Henry reformed the unruly royal household, he streamlined the operations of the legal system, he created a new class of professional administrators, and the Exchequer appears for the first time during his reign. That reign also saw increasing literacy and systematisation in government, a trend exemplified by the survival of the pipe roll for 1129–30. Speaking generally about the reign of Henry I, Sir Richard Southern's view was that 'it is here, we feel, that the history of England begins'.[1] Historians of Anglo-Saxon England would certainly disagree with this, and they would also emphasise the size of the debt owed by the Norman kings to their English predecessors. By contemporary standards, England was already intensively governed in 1066. Moreover, the idea that Henry I and his Norman predecessors were efficient administrators has been challenged as no more than a 'myth'. In a powerful article, Warren argued that the Norman kings relied on English servants until around 1100 and made little if any effort to understand the Anglo-Saxon system themselves. When the English administrators died, the innovations which followed amounted to 'an attempt not so much to improve upon the Anglo-Saxon system as to shore it up and stop it collapsing'. The standard of the coinage declined under Henry I, Warren claims; underlying Henry's famous writ of c.1108 concerning the holding of shire and hundred courts is the suggestion that the system was falling apart; the shiring of England, one of the great Anglo-Saxon achievements, came to an abrupt halt after 1066; the opportunity to reassess liability for geld was never taken. Warren does not deny that Henry I's financial system was 'precocious', but overall he concludes that, 'Under the Normans the Anglo-Saxon system became ramshackle. Norman government was a matter of shifts and contrivances.'[2] These are controversial views, and most historians would not agree with them. However, they do provide an important corrective to the idea that England's path towards strong, centralised government was a smoothly untroubled one.

1 R.W. Southern, 'The Place of Henry I in English History', *Proceedings of the British Academy*, 48 (1962), pp. 128–9; reprinted in *Medieval Humanism and Other Studies* (Oxford, 1970).
2 W.L. Warren, 'The Myth of Norman Administrative Efficiency', *Transactions of the Royal Historical Society*, 5th series, 34 (1984), pp. 113–32.

court when they wished and not according to the traditional customs. Only 'I myself', the king said, 'if ever I shall wish it, will cause them to be summoned at my own pleasure'.[22] His policy of making loyal courtiers sheriffs has already been mentioned; this was supposed to ensure that shrievalties remained within his ultimate control, as was his expressed wish that the office should not become hereditary.

Shires remained subdivided into hundreds and wapentakes after 1066, just as they had been before. The role of the hundred remained largely the same, too. Domesday Book records about 730 hundreds and wapentakes. The hundred had its own court which met every month. It was presided over by a reeve appointed by the sheriff (or by the lord's reeve if the hundred was in private hands), and was attended by local landowners who were obliged to appear. Twice a year a special meeting of the hundred court was presided over by the sheriff himself. His principal job was to check that the tithing system was working properly and that every free adult male was a member of a tithing. By the early twelfth century, too, it had acquired the responsibility for the operation of the *murdrum* fine, the penalty payable when a Norman was found dead within its boundaries.

Royal wealth

According to William of Poitiers, Duke William of Normandy's motive for invading England in 1066 'was not the increase of his own wealth and glory but the reform of Christian practice in that land'.[23] Pious though the duke might have been, however, he certainly knew how valuable a prize England was. One indicator of the kingdom's wealth is the amount of money in circulation during the eleventh century. Amounts of geld allegedly levied in the seventy-five years before 1066, which were discussed in Chapter 2, suggest that there were mountains of silver pennies in the kingdom. Indeed, it has been estimated that, in 1086, there were approximately nine million silver pennies in England, worth roughly £37,500. But there was more to England's wealth than coins. Especially in the southern and central regions, the country was fertile and productive. Famines and poor harvests did occur, but in a normal year England produced more grain than it needed to feed its population, and where arable farming was impossible, thousands of sheep grazed on good-quality pasture land and produced meat, milk, cheese and, above all, wool. Other natural resources were available, too: tin from Cornwall, lead from Cumbria, iron ore from the Forest of Dean.

Most of this food and these materials were used to meet the needs of the native English population. Estimates are notoriously unreliable, but there were probably between 2 million and 2.5 million English men, women and children at the time of the Norman Conquest. Something between 6 and 10 per cent of them would have lived in towns, making England a highly urbanised kingdom by contemporary standards. A 'town' in this eleventh-century context has been defined as 'a permanent concentration of population, some hundreds at least, who made their living from a variety of non-agricultural occupations'.[24] The 200 years before 1050 had been a time of urban expansion: more towns were established and more people left the countryside to live in them. Sometimes a town had grown up around one of the fortified *burhs* established by King Alfred and his successors to meet the threat of the Vikings in the ninth and tenth century; others might have become established around a royal mint or near an important church. Royal legislation stipulating that certain types of goods could only be traded in specific places under the supervision of royal officials might also lead to urban development. By 1066, England had more than a hundred towns, about thirty of which had populations of between 1,000 and 5,000. Most were concentrated in southern and particularly eastern England. The most northerly was York. The five most important towns in England in 1066 were Winchester, Norwich and Lincoln, with populations of between 5,000 and 10,000; York with probably more than 10,000 inhabitants; and London with perhaps as many as 25,000.

The Norman Conquest may have interrupted urban expansion in the short term. After the Harrying of the North, for example, the population of York plummeted. Other towns were destroyed at least in part, either as part of the invaders' ravaging tactics or in order to make space for new castles. At Lincoln, for example, 166 houses were demolished in order to build the new castle there. However, in the longer term, the impact of the conquest on English towns was probably a positive one and the brake it put on urban growth only temporary. New towns grew up around post-conquest churches, at Battle in Sussex, for instance, and castles (Newcastle is an obvious example). Newcomers were attracted to English markets because of the commercial opportunities they offered. England's first Jewish community came from Rouen to settle in London shortly after 1066, for example. A hundred years after this, by which time they had settled in towns across England, their main occupation was money-lending; initially, however, they dealt in bullion, bought and sold silver plate and exchanged foreign coins for English ones. And towns along the south coast, Southampton, Pevensey, Sandwich and Chichester, all benefited from an increase in cross-Channel trade. London also grew in part as a consequence of the expansion of England's trading horizons. The increase in the number of towns was to be a marked characteristic of England in the twelfth century.

The range of occupations followed within towns was extensive. With their blacksmiths, leather-workers, potters, tailors, dyers and goldsmiths, they were centres for manufacturing. Because there were also butchers, bakers, brewers and fishmongers among the inhabitants, they were centres of food distribution, both for fellow townspeople and those of their country cousins who came to town to sell their surplus agricultural produce. Most trade was of this kind, locally-based. The towns required food and this led to increases in agricultural production. In return, the traders and craftsmen in the towns met the countryside's needs for professionally-made tools, clothes and the occasional luxury. But there was international trade, too. England exported tin and surplus grain, hides and herrings. Cloth was another export: dyed woollen fabrics as well as luxury hangings and embroidered garments for which England was famous. It was the seamstresses of Kent, after all, who were responsible for the Bayeux Tapestry. However, the most important English export was wool, which was carried across the Channel to be used mainly by the Flemish textile industry. There were imports as well, mostly consumer goods for the better-off: silks, spices and furs had to come from abroad, as did wine and much finished cloth. Such commodities might be brought into the kingdom by foreign traders and merchants, or by Englishmen who had travelled abroad themselves. The demand for such commodities led in turn to the development of ports, not just along the coastline but inland, too, where rivers flowed in from the sea. York, Lincoln and Exeter were all ports at this time.

Important though towns were, most of England's wealth was generated in the countryside, where probably nine out of ten people lived and worked. In Yorkshire, Lincolnshire, eastern England and Kent so-called 'multiple estates' predominated. In these there was a central settlement to which the inhabitants of outlying subsidiary settlements were obliged to render goods, money and, less often, labour services. In much of southern and midland England, by contrast, most people lived on a 'manor'. This typically consisted of a number of houses grouped together, a church or chapel and perhaps a large house belonging to the lord. Such an arrangement constituted the classical 'nucleated' village. The village would have been surrounded by two or three large fields, one of which would be left uncultivated or 'fallow' every year. The fallow field would serve as grazing land for the villagers' livestock; the animals in their turn would restore its fertility with their manure. Most of this land would have been the lord's. He would have farmed some of it himself to obtain food and saleable surplus produce. This was his 'demesne' land – the land he kept 'in hand'. Other parts of the lord's land would be leased out to tenants, whose lands, like the lord's demesne, would be spread across the three open fields. They would pay him rent, in cash, produce or labour. All of those tenants who worked the land with their own hands can be described as 'peasants', but there were different designations within this general term. *Villani* or 'villeins' make up 40 per cent of the rural population recorded in Domesday Book. A typical villein would hold a 'yardland' (thirty acres) or half a yardland (fifteen acres). He would produce enough food for himself and his family, as well as a small surplus which he could sell. The 'cottagers' were the next largest group recorded in 1086 – about 30 per cent of the total. Each cottager would probably hold between three and five acres. He would not be self-sufficient, and would hire himself out to work on the lands of better-off neighbours. The lowest group of all were the slaves, who made up probably 10 per cent of the rural population in 1086. All of these men were 'unfree' to some extent. Attendance at the manorial court, presided over by the lord's bailiff, would have been compulsory. The villeins and cottagers would be obliged to work on their lord's demesne lands for perhaps two or three days a week; more at harvest time. The slaves had to do what they were told; if they did not they could be punished by their lord with mutilation or death. The number of slaves was declining by the end of the eleventh century, both because the Church disapproved of enslavement and because it cost the lord money to support them. Slavery had all but died out in England by the middle of the twelfth century.

It was the king's task to exploit the resources of his kingdom as effectively as he could. After all, no matter what his powers might be in theory, he could do little without money. His daily needs had to be met: food, clothes and the like. A king was constantly on show, too: ceremonial, display and the luxuries associated with courtly life were expensive. The king also had to reward his followers and act charitably, and sometimes there were unexpected costs, such as the £6,666 William II agreed to pay his brother Robert for control of Normandy in 1095. Most importantly, though, the king needed money to meet the cost of warfare of one kind or another. There were regular outgoings, such as the wages of the king's knightly *familia*. But all of the kings of this period spent lengthy periods on campaign, and when a campaign was under way and mercenary troops needed payment, the king's costs rocketed. There was more to it than the payment of troops, however. Castles had to be built and maintained, alliances had to be paid for and diplomatic expenses had to be met. In 1101, for example, Henry I agreed to pay the count of Flanders an annuity of £500 in return for the service of 1,000 knights in time of war.

According to Judith Green, 'Henry I was an extremely wealthy king.'[25] And, indeed, the pipe roll for 1129–30 shows that the Exchequer collected approximately £23,000 for the king in that year. Such sums were probably more than adequate to meet Henry's needs in times of relative peace, and the surplus would have been available in a time of war or for other emergencies. So where did the post-conquest kings get their money from and how did they collect it?

The royal lands

The king was the greatest landholder in the kingdom, and most of his regular income was derived from this source. As has been seen already,

William the Conqueror had Harold to thank for his massive landed wealth; the latter had united the Godwin family lands with the royal lands when he became king in 1066. In the Domesday survey of 1086 the king possessed over 18 per cent (by value) of the landed estates listed. There were four shires in which the king held more than 30 per cent of the land, and another eight in which he held between 20 and 30 per cent. Almost everywhere he held more than 10 per cent. This gave the king money and power, and 'meant that the monarchy was drawing revenue from every part of the kingdom and that royal estates gave a local physical focus of royal power everywhere'.[26]

The king could collect the profits and rents from the farms and income from the sale of crops and livestock on his demesne lands. But it would have been a job of almighty complexity for the king personally to manage all his lands throughout the country. The usual practice, therefore, inherited from the Anglo-Saxon kings, was for him to devolve responsibility for the administration of the royal lands and the exercise of royal rights within individual counties to the sheriff. In return for this privilege, the sheriff paid his annual 'farm'. As has been seen, he often collected more than he owed and kept the surplus for himself. The advantage of the system for the king was that the county farms provided him with a regular and predictable income without the problems of having to administer the lands themselves. According to the pipe roll for 1129–30, over £9,000 was due to the king from this source from the year in question and over £6,000 of this was actually paid.

Feudal dues

After 1066, the king drew a significant proportion of his regular revenue from the exercise of his rights as a feudal lord. This was a quite new source of revenue for the English kings, and derived from the nature of the landed settlement imposed by the Normans. Used wisely by the king, the system could foster ties of loyalty and dependence. However, royal failure to exploit these sources of income fairly could cause anger, create tension and, ultimately, provoke opposition.

Like all feudal lords, the king was entitled to raise a so-called 'gracious aid' from his tenants for three specific purposes: when his eldest son was knighted, when his eldest daughter got married and when he needed to pay a ransom. Henry I made use of this prerogative in 1110 when his daughter Matilda was betrothed to Emperor Henry V. There were other more regular ways the king could raise money from his tenants, too. In place of actual military service, for example, and because ready cash was often more useful in war than someone else's mounted knights, a money payment known as scutage (literally 'shield money') was often substituted by tenants. Such payments are first recorded during Henry I's reign, but were probably being made before then. Consent was not required before a scutage was levied by the king, although there was supposed to be an immediate military necessity which needed to be met. At other times, if a tenant-in-chief rebelled or died without heirs, his lands would return or 'escheat' to the king. He could run them, grant them away as a gift or sell them off as he pleased, thus creating new bonds of loyalty but also fresh resentment in the minds of those dispossessed and their heirs; many quarrels between families claiming the same lands were played out during the civil war of Stephen's reign. And there were other controls exercised by the king over the lives of his vassals' relatives. If a tenant-in-chief died leaving an heir, that heir could not enter into his inheritance until he had paid a so-called 'relief' to the king; the amount of the payment was negotiable but often large so as to keep the new tenant in debt and under royal control. Further, if the tenant-in-chief died when his heir was under age, the king was entitled to take possession of the lands, administer them and take their profits until the heir was old enough to succeed. He could also sell the right to exploit the lands to someone else. These were the king's rights of 'wardship'. Royal permission had to be sought by a tenant-in-chief, too, before he could marry off his daughter. A small payment would make the granting of that permission more likely, and if permission was not sought, a financial penalty would be imposed. And if the tenant-in-chief died leaving a widow of marriageable age or unmarried sons and daughters, it was the king's prerogative to arrange (or sell) their marriages.

The way William II in particular administered this system gave rise to grievances and complaints. Consequently, in his coronation charter, Henry I promised that reliefs should be 'just and lawful' and that other feudal dues would be levied fairly.[27] In practice, the amounts paid and payable continued to depend on the bargain an individual could strike with the king. The pipe roll for 1129–30 shows that Geoffrey de Mandeville owed Henry I a relief of £866, and Ranulf II, the new earl of Chester, owed £1,000 from the relief his father had promised. Both of these men chose to oppose the next king when he showed signs of weakness, as did other men who felt aggrieved by the way Stephen's predecessors had exploited their feudal powers. He was unable to satisfy all the demands for redress which followed his coronation, and as other pressures mounted on him, disgruntled individuals soon became bold enough to help themselves to whatever they could get.

Royal justice

The king's interest in the administration of justice did not stem purely from his role as peace-keeper and judge. More will be said about this in the next chapter when the legal system is examined more closely. Suffice it to say here that royal justice was highly profitable. Payments might be made to the king to secure his assistance in a particular lawsuit. The pipe roll for 1129–30 records that nearly £800 was demanded by the king for his help in judicial matters; just over £100 of this was actually paid. The royal writs which came to dominate civil cases in the royal courts as this period went on had to be paid for, too. Tithings were fined if they failed to carry out their local law enforcement responsibilities. Those who acted as sureties for the appearance of a party in court were fined if that party failed to appear. The belongings of convicted criminals were confiscated by the king's officers and sold. Most sums from such sources were small, but because there were so many of them, large amounts could be raised for the royal coffers. In Bartlett's words: 'The king was the fount of justice, but his waters did not run freely.'[28]

The royal Forest

Kings had always hunted; the activity was seen as good training for warfare. Edward the Confessor is reputed to have been a very keen huntsman, but the importance of the royal hunting lands took on a new importance after 1066. Areas suitable for hunting were designated by William I and his sons as royal preserves, 'forests', and collectively as 'the Forest', where the beasts of the chase (the red deer, fallow deer, roe and wild boar) were protected for the king's benefit. Some of the Forest was on the king's own land, but much of it was on the lands of other lords, whose rights over those lands were consequently restricted. The largest concentration was in Hampshire (the 'New Forest'), Wiltshire, Dorset and Somerset. Eventually, most of Essex was Forest and there were other extended areas in Nottinghamshire ('Sherwood Forest').

The Forest supplied the king with food and timber. It also supplied him with money. In 1129–30, according to the pipe roll for that year, more than £400 of Forest income was demanded by the king, and over half of this was paid. Rights to graze cattle or feed pigs had to be paid for, as did the right to cut down trees. The Forest soon developed its own system of law and law enforcement, too. It was harsh and arbitrary, a matter purely for the king's will. Landholders could not hunt deer on their own lands if they were within the Forest, and they could not farm their lands in the same way as other landholders. Breaches of Forest law were punished with large fines. Whilst it was a source of valuable funds, therefore, because of the harshness and unpredictability of the Forest system, it was also a source of criticism and a focus for resentment. It was also an obvious source of concessions for a king with his back to the wall. As part of his bid to gain popular support against the rebels of 1088, for example, William II 'forbade every unjust tax and granted people their woods and hunting rights'. The royal Forest only covered certain parts of the country, of course; nevertheless, for those living within its boundaries, Warren's comment rings true: 'For a century and a half the Forest law and its enforcement must have been for all ranks of society the most persistent and alarming expression of the wilful authority of post-conquest kings.'[29]

Geld and coinage

The Norman kings were extremely fortunate in having gained control over a system of government, integral to which was the only approximation to a nationwide system of regular taxation in western Europe. They may not have levied geld every year after 1066, but it was a reliable and regular source of income for them. William I almost certainly levied it from the start of his reign; indeed, heavy taxation was probably one of the reasons why the north of England resisted the Normans so determinedly in the early years after Hastings. The burden could certainly be heavy. In 1084 William imposed a national levy of six shillings on the hide; he probably levied it more often at the lower rate of two shillings. This is what Henry I did, and this appears to have been the standard rate for the rest of the Norman period. The pipe roll for 1129–30 records that, of £4,355 demanded in that accounting year, £2,374 was paid. However, the importance of geld soon began to wane. Many individuals or institutions were exempt from payment (favoured courtiers or religious houses, for example) and tenants-in-chief did not have to pay geld in respect of their own demesne lands. The tax was also difficult to collect and unpopular, and there are signs that it was producing ever smaller yields. How far it was collected at all during Stephen's reign is unclear. It may have been collected during his early years as king and within the areas he controlled towards the end. As Crouch has said, 'Henry II's administration restored this source of revenue suspiciously quickly.'[30]

The Norman kings also continued to manipulate and profit from the English coinage in much the same way as their Anglo-Saxon predecessors. Control of the coinage remained a royal monopoly and no foreign coin was allowed to circulate within the kingdom. After 1066 silver pennies of standard weight and design were produced, and every three years until at least 1125 a new coinage was issued and the king pocketed the profits. New mints were opened, too, as royal authority spread to the remoter parts of England. Before 1066, there was no mint further north than York, but one was opened after in Durham, and several in Wales, at Rhuddlan and St David's, for example. Significantly, the moneyers who produced the coins remained overwhelmingly English, certainly until at least 1100. The king needed good-quality silver pennies to meet his expenses, and he needed to maintain royal control over the coinage as a demonstration of his authority. This explains why the Norman kings were so harsh to those who abused the system. In 1100, Henry I announced that anyone found in possession of false coin should lose a hand and be castrated. In 1108 he extended the punishment to loss of eyes and lower limbs. And in 1124, after complaints from his mercenaries about the quality of the coin with which he was paying them, Henry ordered that all the moneyers in England should have their right hands cut off.

Despite such measures, there are signs that by the end of Henry I's reign the quality of the English coinage was declining somewhat. Silver may have been in short supply generally, so the moneyers of 1124 may be considered unfortunate. And Henry's problems with the coinage were as nothing to those faced by Stephen. As England was divided between rival camps in the civil war from the late 1130s, the national system of coinage collapsed. Stephen continued to issue coins within his area of direct control, the south-east and East Anglia; he even ordered two recoinages, one in the late 1140s and another in the early 1150s. However, pennies were issued in the Empress's name and circulated within her south-western power-base, and individual magnates, men such as Earl Robert of Gloucester and Earl Henry of Northumbria, issued their own coins, too. That this was possible speaks volumes for the extent to which Stephen's authority had shrunk by the second half of his reign.

Vacant churches

In the same way as the king controlled succession to the lands of his tenants-in-chief in his capacity as a feudal lord, he controlled the lands of bishoprics and abbeys during 'vacancies'. Like any other tenant-in-chief, when a bishop or an abbot died, the lands his church held from the king were administered by their royal lord until a successor was appointed. The king was supposed to allow the church as much money as it needed to function properly, but he kept any profits for himself. Given that it was the king who appointed the next bishop or abbot, the system was clearly open to abuse by an unscrupulous ruler. William II, aided and abetted by Ranulf Flambard, acquired a reputation for allowing churches to remain vacant for unreasonably long periods so that he could keep the profits. According to Orderic Vitalis, 'When bishops and abbots died the king's officers seized all the property and wealth of the churches, and for three years or more administered them entirely as part of the royal demesne.' William of Malmesbury tells a similar tale: King William bestowed ecclesiastical honours 'only after long deliberation . . . so that, on the day he died, he held in hand three bishoprics and twelve abbeys without shepherds'.[31] Such claims may have been exaggerated, although there is no doubt that William II did obtain funds by such means: he retained custody of Canterbury's estates from after Lanfranc's death in 1089 until 1093, and from 1097 until his own death whilst Anselm was in exile. And, as Barlow has said, 'Rufus' wars were largely financed by the church.'[32] Henry I for his part promised in his coronation charter of 1100, and again as part of his settlement with Anselm in 1106, that such practices would end, but he was as guilty as his brother of exploiting the churches which came under his control. He took the profits from Canterbury (1109–14), Durham (1128–33), Hereford (1127–31) and Chester (1117–21 and 1126–9).

The Exchequer

Subjects had always complained about royal financial demands. The *Anglo-Saxon Chronicle*, for example, makes repeated protests about the heavy taxes imposed on the people by William I and his sons. Only the pipe roll for 1129–30 allows a realistic estimate of royal revenue during this period to be made. As has been seen, the Exchequer collected nearly £23,000 for the king in that year. This does not give the whole picture, and there were certainly other funds received by the king which were not included on the pipe roll. Moreover, it is always possible that 1129–30 was an unusually profitable, and therefore not necessarily representative, year. However, the importance of the pipe roll lies not just in the sums it records; it is the only surviving record of the greatest of all Norman innovations in royal government – the Exchequer.

The Exchequer in its fully-developed form was the central financial department of royal government. A great deal is known about it because of the surviving records relating to it. First are the pipe rolls. A pipe roll is a record of an audit of the accounts of each sheriff held at Michaelmas every year at the Exchequer. The 1129–30 roll is the only one which survives from Henry I's reign, but they survive in a continuous series from 1156. They set out in great detail the amounts of money paid into the royal coffers by the sheriffs and the amounts owed to the king from a whole range of sources. Thus they reveal where much of the king's income came from as well as the inner workings of the royal administration. The second source is a handbook of Exchequer procedure compiled by Richard FitzNigel in about 1179 known as *The Dialogue of the Exchequer*.[33] Richard was the son of Nigel, bishop of Ely, who had been royal treasurer under Henry I. Richard became treasurer himself under Henry II and bishop of London under Richard I. It is a unique source: an insider's guide to the mechanisms of royal government.

'The Exchequer, perhaps the best known cogwheel of Henry [I]'s evolving administrative system, emerges from the mist around 1110 under the direction of Roger of Salisbury.'[34] Why 1110? In that year Henry I had specific financial needs, the most important of which was a dowry for his daughter Matilda, who had been betrothed to Emperor Henry V. The king levied a gracious aid, as he was entitled to do, at the rate of three shillings per hide. This money had to be collected and dealt with at the centre, and this may have been the spur to the emergence of the Exchequer in its recognisable form. More generally, as the king's commitments in and outside England had increased after 1066, so had his need for ready cash; and as the number of debts owed to the king grew out of the new mechanisms of feudalism, an office dedicated to the thorough collection and auditing of his revenues became increasingly desirable. It needs to be emphasised, however, that the Anglo-Saxon kings had collected vast quantities of geld before 1066, and that some mechanism for dealing with the huge piles of silver pennies brought to the treasury at Winchester by their sheriffs must have been used by them. The *Dialogue* certainly implies that before 1110, and perhaps even before 1066, there was already a place where royal revenues were audited and collected. The year 1110 may be important, therefore, but only as the point at which the Exchequer began to be referred to by that name.

In its most basic form, in Clanchy's words, 'the Exchequer was not a government department but an object'. According to the *Dialogue*, 'It is a quadrangular board about ten feet in length and five in breadth', and it derived its Latin name, *scaccarium*, from the chequered cloth which covered it.[35] The cloth served as a gigantic abacus, and different columns and squares on the cloth represented different amounts of money. When the sheriff handed over his money it was set out on the cloth alongside what he owed. Surpluses and deficits could then be calculated. The system was simple and allowed for thorough accounting of the monies owed to the king. The sessions of the Exchequer were held twice a year, at Easter and Michaelmas, at the royal treasury at Winchester and, later, Westminster. What happened at these sessions is described in great detail in the *Dialogue*. Presiding over the sessions would be the chief justiciar (or Bishop Roger of Salisbury under Henry I), who would be assisted by numerous other royal officials, the chancellor, the constable, the marshal, the treasurer, two treasury chamberlains and several clerks. At the Easter session, the sheriff would appear and a preliminary 'view' of his accounts would take place. He would pay over such money as he had and would receive a receipt in the form of carved wooden tallies in return. At Michaelmas the main account was held when the sheriff presented himself before the barons to be examined, first by the treasurer about the county farm, and then by the chancellor's clerk (who later evolved into the Chancellor of the Exchequer) about 'pleas and agreements', money which the sheriff had been ordered by the king to collect from individuals. Such sums may have been feudal dues owed to the king, whilst others might be sums offered to the king by individuals looking for royal support in some legal dispute or other. Those sums which the sheriff had been ordered to pay out by the king during the course of the year were then subtracted from the sums he owed. Then, when all the sheriff's debts had been calculated, a final calculation of what he still owed or of what he was owed by the king was worked out on the chequered cloth. The money the sheriff had brought to the Exchequer was put into sealed bags, and he was given more wooden tallies as receipts. The quality of the coin he had produced was then tested, either by measuring it against a standard weight, or by the process of 'assay', melting it down to ascertain its precise silver content.

Details of everything accounted for and either owed by or owing to the sheriff were entered on the pipe roll for that year. The roll for 1130 has been described as 'by far the earliest surviving kingdomwide financial survey in the history of humankind'.[36] It records the amounts paid into the Exchequer, some of which were owed in respect of the financial year 1129–30 and some of which were left owing from previous years. Any debts left unpaid at the end of this year were carried forward to the next and added to the debts still unpaid which had been carried forward from previous years. In total, at the end of the 1129–30 audit, the outstanding debt owed to the government was a colossal £68,850. It was through the Exchequer that the king and his officials could keep track of these sums and maintain pressure on those who owed them. It was also through the Exchequer that the king kept his officials honest and accountable. The Exchequer 'was central to the exaction of revenue, the control of local officials and the web of political control the king could spin over the country'.[37]

Military organisation

Military organisation was crucial to the success of the Norman Conquest. With strong armies, the kings could defeat their internal and external enemies on campaign. With enduring symbols of military power and might, they could intimidate them into lasting submission. The most potent of such symbols was the castle. Orderic Vitalis famously stated that 'the fortifications called castles by the Normans were scarcely known in the English provinces and so the English – in spite of their courage and love of fighting – could put up only a weak resistance to their enemies'.[38] There may have been some castles in Anglo-Saxon England, but the only one known about for certain was built by a Frenchman, Earl Ralph, at Hereford. For Duke William, it was natural that his first acts on landing in England were the erections of fortified structures at Pevensey and Hastings. More castles were then built as he proceeded to London after his victory over Harold. In 1068–9, castles were constructed on the king's orders as far apart as Exeter and York, with many in between, as William travelled across England. Still more were built by the Conqueror's sons, by Robert Curthose at Newcastle in 1080–1, for example, and by William II at Carlisle from 1092. However, castles were not exclusively royal creations. In the marcher earldoms and in the Sussex rapes, castles were built by the men with delegated responsibility for the areas. Great men in general, too, preferred to set the seal on their local power with the construction of a castle. Not just laymen, either, as Bishop Roger's castle at Shrewsbury and Bishop Henry of Winchester's at Farnham showed. The king, of course, had to try and ensure that private castles were constructed only within limits set by him.

Most early castles would have been little more than wooden stockades on hastily-built earth mounds, but stone soon replaced timber. Castles thus became permanent signs of Norman domination to a hostile and restless native population. Included in the *Anglo-Saxon Chronicle*'s obituary of William I is the comment that 'He had castles built and poor men hard oppressed.'[39] However, there was more to castles than this. Managed by a reliable castellan and manned by a professional garrison often made up of household troops, they were important as places which could be retreated to and defended in times of revolt, as centres of local government and administration, as focal points for settlement and as storehouses for royal treasure. But castles came into their own in wartime: controlling one's own and taking control of the enemy's were essential if victory was to be achieved, as William II found in 1088, Henry I in 1101 and Stephen for most of his reign. By 1135, there were hundreds of royal and private castles across England, and during the civil war of the next twenty years, control of any area could not be claimed unless its most important castles had been taken.

The core of the royal army in wartime was provided by the knights of the king's household and the household knights of his great men. This system would have been familiar to the Anglo-Saxon kings, as would the service of the *fyrd*, which the Norman kings, like William II in 1094 and Henry I in 1101, continued to use. But the Norman kings introduced significant new elements into the ways English armies were organised. After 1066, all those who held land from the king (his 'tenants-in-chief') were obliged to provide him with mounted knights to fight in the royal army or garrison royal castles. The total number of knights owed by all the king's tenants-in-chief was the *servitium debitum* (literally 'service owed'). The number of knights expected from lay tenants-in-chief was ill-defined and flexible in the immediate aftermath of 1066. However, as will be seen in Chapter 8, a fixed, specified number of knights (a 'quota') was requested by William I early on in his reign, perhaps by 1070, from his ecclesiastical tenants-in-chief, the great cathedrals and abbeys. As for the king's lay tenants-in-chief, the process of establishing quotas was a much slower business. As land came into the king's possession, he could distribute it and make individual arrangements as to the amount of 'knight service' due from his new tenants. But by 1100 there was almost certainly a more or less fixed number of mounted knights whose service the king was 'owed' by his tenants-in-chief. Orderic's estimate that the king was owed 60,000 knights on this basis is almost certainly a gross exaggeration; the real figure was probably no higher than 5,000.[40]

In practice, some tenants-in-chief would serve in the king's army having brought with them the knights they owed. But the *servitium debitum* was

DEBATE 6
Did the feudal system ever exist?

The Norman Conquest affected England in profound and diverse ways. After 1066, a new élite speaking a new language ruled the kingdom; new styles of military and ecclesiastical architecture were imposed on the English landscape; England was linked to continental Europe more directly than before. Most importantly, however, according to J.H. Round in 1891, the Normans introduced 'the feudal system' into England.[1] By this, Round meant a structure of landholding and of military and social obligation wherein a 'vassal' received land from a 'lord', performed homage to him and undertook to provide the lord with military service expressed in terms of a fixed number of knights. The vassal could in turn grant his land in similar ways to his own 'sub-tenants'. For over half a century after Round put forward his famous thesis, historians accepted and enlarged upon it. However, since the 1970s, serious doubts have been raised about the validity of 'feudalism' as a concept; and the idea that the Normans simply imposed a wholly new system of landholding and military obligation on England has looked increasingly unconvincing. The members of the ruling classes of Anglo-Saxon England and pre-conquest Normandy owed obligations to each other as lords and tenants, including military ones; and after 1066, kings and lords relied more on the troops of their households and on mercenaries than they did on soldiers raised 'feudally' from their tenants. The Normans may have defined obligations more precisely, but, according to Gillingham, 'the notion that the Normans introduced a new framework of lordship, the "feudal system" or "feudalism", is a myth.'[2] With such powerful denunciations dominating it, the debate over feudalism appeared to have been closed. However, Carpenter may have reopened it with his recent references to 'the introduction of feudalism to England' after 1066, and to a 'feudal structure' being in place by 1100. He does not deny that kings and lords in pre-conquest England may have 'enjoyed in some respects equivalent powers' to their post-conquest successors, but the tenurial and social changes introduced by the Normans were 'still immensely significant'.[3] Thus whilst the idea derived from Round and others that William I introduced a 'perfect feudal pyramid' into England no longer stands up, 'feudalism' is still a useful concept if it is used carefully and on the understanding that a single word cannot do justice to the political, social and military complexities of post-conquest England.

1 J.H. Round, *Feudal England*, 3rd edn (1909, repr. 1964), p. 182.
2 J. Gillingham in *From the Vikings to the Normans*, ed. W. Davies (Oxford, 2003), p. 218.
3 Carpenter, *The Struggle for Mastery*, pp. 81–7.

probably considerably greater than any force the king in wartime would actually need. There is certainly no evidence that the entire *servitium debitum* ever turned up for service in England or Normandy. It fulfilled another purpose, however, as the basis upon which payments of scutage could be assessed, and the king's position as a feudal lord enabled him intensively to raise those feudal dues discussed above. In Carpenter's words, 'What feudalism gave the king was thus military service, money, sources of patronage (in the marriage of widows and – best of all – of heiresses), and also social and political control . . . The king's exploitation of his new feudal rights was absolutely central to the workings of politics and society in the century and a half after the Conquest.'[41] The king's need for money remained paramount, however: money which the king was apt to spend on that other essential part of any royal army of this period – the mercenaries. The men in the contingents from Maine, Brittany and Flanders who had fought with Duke William at Hastings had been paid. As has been seen, William II was notorious for lavishing huge sums on his mercenaries; and hired contingents from Brittany and Maine were crucial to Henry I's success at the battle of Tinchebrai in 1106. There was nothing dishonourable or inappropriate about this: it was realistic military leadership. Experienced professional soldiers would always be more attractive to the king than the potentially ramshackle outfits which his tenants-in-chief might produce.

Government in writing

The Anglo-Saxon kings had issued orders in writing, and other information about estates and tax obligations was also written down before 1066. However, a notable feature of the post-conquest period was the increased use of documentation by the king's government. Various reasons lay behind this. The king was separated from his household and his officials regularly after 1066 and he needed to keep in touch with them; they in turn needed to communicate with officials in the localities. Records also had to be more systematic if a track of the debts owed to the king was to be kept. At the heart of this development was the king's chancery, staffed, as has been seen, by his priests under the supervision of the chancellor, and the Exchequer.

Until the early twelfth century the royal chancery was small and its organisation rudimentary. How far the priests of the chapel continued to draft documents as simply one amongst a number of other duties is difficult to tell. The most important documents they prepared were the king's writs. For the first few years after 1066 they continued to be written in English, almost certainly by English scribes. One of the most famous was William I's writ of 1067 confirming the ancient privileges of the city of London.[42] But from 1070 onwards Latin became the official language of royal government and England was brought into line with the continental standard. Why this happened at this time is unclear, but it may reflect William I's loss of patience with his restive English subjects after the rebellions of the previous years. There were other changes to the form of the writ, too. They carried the name of at least one witness from the early 1070s, and by the end of the eleventh century places and dates of issue were regularly included.

The uses of the writ were extended by the Norman kings, as well. Before 1066, it had served as a title-deed to land, announcing a new grant or confirming a previous one. William I and his sons used writs in this way, but they also used them as a means of giving orders and instructions to royal officers and private individuals. A rough comparison of what survives from the pre- and post-conquest periods suggests how much more documentation was being produced by the royal government after 1066. Fewer than 2,000 writs and charters survive from the entire Anglo-Saxon period, but for William II's reign there is an average of fifteen extant documents per year and for Henry I's the figure rises to forty-one. Many hundreds more were certainly issued and have been lost. The pipe roll for 1129–30 alone refers to the issue of nearly 300 writs authorising expenditure, and it has been suggested that Henry I's government may have been producing as many as 4,500 letters per year by the 1130s.[43] Even Stephen's truncated administration managed to produce an average of about thirty-eight charters per year across the whole of the reign.

However, two written records stand out from this period, both of which testify to the power and reach of royal government after 1066. One of these, the pipe roll for 1129–30, has already been mentioned. But more important even than the pipe roll, and unique in medieval Europe, is Domesday Book. After discussing matters with his counsellors at his Christmas court at Gloucester in 1085, William I ordered a great survey of England to be carried out. According to John of Worcester, the king wanted to know 'how much land each of his barons possessed, how many enfeoffed knights, how many ploughs, how many villeins, how many animals and what livestock everybody had from the highest to the lowest in all his kingdom, and what rent could be obtained from every estate'. The *Anglo-Saxon Chronicle* went further: so detailed was the survey 'that there was no single hide nor virgate of land, nor indeed (it is a shame to relate but it seemed no shame to him to do) one ox nor one cow nor one pig which was there left out, and not put down in his record, and all these records were brought to him afterwards'.[44]

To carry out the survey, as has been seen at the end of Chapter 2, the country was divided into at least seven circuits, each with its own commissioners. Material was collected from tenants-in-chief and juries of local men and was presented at the shire court. The name of each manor had to be given, the name of its holder before the Conquest, the name of its present holder and, if one account is to be believed, detailed information on a range of other matters.[45] How many slaves and freemen did the manor contain, for example, how much woodland and pasture? What was it worth in 1066 and what was it worth at the time of the survey? And in addition, all this information had to be given for three separate dates: when Edward the Confessor died, when William I re-granted the land and in 1085. The first volume of Domesday, 'Great Domesday', contains surveys of all the English shires south of the Tees except Norfolk, Suffolk and Essex. The returns for these three counties make up volume two, 'Little Domesday'; they were never written up in their final form. There are other gaps, too: London was never surveyed, for example, neither was Winchester, probably because such projects were too complex to undertake in the available time. Despite this, the wealth of detail the survey gives about landholding both before and after the Norman Conquest is extraordinary. The information in Great Domesday is arranged county-by-county, and within each county by landholder. A list of the king's lands in the county always comes first, followed by those of the churches and then the lay lords in ranking order. It thus gave the king an accessible and beautifully-arranged record of his own estates, those of his vassals and their own tenants, and it recorded their value. This is probably why he wanted the survey carried out: it recorded in unambiguous and exhaustive detail the impact of the Norman Conquest on England, and it gave the king the information he needed to control his people and exploit the resources of his kingdom. It is no wonder that it acquired its ominous name: contemporaries could think of nothing as final and conclusive other than the Last Judgment itself.

Conclusion

Although much remained the same within the system of English royal government after 1066, the following ninety years or so also saw innovation and evolution. However, change rarely came about as a result of any preconceived royal plan; it usually happened pragmatically in response to circumstances and events. Thus, since the Norman kings liked hunting so much, a system of Forest administration gradually emerged; because parts of England were more vulnerable or valuable than others, special administrative units like the marcher earldoms and the Sussex rapes developed; because the king could not always be in England, someone had to run the country in his absence. But even this description risks crediting the kings and their servants with too much conscious planning. The keynote of this period was not the deliberate creation of institutions and administrative systems but the extension and intensification of royal activity. This served to consolidate the gains made by William I in 1066, but, most importantly, it served to increase royal revenue. All the kings of this period were concerned with accumulating the resources required to defeat their enemies. William I and his sons won their victories in part because they were able soldiers, but largely because they were rich. And despite his abilities on the battlefield, Stephen was a military failure;

DEBATE 7
What was the purpose of the Domesday survey?

No contemporary explained why the Domesday survey was undertaken in 1085–6, and historians still argue about its purpose. One view is that William I wanted to use the information to reassess liability for geld across England. However, no reassessment ever took place and, in any event, the survey gathered more information than such an exercise would require, and the manner of its arrangement in Domesday Book did not facilitate individual geld assessments. More likely, the survey was designed to give the king and his officials information about land and landholders. Reliable and up-to-date details on such matters would enable the king to exploit the resources of his kingdom more efficiently; if he knew precisely what lands his tenants-in-chief held he would be better-placed to raise the sums they owed him as their feudal lord, and to administer their lands when they came into his possession. The records produced by the survey also allowed lines to be drawn under twenty years of Norman rule in England. A massive transfer of landed power had taken place since 1066, and, once set down in Domesday Book, the records of the survey served as legal title to land and as evidence in the event of disputes. However, it can be no coincidence that the Domesday survey was undertaken immediately following a time of acute national crisis, when a Danish invasion of England had appeared imminent, and during which a massive French army had been billeted on the kingdom. To be sure, once the invasion had failed to materialise, the king wanted to know what the resources of his kingdom were and who held them. But he also wanted to know to whom the landholders of England owed their allegiance. So in 1086, when the Domesday commissioners had completed their task, 'all the people occupying land who were of any account over all England, no matter whose men they were' came to William at Salisbury, and they pledged their loyalty to the king 'against all other men'.[1] According to Bates, this 'was probably the planned climax of the Domesday survey'; and the awed tones in which contemporaries commented on its oppressive intensity vividly suggest that, for all its usefulness as a fiscal tool and as a guarantor of title, its primary purpose was to provide information which would allow the Normans to tighten their grip on the land and people of England.[2]

1 *NC*, p. 78.
2 Bates, *William the Conqueror*, p. 200.

confined in his restricted area of authority, he lacked funds and was, as a consequence, 'cataclysmically less powerful than Henry I'.[46] Kings could not win their wars without money, and according to Warren 'the king's wealth was the product of a vast foraging operation'.[47] More specifically, they administered their lands efficiently, exploited their feudal tenants ruthlessly, and supervised the legal system closely. To do all these things successfully, moreover, records had to be kept of what the king was owed and by whom, and instructions had to be given to royal officials more often and in more detail than ever before. The more sophisticated and thoroughgoing the system of royal government became, therefore, the more effectively the king's subjects could be fleeced. The king was in theory concerned with the welfare of his people; in practice, he preyed upon them in the selfish pursuit of his own political and military interests. In other words, 'The pressure that the kings of England felt to defend their territories was transmitted to their subjects as a painstaking and unwearying pursuit of their silver pennies'.[48]

Notes

1 John Prestwich in *Anglo-Norman Warfare,* ed. Strickland, p. 76.
2 *EHD II,* pp. 432–6.
3 *NC,* p. 79; *WMK* i, p. 279.
4 Carpenter, *The Struggle for Mastery,* p. 90.
5 *NC,* p. 79; *EHD II,* pp. 184, 209, 318.
6 *WMHN,* p. 16.
7 *NC,* p. 78.
8 *OV* iv, p. 122.
9 *OV* vi, p. 454.
10 Crouch, *The Normans,* p. 140.
11 *OV* v, p. 311.
12 *OV* vi, p. 16.
13 Carpenter, *The Struggle for Mastery,* p. 91.
14 *EHD II,* pp. 454–60.
15 Hollister, *Henry I,* p. 258.
16 *OV* vi, pp. 346–50.
17 Gillingham, *The Angevin Empire,* p. 69.
18 Crouch, *The Reign of King Stephen,* pp. 325–7.
19 Green, *The Government of England under Henry I,* p. 126.
20 Golding, *Conquest and Colonisation,* p. 105.
21 *OV* vi, p. 16.
22 *EHD II,* p. 465.
23 *NC,* p. 28.
24 Dyer, *Making a Living in the Middle Ages,* p. 58.
25 Green, *The Government of England under Henry I,* p. 51.
26 Bartlett, *England under the Norman and Angevin Kings,* p. 160.
27 *EHD II,* p. 433.
28 Bartlett, *England under the Norman and Angevin Kings,* p. 168.

29 *EHD II*, p. 174; Warren, *The Governance of Norman and Angevin England*, p. 164.
30 Crouch, *The Reign of King Stephen*, p. 335.
31 *OV* v, p. 203; *WMK* i, p. 577.
32 Barlow, *The Feudal Kingdom of England*, p. 121.
33 *EHD II*, pp. 523–609.
34 Hollister, *Henry I*, p. 356.
35 Clanchy, *England and its Rulers*, p. 49; *EHD II*, p. 527.
36 Hollister, *Henry I*, p. 369.
37 Carpenter, *The Struggle for Mastery*, p. 154.
38 *NC*, p. 101.
39 *NC*, p. 80.
40 *NC*, p. 106.
41 Carpenter, *The Struggle for Mastery*, p. 85.
42 *EHD II*, p. 1012.
43 Clanchy, *From Memory to Written Record*, p. 58.
44 *NC*, p. 78.
45 *EHD II*, p. 946.
46 Carpenter, *The Struggle for Mastery*, p. 175.
47 Warren, *The Governance of Norman and Angevin England*, p. 85.
48 Bartlett, *England under the Norman and Angevin Kings*, p. 177.

7

The Kings and the Law, 1066–1154

As in government, there was a good deal of continuity between the legal systems of pre- and post-conquest England. William I and his successors preserved the Anglo-Saxon system of shires and shire courts, hundreds and hundred courts and they also accepted important elements of English custom. Partly this was a question of pragmatism: the system worked well. But the stress upon continuity suited the Norman kings' view of their own legitimacy, too: they were the rightful heirs of Edward the Confessor, they argued, and part of their inheritance was the extant system of law. In the so-called *Laws of William the Conqueror* (probably a twelfth-century document, reflecting the laws it was thought William had made), it was proclaimed that 'all shall have and hold the law of King Edward in respect of their lands and all their possessions, with the addition of those decrees I have ordained for the welfare of the English people'. And, at his coronation, one of the promises made by Henry I was to restore to his people 'the law of King Edward, with such emendations as my father made to it with the counsel of his barons'.[1]

But although many of the elements of the post-conquest legal system were of Anglo-Saxon origin, there were important advances in legal thought and practice under the Norman kings. The main trend was towards an increasing involvement for the king and his representatives in the everyday administration of justice through, amongst other things, an extension of royal jurisdiction over nearly all types of civil and criminal cases, an increase in the number of royal judges who were able to supervise those cases, and the increased readiness of the king's subjects to seek the benefits of royal justice. Just as significantly, new *types* of law were introduced alongside the new systems which administered it. The traditional view is that 'feudal' law was brought to England by the

Normans and operated in tandem with and alongside traditional Anglo-Saxon 'customary' law. Matters were not as straightforward as this, but the maintenance and protection of Norman rule did necessitate innovations in the criminal law, whilst a new system of landholding after 1066 meant that ways had to be found to regulate the relations between landlords and tenants and to solve problems concerning land. Underlying both of these dynamics, meanwhile, was the king's need for money to fight his wars: royal justice was profitable, and this in itself was a powerful stimulus to experiment.

It is usual to speak of the second half of the twelfth century and the reign of Henry II in particular as having been the formative period as far as the development of the English Common Law is concerned. As will be seen in Chapter 11, the advances which took place then were considerable; however, Henry II had much to work with. The developments which occurred in the century after the battle of Hastings, and particularly during the reign of Henry I, provided the Angevin kings with essential building blocks: without them, the edifice they constructed (if they had been able to build it at all) would have lacked firm foundations. In Hollister's words, 'In the history of the development of the English common law, these innovations from the first third of the twelfth century reveal an advancement toward coherent, centralised government, which challenges the long-standing assumption of a fundamental disjunction between the legal history of the reigns of Henry I and Henry II.'[2] Even during Stephen's troubled reign, the structures and mechanisms of royal justice continued to function, albeit under strain and within restricted geographical areas, and they remained intact and ready to be revived in 1154. If the civil war damaged the tree of English justice, its roots remained very much alive. They lay deep in the soil, after all.

The principal courts

Legal judgments were delivered in a court of some kind. But court sessions were also social occasions and meeting places. Disputes of national or local significance were mediated there, transactions were witnessed and important announcements were made. The courts themselves were composed of the court-holder (the individual, or his representative, with the power to convene the court), and the court's 'suitors', that is those who had an obligation to attend the court or who chose to do so. Whilst the court-holder presided over the court, it was the suitors who gave judgment in the cases.

After 1066 just as before, the most important courts were the king's own court, the shire court and the hundred court. A new type of court also appeared after the arrival of the Norman kings, the court of the local lord. Kings made some attempts to clarify which courts should hear particular types of cases. In the early 1070s, for example, William I issued a writ stating, amongst other things, that ecclesiastical cases (which encompassed disputes about marriages, wills and legitimacy) should not be heard in hundred courts or by lay judges; rather they should be heard in church courts before ecclesiastical judges. And in about 1108 Henry I issued a writ which purported to set out the limits of the jurisdiction of certain courts.[3] Shire courts and hundred courts were to meet at the same places and at the same times as they had done in the time of Edward the Confessor 'and not otherwise'. If there was a dispute about land between two of the king's tenants-in-chief, it went on, the hearing should be in the king's court (because he was their lord); if the dispute was between two of the vassals of one of his tenants-in-chief, it should be heard in their lord's court; and if the dispute was between the tenants of different lords, it should be heard in the shire court. In practice, though, matters were more fluid than this and there were no hard and fast rules dictating the court to which every dispute should come. At the start of a case, the choice of court depended on a number of factors. Who were the parties? Where did they live? Who was their lord? What was the case about?

The king's court or *curia regis*

Fundamental amongst the duties of the medieval king was the doing of justice, both between his immediate vassals in his capacity as their lord and between his subjects in his capacity as their king. The king was the ultimate fount of justice in his kingdom, and his decisions were binding and authoritative potentially on all matters. Thus he was sought out wherever he went by those eager for an audience and for a conclusive decision in their favour. There was nothing new about this, but developments were afoot. By the start of this period, the concept of a national 'peace' which it was the king's duty to preserve was a familiar one. In his coronation charter, for example, Henry I promised to 'establish a firm peace in all my kingdom, and I order that this peace shall henceforth be kept'.[4] The thirty-three years of unbroken peace which Henry I brought to England was remarked upon by contemporaries: 'He made peace for man and beast', said the *Anglo-Saxon Chronicle* on his death; and according to Orderic Vitalis, 'He always devoted himself until the end of his life to preserving peace.'[5] Also, at least by Henry I's reign, certain types of case ('royal pleas' or 'pleas of the crown') were considered to be a special royal preserve, and could only be heard by the king or his representative. A list of these (by no means definitive) was given in the *Laws of Henry I*, a legal tract dating from about 1115, and included all the most serious offences, such as murder, treason, arson, robbery, rape, and 'theft punishable by death'. Other matters (treasure trove, rights over wrecks, destruction of the highway) were also included in the list as, significantly, was the royal right to hear appeals from other courts over claims of unjust judgment or 'default of justice' in other courts.[6] In other words, the king claimed a supervisory jurisdiction over the decisions reached by and between his subjects in lower courts.

Obviously, the king might hear cases brought before him in person, but royal courts had to be held in the absence of the king, too. When the king was absent from England, as he frequently was after 1066, his deputies or his officials heard cases in his name. So that the king's pleas could be heard across the country, moreover, it was necessary that there be local officials to hear them. Anglo-Saxon kings had sent men into the shires to hear particular cases, and the Norman kings continued to do something similar, sending specially-appointed justices out into the localities to deal with cases which required royal involvement. However, the Norman kings also began (it is not clear precisely when, but it was certainly happening under Henry I) to use so-called 'local justices', men permanently resident in particular shires whose job it was to hear cases in the king's name. More importantly still for the future, the reign of Henry I saw the developing importance of 'itinerant' (travelling) justices, who were sent to particular counties to hear a wide variety of cases. These men were the forerunners of the 'justices in eyre' of Henry II's reign, and more will be said about these men in Chapter 11. However, it is important to remember that at this stage these royal judges did not give judgments in the courts they supervised; this remained the job of the suitors to the court. Moreover, each shire court continued to have its own customs which were applied even when a royal judge presided; as yet these were not local sessions of a national royal court.

The shire court

Shire or county courts were well-established features of the English legal landscape before 1066, and they continued to function much as they had always done after the conquest. However, they came to sit more frequently during this period; every four weeks by the early thirteenth century, as opposed to twice a year before 1066. This in itself is strongly suggestive of their popularity and effectiveness.

Usually, the shire court was presided over by the local sheriff. The local bishop may occasionally have presided, too, but for reasons which are discussed in chapter 12, his influence was probably reduced during the 12th century.[7] And, as has been seen, a royal justice may occasionally have supervised sessions of the shire court. There were no fixed rules about who had to attend the court. The *Laws of Henry I* stipulated that, amongst others, bishops, earls, sheriffs, hundredmen, reeves, barons, village reeves and other lords of lands should attend, but in practice there was probably much local variation concerning attendance, and an obligation to attend the court probably rested more than anything else on status as indicated by landholding.

The shire court dealt with a wide range of matters, many of which concerned non-legal business. Important royal announcements might be made there, and high-status land transactions witnessed. The bulk of the disputes heard there concerned land claims and offences involving violence or theft. If the offences involved breaches of the king's peace, a royal representative would need to be present.

The hundred court

In the early twelfth century there were probably about 600 hundreds or wapentakes in England. Some counties contained more than others, and the hundreds themselves varied considerably in size. Many of these hundreds, moreover, were in private hands, having been granted to individuals by the king. Each in theory had its own court.

Like the shire court, the hundred court was a legacy of pre-conquest England, where it was probably held once a month. 'However, by the early thirteenth century, hundreds were apparently held every fortnight.'[8] Presiding over the court, which sat for one day at a time, was a bailiff, appointed by the sheriff, or by the lord if the hundred was in private hands. The obligation to attend rested on the larger landholders of the hundred. It has been calculated that 20,000 men (perhaps 1 per cent of the estimated population in 1086, or one in twenty adult males) were obliged regularly to attend the hundred court.

The shire and hundred courts had similar jurisdictions, and the same case might be dealt with at different stages in both courts. Generally, the hundred probably dealt with less serious disputes than the shire court. And for most people, especially if they had different lords but lived in the same hundred, the hundred would be their court of first resort. Twice a year, there was a special session of the hundred, which was to be attended by all freemen of the hundred. These sessions were presided over by the sheriff himself and, amongst other things, he checked the functioning of the tithing system.

Lords' courts

These courts, also called 'honorial' or 'seignorial' courts, were a Norman innovation in England after 1066. Unfortunately, very little is known about how they worked. In theory, every lord held a court for the men of his lordship or 'honour', where disputes between them could be settled. The giving of such judgment between vassals was a vital requirement of good lordship, and an obvious example of one aspect of the 'feudal system' in operation. On one level, indeed, when hearing disputes between his tenants-in-chief, the king's court was functioning simply as the grandest lord's court of all.

The lord did not simply hear disputes and make judgments on them. His tenants were the suitors to his court and obliged to attend, and they had an important role to play. After all, 'honorial courts were the key venue for the management of seignorial resources and personal relations'.[9] The lord made important announcements to his tenants there, they gave him advice and witnessed his transactions and their own. After all, the lord–vassal relationship entailed reciprocal responsibilities. Just as the king's tenants-in-chief expected their lord to listen to and heed their counsel, so the vassals of lesser lords expected that justice would be done to them and that their opinions would be given due weight.

The lord's court could also be used to deal with certain types of offence against the person or goods, if the lord had acquired the right to have such cases heard there. Sometimes these rights were expressly set out in the documents recording the grant of land to the lord; at other times, the origins of the rights claimed were more obscure. Most important amongst these were the Old English forms of jurisdiction called 'sake and soke' and *infangentheof*. The latter gave the lord the right summarily to execute thieves caught red-handed on his lands. The former gave the lord a wider, less precisely-definable right to enforce order within his lands. Such rights do not appear to have encroached on the hundred's rights to impose capital punishment, and they certainly did not cover any royal pleas.

The criminal law

Enforcement and policing

In the twelfth century, the threat and reality of violence permeated society at all levels. The aristocratic élite was brought up to fight, and lower down the social scale the rigours of daily life, and the inescapable grind of poverty made a high degree of criminality inevitable. This was a knife-carrying society, too. Trivial arguments could easily turn nasty and brutal, and minor wounds sustained in a fight could prove fatal in an age where treatment options were limited. Thus a minor disagreement could ultimately lead to the most serious charges.

The biggest problem for those interested in keeping violence and disorder to a minimum was the difficulty of apprehending offenders. Unless they were caught red-handed, it was all too easy for them to escape undetected, and other methods of instilling respect for the law had to be found. William I, for example, introduced the *murdrum* fine, a penalty imposed on a local community (the hundred or village or perhaps the lord of the land where the killing took place) for failure to produce the secret killer of a Norman. Such penalties gave an incentive to produce murderers after the event, but also to prevent killings in the first place. The introduction of the *murdrum* fine probably tells us much about the native hostility faced by the Norman newcomers in England after 1066, but in setting out to deal with such problems William was only extending a principle that would have been familiar to the local communities of Anglo-Saxon England, that of communal responsibility for the wrong-doing of individuals. This principle was best expressed through the operation of the tithing system, which continued to function after 1066 probably much as it had done before.

There is no quantifiable evidence by which to judge the effectiveness of this system of local policing. When the identity of the offender was unknown, it could not have been helpful at all. Plenty of offenders must have fled, too, even though they believed that they had acted violently in self-defence or that death or injury had been caused by accident. An alternative option for the offender was to seek sanctuary in a monastery or church. This provided a respite, usually of thirty or forty days, but then it was likely that he would have to leave the country anyway. Otherwise, if the identity of the offender was known, but he had not been apprehended, he would be summoned repeatedly to appear in court and, when he failed to do so, he would be formally outlawed. This placed him outside the normal workings of the law. If captured, he could be executed immediately upon outlawry being proved, and if he resisted arrest he could be killed with impunity.

Trial and proof

Depending upon the nature of the offence in question, a trial would usually take place either in the court of a lord with sake and soke, the hundred or shire court. The most serious cases, where breaches of the king's peace or royal pleas were concerned, would be heard in the presence of a royal justice or perhaps of the sheriff acting in that capacity. There was no national prosecuting authority, and most accusations were brought by an individual (usually the victim or a member of their kin) through the process of 'appeal'. If both parties appeared on the appointed day, the accuser would formally state the charge and offer to prove it; the defendant would formally deny the accusation. Claims and counter-claims would then be made (an alibi, perhaps, or a claim of self-defence) and evidence brought forward. The defendant's reputation would then be considered: notorious wrongdoers had a much more difficult job than men of previously good character.

In hard cases, a form of proof had to be decided upon by the suitors. Three main methods were used: oath, ordeal and battle. Oaths were another legacy from pre-conquest England, but their popularity in relation to serious offences appears to have diminished over this period. The ordeals of fire and water were regularly used in criminal cases after 1066, and belief in their effectiveness as a sign of God's judgment did not diminish. The prospect of undergoing the ordeal may also have acted as a deterrent or as a reason for pleading guilty. Fear of God and of execution upon failure may have persuaded many accused to opt for submission and a lesser penalty: mutilation, perhaps.

In addition to water and fire, the Normans introduced a new form of the ordeal to England: trial by battle. Trial by battle had a long history in Europe but was unknown in Anglo-Saxon England. However, by the later twelfth century it had become the preferred method of proof in appeals concerning serious offences. The battle was fought between the accused and the accuser if both were fit and, unlike in battles concerning land where swords were used, the combatants in criminal cases would have employed hammers or staffs with sharpened and reinforced ends. The popularity of this method of proof testifies once again to a genuinely-held belief that God would intervene on the right side.

Punishment

If the accuser failed to prove his case against the accused, he would be punished for having brought a false claim. He would have to pay a sum to the king, and probably something by way of compensation to the accused. More seriously, if the accused failed to establish his innocence, he would have to face the appropriate penalty. For lesser offences, a system of compensation, familiar to the Anglo-Saxons, continued to operate. However, the Norman kings did much to sweep away the Old English system of compensatory justice. For serious offences, the accused would face death, usually by hanging; or occasionally, if he was luckier, physical mutilation of some sort, perhaps the loss of a limb, blinding or castration. At Christmas 1124, the royal justice Ralph Basset hanged forty-four thieves in one sitting of his court in Leicestershire, whilst he had six others blinded and castrated. Punishments were so severe because, first, it was thought that the perpetrators deserved such treatment, and, second, to act as a deterrent to others.

Civil cases

In medieval England, land was the ultimate source of wealth and prestige. The more land a man had, the greater his standing in local society and the greater his influence within political society. In other words, together with the possession of land went power and influence over individuals and communities. Not surprisingly, therefore, rights over land were jealously guarded and fiercely coveted.

Landholding

Land could be held in various ways. Laymen might grant land to a church 'in free alms' or *frankalmoin*. This meant that nothing was expected from the church except prayers and an enhanced chance of salvation. As for grants between laymen, one form of tenure was socage, that is land held from a lord in return for a regular money payment or other specified dues. Other lands might be held on a lease in return for a periodic payment for a specified term, a lifetime perhaps or a number of years. More usually after 1066, though, where a transfer of land took place between one layman and another, the land in question (the 'fee' or 'fief') was held by the grantee (the 'vassal') in return for services, usually military, to be performed by him to the grantor (the 'lord'). On receiving the lands, the vassal would perform homage to his lord, promising the loyal performance of the agreed service. Thus if a vassal is said to have held three knights' fees of his lord in a particular area, he held the lands in question on the understanding that he would provide his lord with three knights in time of war. The words 'fee' and 'fief' in this context are derived from the Latin word *feudum*, and explain why vassals are described as having been 'enfeoffed' with lands by their lords. The Latin *feudum* is also the root of the word 'feudal', and land held in return for homage and military service is of the essence of the so-called 'feudal system'.

When control over land was transferred in this way, the vassal did not 'own' the land. Rather he 'held' the land of his lord, and he was safe in his holding and free to deal with it largely as he pleased as long as he continued to perform the stipulated services. There was nothing to stop him granting away the lands he held from his lord to tenants of his own and creating new relationships where he was the lord: this is known as 'subinfeudation'. Increasingly over this period, too, the notion hardened that the lands held by a tenant should pass directly to his heirs; in other words, fiefs became 'heritable'. If there was no dispute about who the correct heir was, and once the requisite payment (the 'relief') had been made to the lord and homage performed by the new vassal, there was usually little problem.

Disputes

Nevertheless, there were still innumerable disputes about land. A new lord might seek to introduce his own followers into lands already held by others, for example, or there might be controversy about who the closest heir to a deceased tenant was. Sometimes grantors even gave the same lands to more than one person. Such disputes could involve violence, which gave rise to subsidiary legal issues.

The forum for the hearing of such disputes depended on a variety of factors, and disputes over land could be held in all of the courts mentioned above. Henry I's writ of 1108 is helpful here, but it is not exhaustive. A lord's court could deal with disputes between his men, for example, but also with complaints made by a tenant against the lord himself and with disputes between the lord's tenants and their own men.

Royal involvement in lower courts was increasingly common, too, and a litigant could obtain a royal writ issued to the court-holder ordering him to 'do right' in a certain matter. If a disappointed party complained of the justice he had received in a lower court, moreover, he could obtain a royal writ ordering the case to come before the king or his justices. Once the parties were both in court, claims would be made and denied; sworn testimony or documentary evidence might be used, custom and land-holding practice might be referred to. Where the merits of the dispute were unclear, a method of proof again had to be decided upon. Ordeals by fire or water were very unusual in disputes over land, but trial by battle was once again an option. It may have been a more dignified affair than the procedure used in criminal cases: swords were used, for example, rather than staffs or hammers, and the parties could employ champions to fight on their behalf. The winner of the case ended up in possession of the land, although settlements made 'out of court' were by no means unusual.

Conclusion

Between 1066 and 1135, the hold of the English kings over their king-dom's legal system became tighter. At the same time, procedures became more regular and, through the use of royal writs, for example, more centralised. This was inevitable in a country which was still being conquered and colonised in 1100. However, developing notions of the king's peace and clearer ideas about which types of case were the king's business also prompted this shift. The Norman kings were happy to use pre-conquest mechanisms and procedures, such as the shire and hundred courts and the tithing system, but they also introduced changes of their own, such as the *murdrum* fine and trial by battle. While evidence from Stephen's reign is lacking, moreover, it is generally accepted that, within the areas of England he controlled most fully (Essex and the south-east), the principal courts continued to function and royal justice continued to be exercised. Elsewhere, responsibility for the routine administration of justice may have devolved of necessity to local lords. Nevertheless, it is not unreasonable to speculate that the courts of the shire, the hundred and the local lord operated more or less as they always had in the areas controlled by Stephen's opponents. Henry II would not have found it too difficult to breathe new life into the damaged but robust system which he inherited in 1154.

Having said all this, it would be unwise to overstate the degree to which the English legal system had achieved uniformity and coherence under the king by the mid-twelfth century. One Norman innovation, indeed, the lord's court, may actually have served to restrict the reach of royal justice by taking business out of the shire and hundred courts.

And even where royal justice was exercised most effectively it was still developing, and large parts of the kingdom remained outside the system altogether. The Church and the royal forests had their own laws and procedures. Many hundreds remained in private hands; probably more after 1066 than before. And other individuals or institutions had special powers which reflected the realities of royal power after 1066. The abbey William I founded on the site of the battle of Hastings, for example, had the right to exclude royal justices from its lands. And more extensively, in vulnerable frontier areas such as the county of Chester or the bishopric of Durham, the earl and the bishop possessed what were, in effect, royal powers: they appointed their own sheriffs who did not account at the royal Exchequer, and royal justices could not operate within their jurisdictions. Nevertheless, in the first century after the Norman invasion, political and military necessity had combined with a continuously evolving sense of the king as supreme judge and the guarantor of a national peace to ensure that royal influence within and over the legal system continued to increase. In Judith Green's words: 'the scope of royal justice was expanding in the early twelfth century, with a continuing enlargement of its powers over crime and a vigorous interventionism in the land law.'[10] As a result of such developments, wider respect for royal authority was fostered, and the king's control over his subjects was reinforced. Just as importantly, the courts were a source of revenue for the king. Financial penalties were imposed on tithings which failed to meet their responsibilities; there were penalties if a party failed to appear in court; accusers who failed to prove their case were fined and royal writs had to be paid for. Lesser offences could still be punished financially as well. The more the operation of the legal system could be brought under royal control, the greater the opportunity for profit as well as power.

Notes

1 *EHD II*, pp. 432, 434.
2 Hollister, *Henry I*, p. 359.
3 *EHD II*, pp. 647–8, 465. See also p. 127 for further consideration of William I's writ.
4 *EHD II*, p. 434.
5 *EHD II*, p. 209; *OV* vi, p. 99.
6 *EHD II*, pp. 491–5.
7 See below, p. 191.
8 Hudson, *The Formation of the English Common Law*, p. 38.
9 Ibid., p. 43.
10 Green, *The Government of England under Henry I*, p. 105.

8

The Kings and the Church, 1066–1154

As has been seen in Chapter 4, the English Church on the eve of the Norman Conquest was by no means moribund. However, the duchy of Normandy had been a centre of ecclesiastical reform since the turn of the eleventh century, and to Duke William and his Norman followers in 1066 the English Church would have appeared old-fashioned and in need of modernisation. From about 1070 onwards, therefore, significant changes were made to the structure and personnel of the English Church, and other innovations were introduced, into the way monastic life was conducted, for example. There were significant elements of continuity as well, most importantly in the ways the king continued to exercise control over ecclesiastical affairs. If the king was to govern his kingdom effectively, he had to govern the Church within it. So the changes made to the English Church between 1066 and 1154 will be analysed here to discover the extent to which they impacted on the effective exercise of royal power.

The Church in Normandy

William I wanted to dominate the English Church because doing so would help him dominate the kingdom. Such domination was also what he was accustomed to from his rule in Normandy. Writing at Canterbury in the early twelfth century, the monk Eadmer claimed that William I's aim after Hastings was 'to maintain in England the usages and laws which he and his fathers before him were accustomed to have in Normandy'.[1] Monasticism in Normandy had been reinvigorated during the first half of the eleventh century. Established monasteries were revived and new ones were founded by the duke and his aristocracy. Duke William himself and his wife made a 'double foundation' at Caen in the years before 1066, the duke's dedicated to St Stephen (the 'Abbaye aux Hommes') and Matilda's (the 'Abbaye aux Femmes') to the Holy Trinity. The duke's right to appoint to bishoprics and abbacies was acknowledged well before 1066, and although many candidates came from the ranks of the ducal chapel, and others (Odo, bishop of Bayeux and Geoffrey, bishop of Coutances, for example) were members of William's family, as a group William's choices were good, loyal administrators and morally accept-able. Perhaps the most important appointment of all was that of Maurilius, archbishop of Rouen (1054–67), a Lotharingian. He and William, who presided over them, summoned a series of councils of the Norman Church, at Lisieux (1054 and 1064), Caen (1061) and Rouen (1063), with the aim of streamlining its organisation and improving its discipline. The intensity of such conciliar activity in Normandy contrasts sharply with the situation in England during this period, where no such reforming councils met.

By 1066, therefore, the Norman Church was tightly-organised and well-regulated, with the duke in overall control of its affairs. It was also a centre of reform, a state of affairs gratefully recognised in Rome. As duke and then king, William was properly respectful towards the popes, but he always remained clear about his own dominant position towards the churches he controlled. And until about 1075, the popes went along with this. In 1061, therefore, Alexander II (1061–73) acknowledged that William should be allowed to appoint the archbishop of Rouen and, in the same year, when the duke refused to allow papal legates to examine the case of the abbot of St Evroult, whom William had deposed, the papacy meekly submitted. Papal approval of William's rule is best evid-enced by the banner provided for him by the pope on the Hastings campaign.

Controlling the English Church

Every king needed the support of the Church before he could be crowned. It was Lanfranc who ensured that William I's wishes were carried out in 1087, for example, and who smoothed the path to William II's accession. For his part, William I had not set about imposing his will on the English Church immediately after Hastings. Partly this was because he had to deal first with the opposition which faced him after 1066. But he also needed to obtain the backing of the established English Church and the stamp of legitimacy which that would give him. In 1069, however, Arch-bishop Ealdred of York died, leaving an important vacancy to be filled, and by early 1070 William appeared to have dealt with a major Danish invasion and to have brutalised northern England into submission with the Harrying of the North. At Easter 1070, therefore, at Winchester,

William set about addressing the shortcomings of the English Church. A papal deputation, led by Ermenfrid, bishop of Sion, had arrived in England, and he re-crowned the king before several English bishops were deposed. The bishops of Selsey, Lichfield, Durham and Elmham were all removed from their posts as, most notably, was Stigand, archbishop of Canterbury and bishop of Winchester. The vacancies were filled mostly by Normans. Thomas became archbishop of York, Walkelin bishop of Winchester, Herfast bishop of Elmham and Walcher bishop of Durham. But most important of all was the appointment of Lanfranc, an Italian and abbot of William's foundation of St Stephen's, Caen, as archbishop of Canterbury. After the Winchester council, only three English-born bishops remained in place – Leofric of Devon and Cornwall (d. 1072), Siward of Rochester (d. 1075) and Wulfstan of Worcester (d. 1095). The other three bishops of English sees in 1070 were either Lotharingian (Giso of Wells and Herman of Sherborne) or Norman (Walter of Hereford). As for the English abbots, only those of St Augustine's Canterbury and St Albans were deposed in 1070. There were other depositions later (Wulfric of the New Minster, Winchester in 1072, for example), but William seems to have been content to replace Anglo-Saxon abbots with Normans as they died. Of the twenty-one abbots who attended Lanfranc's council at London in 1075, thirteen were Anglo-Saxons; in contrast, by 1086, only three Anglo-Saxon abbots remained. In all, between 1066 and 1135, approximately sixty foreigners became abbots of English monasteries.

The depositions of 1070 sprang from William I's need to, in John of Worcester's words, 'strengthen his position in the newly acquired kingdom'.[2] By the end of his reign, this process had gone even further: eleven of the fifteen English bishops were Normans, and only one, Wulfstan of Worcester, was English. The Church's control over land and people was the key reason behind the king's determination to control appointments. When a bishop was elected, he 'would immediately become a major landlord, a local, perhaps regional, and possibly national potentate, and a master of knights, castles, and money as well as religious director of his see'.[3] At the time of the Domesday survey, 1086, between a quarter and a third of the landed wealth of the kingdom was held by the Church, and it is obvious that the king would want reliable men in charge of such extensive and widely-scattered resources. By the early 1070s, therefore, the obligations of these religious houses to the king were already being clearly defined. According to the twelfth-century *Book of Ely*, 'At this time [1072] . . . king William . . . commanded both the abbots and bishops of all England to send their due knight service and he established that from that time forward contingents of knights should be provided by them to the king of England in perpetual right for their military expeditions.'[4] The bishops and abbots were the king's ecclesiastical 'tenants-in-chief' and a fixed, specified quota of knights was demanded by William in return for their lands. Another example of the system in practice is given by a writ addressed by the king to the abbot of Evesham, probably in about 1072, instructing him to come to the king with the five knights that he owed.[5] The size of a quota for a particular church, usually in multiples of five or ten, appears to have been fixed arbitrarily by the king. It would have depended on a number of factors: the extent of the land in question, the wealth of the church, its strategic significance and favouritism. Glastonbury and Peterborough may have owed sixty knights each because they were the main centres of authority in the potentially turbulent Somerset marshes and fenlands of East Anglia. However, it is not clear why Abingdon and Evesham owed only five knights, whilst Winchester owed twenty and Bury St Edmund's forty. Nevertheless, the king clearly took his tenants' obligations seriously. When in 1082 Bishop Odo of Bayeux was accused of treason against William I, he claimed that his status as a bishop meant that he could only be tried by the pope. Archbishop Lanfranc replied that, on the contrary, he would be tried just like any other tenant-in-chief in the royal court. Similarly in 1088, when William of St Calais, bishop of Durham was accused of having supported William II's opponents during the revolt of 1088, he denied that the king's court had any jurisdiction over him. Lanfranc insisted that it was Bishop William's status as a tenant-in-chief and therefore his lay estates that were at stake, and the royal court proceeded to pronounce judgment against him.

As well as legitimacy, political support and military resources, the Church also provided the king with funds. Rufus for one, it has been said, 'had absolutely no interest in the church save as a source of profit'.[6] Individual religious houses paid geld, of course, and this was levied frequently by the Norman kings, much to the distress of the English sources. Alternatively, the king might simply help himself to whatever he could get. According to the *Anglo-Saxon Chronicle* and John of Worcester, for example, in 1070 William I ordered that every English monastery should surrender its cash reserves to the king.[7] Kings could take money from ambitious churchmen, too. Notoriously, Herbert Losinga paid William II for the privilege of becoming bishop of Norwich in 1091, and in 1095, on the death of Bishop Wulfstan of Worcester, the same king demanded a payment from all of the bishop's tenants. Roger de Clinton was accused of paying Henry I £2,000 in 1129 so that he would be 'more worthy' of the bishopric of Chester. A more regular source of royal income, as has been seen in Chapter 6, were ecclesiastical vacancies. William II, assisted by Ranulf Flambard, and Henry I were particularly assiduous in their exploitation of this source of revenue.

English monastic chroniclers universally criticised Ranulf Flambard because he was so successful in raising money for the king. William of Malmesbury, for example, described how he 'skinned the rich, ground down the poor, and swept other men's inheritances into his net'. However, for the *Anglo-Saxon Chronicle*, he was more than a mere financial enforcer; it was Ranulf 'who had managed [the king's] councils over all England and superintended them'.[8] Flambard's reward for his loyal service was the traditional one of a bishopric: in 1099 he became bishop of Durham, albeit after paying £1,000 to the king for the privilege. Thus the Church was also a source of patronage for the king as well as funds. Of the fifteen bishops appointed by William I, ten were royal clerks. According to Orderic Vitalis, William II 'bestowed ecclesiastical honours, like hireling's wages, on clerks and monks of the court, looking less for piety in these men than for obsequiousness and willing service in secular affairs'.[9] In fact six out of the eight appointments to bishoprics made by Rufus were of royal clerks. Then, between 1100 and 1125 every new bishop was appointed from amongst the ranks of the king's servants. Posts within the royal administration were sought after by the ambitious because this was an avenue to status and wealth in the highest reaches of the English Church; and their success in obtaining bishoprics is evidence of how highly valued they were by the king. Royal priests ministered to the king's spiritual needs, but they also drafted his documents. As has been seen in Chapter 6, the chancellors of the Anglo-Norman kings were almost certain to obtain bishoprics, the most notable example being Gerard, chancellor of William I and Rufus, and bishop of Hereford (1096–1101) and archbishop of York (1101–8). And by 1110 a bishop, Roger of Salisbury (1107–39), was in overall charge of royal government. Elevation to a bishopric did not inevitably mean that the individual in question gave up his secular responsibilities. Indeed, by 1135, the administration was under the close control of not just Roger of Salisbury, but of his nephews Alexander, bishop of Lincoln (1123–48) and Nigel, bishop of Ely (1133–69), the royal treasurer.

As well as running the royal administration itself, the leading churchmen of the day were also expected to advise the king on great affairs of state as well as on matters of direct relevance to the Church. Archbishop Lanfranc performed all of these functions for William I – regent, judge, counsellor, his closeness to the king is most obviously revealed by the series of letters he wrote to William in Normandy in 1075, which kept the latter informed of the progress of the revolt of that year. Later, in 1085 at Gloucester, the leading churchmen as a group contributed to the discussions which led to the commissioning of the Domesday survey, and several, such as Remigius, bishop of Lincoln (1072–92) and Walcher, bishop of Durham (1071–80), took up leading roles in the execution of the survey. And in 1127, Henry I's Christmas court at Windsor was attended by 'all the chief men, both clerks and laymen, that were in England . . . archbishops and bishops and abbots and earls and all the thegns that were there to swear to give England and Normandy after his death into the hands of his daughter [Matilda]'.[10] And it was not just the highest affairs of state with which the leading churchmen were involved. They continued to have local military responsibilities, for example. In 1075, Bishop Wulfstan of Worcester and Abbot Aethelwig of Evesham played a leading role in dealing with the revolt of Earl Roger of Hereford; Gundulf, bishop of Rochester (1077–1108) supervised the building of the White Tower in London; in 1088, the garrison of Worcester Castle was under the command of Bishop Wulfstan and was instrumental in suppressing the rising against William II in that part of the country. And as late as 1138, too, Archbishop Thurstan of York was responsible for organising the forces of Yorkshire which fought against the Scots at the battle of the Standard.

Bishops continued to preside over the shire courts, too, as they had done before 1066, along with the earl or his deputy. But changes were made to the way in which different types of cases were heard locally. Some time between 1072 and 1076, William I and Lanfranc ordered that there should henceforward be a much clearer distinction between the respective jurisdictions of lay and Church courts. In a famous writ, the king announced that 'by the common council and counsel of the arch-bishops, bishops, abbots and of all the magnates of my kingdom' all spiritual offences (which included adultery and incest, for example) and all offences committed by members of the Church should only be heard and judged in 'the place where the bishop shall choose and name', and not in the hundred court.[11] The writ leaves many questions unanswered, of course. It does not mention the shire court, where the bishop was probably still able to hear spiritual cases, and there is no compelling evidence to show whether its terms were observed in practice. Also, it does not amount to the complete surrender of lay rights over the Church which it might superficially resemble. Sheriffs were expressly authorised by the writ forcibly to bring any reluctant accused to the Church court. More importantly, as has been seen, the kings continued to treat the cases of disloyal bishops as their own particular preserve; and William I at least would not allow his tenants-in-chief or his royal servants to be examined or punished by a Church court without his consent. The king was prepared to go some way towards meeting the particular needs of the Church, therefore, but he remained in overall control and insistent that his royal rights prevailed above all others.

Other reforms

William I was an enthusiastic supporter of those who wished to improve standards of observance and moral conduct within the Church. Therefore other reforms were implemented within the English Church during his reign with these goals in mind. However, they also impacted significantly on the king's government and on his ability to rule the kingdom. Changes to the monastic life, such as those introduced by Lanfranc for the monks of Christ Church, Canterbury, and by other Norman abbots elsewhere in England, might mean the dismantling of traditional English customs, habits and forms of worship. New churches in an alien style would be built in place of the old in order to accommodate a new liturgy and to suit the aspirations of the Norman élite. Such impositions furthered the process of Norman domination within England. Another innovation after 1066 was the holding of regular Church councils. Admittedly, none was convened during the reign of William II, but under Henry I councils were held at Westminster (1102 and 1127) and London (1107, 1125 and 1129). But the most important councils of all were those which took place whilst William I was king and Lanfranc was archbishop of Canterbury. After two were held in 1070, another was convened in 1072 where, on the king's instructions, the bishops confirmed that Thomas, archbishop of York and his successors should be subordinate to Lanfranc, 'primate of Britain', and that they should profess obedience to him. Thereafter, councils were convened by William and Lanfranc on seven occasions between 1075 and 1086. Just as in Normandy before 1066, the aim of these meetings was to update the practices of the national Church and to bring them into line with canon law. Thus, repeatedly at the councils of the 1070s, the practice of simony was condemned; and at Winchester in 1076 it was decreed that no one was to be ordained deacon or priest unless his unmarried status or celibacy was first proven. Those parish priests who were already married could remain so, but none could marry in the future. Higher standards were obviously expected of cathedral clergy: if they were already married, they were either to forsake their wives or give up their positions.

These councils were also designed to establish effective, accountable mechanisms for controlling the personnel and the machinery of the Church. During the 1070s, the transfer of several episcopal centres to towns of importance within the diocese was approved. Before 1066 most Anglo-Saxon bishops tended not to have a permanent base within their sees, but to move around from church to church. As has been seen in Chapter 4, some bishops had tried to change this practice before 1066, but under Lanfranc transfers were much more frequent. Thus Bishop Herman moved his see (again) from Sherborne to (Old) Sarum or Salisbury after the London council of 1075, Herfast from Elmham to Thetford, Stigand II from Selsey to Chichester, Peter from Lichfield to Chester and Remigius from Dorchester to Lincoln. There were further transfers under Rufus, too: John moved from Wells to the monastery of Bath in about 1090, and Herbert Losinga moved from Thetford to Norwich in 1095. Such changes were in accordance with canon law, but they also aided the process of centralisation within individual dioceses and within the Church as a whole. It was significant, for example, that one of Lanfranc's councils of the early 1070s ordered bishops to hold their own councils twice a year. Standards needed to be maintained, but so did control. The more regular and consistent the structure of the Church became, the easier it would be to administer; a matter of no little concern to the king as well as the archbishops and bishops.

Another development under the Norman kings was the establishment within dioceses of archdeaconries and rural deaneries. At one of Lanfranc's councils of the 1070s all bishops were ordered to appoint archdeacons; and very soon it seems that individual dioceses were being divided territorially. In larger dioceses, often each shire was made an archdeaconry. There had been archdeacons in the Old English Church, but there is no indication that they administered on a similarly territorial basis. The archdeaconries were divided in turn into deaneries, which tended to correspond with the boundaries of hundreds. Thus new levels of authority were interposed between the parish and the bishop, and it was the responsibility of the archdeacons and deans to 'police' their areas, and to ensure that standards were being maintained and that no offences were being committed against canon law. According to Barlow, 'by 1120 archdeacons had secured an established and important place within the English Church', and the complaints raised against them, in Bartlett's words, 'reflect the fact that the Church was exercising an ever more intrusive and effective government'. Similarly by 1135, according to Loyn, '[rural deans] had emerged as a significant and well-defined element in the ecclesiastical hierarchy, holding courts in the bishop's name, enforcing judgements, collecting episcopal revenues and even collecting fines for breaches of the king's peace when ecclesiastical or spiritual matters impinged on the royal'.[12] Archdeacons and deans, in other words, were essential agents in enabling the bishops to control their congregations. This could only help the king rule more effectively.

Kings, archbishops and popes

Papal influence was by no means unknown in Anglo-Saxon England, as has been seen in Chapter 4. But to Edward the Confessor and Harold, the pope was a remote albeit respected figure. William I and Alexander II (1061–73), by contrast, were on closer terms because their objectives in Normandy and England coincided to a significant degree. The popes of the mid-eleventh century had been concerned to stamp out abuses within the Church, to eradicate simony and to establish a celibate clergy. As has been seen, William as both king and duke was happy to support these reforming principles as long as they did not impinge upon his royal rights. In return, Alexander supplied him with a papal banner at Hastings and sent his representatives to re-crown William in 1070. The relationship changed when Gregory VII became pope in 1073. He adopted a more radical reforming stance than his predecessors and propounded the idea that ecclesiastical authority was superior to secular (in other words, that popes had authority over kings) and that the pope was entitled to enforce direct control over the entire Church in matters of doctrine, discipline and law. Such ideas were bound to find little favour with William I, and during the second half of his reign Anglo-papal relations worsened steadily. Gregory was insistent that English bishops should attend papal councils and that he should be able to communicate freely with them. He also made repeated demands for Lanfranc's attendance at Rome after the archbishop had reluctantly travelled to receive his pallium there in 1071, and that papal legates should be allowed to hold councils in England and Normandy. Most provocatively, he wanted William to perform homage to him for the kingdom of England and declare himself a vassal of the papacy. Gregory claimed that William had agreed to do this before 1066 in order to obtain papal support for his invasion of England. The implications of such a claim for the king's authority within his lands could not be countenanced by William, and in 1080 he firmly but politely rejected the pope's demands. In a letter to Gregory, he said, 'I have never desired to do fealty, nor do I desire it now; for I neither promised on my own behalf nor can I discover that my predecessors ever performed it to yours.' The king did allow the payment of Peter's Pence to be resumed after it had lapsed, because this was a long-standing custom, not a sign of subjection.[13]

After 1080, Gregory VII's interest in England waned as his relationship with Emperor Henry IV became increasingly acrimonious. In 1084 he was driven out of Rome by the emperor and his place was taken by the anti-pope Clement III who had been appointed by Gregory's opponents in 1080. These political difficulties relieved the pressure on William I, and William II was able to take advantage of them, too. Rufus had little time for the claims of the papacy in any event, and he was able further to reduce papal influence in England by refusing to come down on the side of one or another claimant to the papal throne. Pope Urban II, who had to deal with Henry IV and Clement III just as Gregory VII had done, was not recognised by Rufus until 1095, in return for an acknowledgement that papal legates and papal letters could only enter England with royal consent.

By this time, the English Church had a new leader. The see of Canterbury had been left vacant by the king after Lanfranc's death in 1089, but William fell seriously ill in 1093 and appeared to be dying. Amongst his acts of repentance was the appointment of Anselm as the new archbishop. Anselm had a Europe-wide reputation as a scholar and as the saintly prior and then abbot of the great Norman monastery of Bec. Temperamentally, therefore, he and the king could not have been more different, and the cooperation that had characterised the relationship between William I and Lanfranc was never present between William II and Anselm. For one thing, Anselm was much more heedful of the demands of the reform papacy than his predecessor had been. However, it was only after having his traditional rights over the Church acknowledged by Urban II that Rufus allowed Anselm to receive his pallium. More tension arose from the king's unwillingness to hold church councils in England as Anselm repeatedly asked him to do. A final quarrel arose in 1097 after the king's unsuccessful campaign against the Welsh: he criticised Anselm for having supplied him with inadequate knights in his capacity as a tenant-in-chief. This prompted Anselm to seek permission to leave the kingdom and go to Rome, perhaps to resign his archbishopric. Finally, the king gave his consent, Anselm departed and they never met again. This allowed Rufus once more to exploit the revenues of the vacant archbishopric; but whilst this benefited him in the short term, the long-term implications of this dispute for royal authority in England were significant. By 1100 the king was not inevitably the ultimate source of all authority in England; and the papacy, revived by Urban II, whose stock had risen dramatically since he had preached the First Crusade in 1095, was beginning to provide a meaningful and credible alternative focus for loyalty. The English king no longer had an exclusive claim on the allegiance of the English clergy.

Henry I's political weakness at the start of his reign, and his desire to distance himself from the excesses of his brother, led to him immediately recalling Anselm to England in 1100. During his absence, however, Anselm had taken in the latest ideas of the reform papacy, in particular its renewed stress on the unacceptability of 'lay investiture'. In other words, the reformers wanted to eradicate the practice of lay rulers giving the emblems of their office, the ring and the staff, to new bishops at their consecration. The symbolism of this practice, which seemed to imply that a bishop was dependent for his power on his lay lord, was intolerable, and so lay investiture was condemned at the papal councils held at Clermont and Bari in 1098 and at Rome in 1099, as was the performance of homage by a churchman to a layman. Such ideas, if put into effect, would impinge seriously on the king's authority over his ecclesiastical tenants-in-chief, and Henry I was determined to retain what he saw as his traditional rights. For his part, Anselm was determined loyally to enforce the pope's reforming decrees, and on his return he refused investiture at the king's hands and would not perform homage to him. Anselm was thus forced into exile again in 1103, but Henry was brought to the negotiating table after he was threatened with excommunication during his Norman campaign of 1105. By March 1106, a settlement had been reached, and it was publicly proclaimed in a Church council at Westminster in 1107. The king agreed to give up his right to invest bishops with ring and staff, but he retained the right to receive homage from the bishops and abbots before they were consecrated.

The king did well by the compromise of 1107. He lost little of practical value by surrendering the right of investiture. He could still expect his leading churchmen to profess obedience to him and perform their feudal obligations; and he retained huge influence over the choice of bishops and abbots in practice. Henry's chief minister, Roger, became bishop of Salisbury in 1107, and his chaplain Thurstan, archbishop of York in 1114. As has been seen, indeed, every new bishop appointed until 1125 was a royal servant of some kind, and ecclesiastical vacancies continued to be exploited by the king, not least at Canterbury for the five years after the death of Anselm in 1109. The king also managed to retain his control over the holding of Church councils, and he restricted papal influence by regulating the visits of papal legates to England. But, whether he realised it or not, Henry was swimming against the reforming tide, and the theories which justified papal supremacy within the Church were now part of the intellectual mainstream across Europe. He could not keep papal legates out of England entirely; several visited the kingdom during his reign, most notably John of Crema, who, in 1125, held a Church council at London which publicised the latest reforming principles. And in 1133 when a new bishopric of Carlisle was created, Archbishop Thurstan of York obtained papal authority to divide dioceses and establish new ones within his province. More and more English prelates were visiting Rome (by 1135 all but two of those in office had done so); more and more English disputes were finding their way to the papal court for judgment, particularly over the vexed question of the respective rights of the archbishops of Canterbury and York. The English king's power over the Church was still extensive in 1135, but his right to govern it as he saw fit and without interference had been curbed in the seventy years since Hastings. And 'if it was still true that Henry's clergy in 1135 placed more trust in a royal charter than a papal privilege, and preferred the king's court to the Pope's Curia, by then they certainly recognised the alternative.'[14]

The reign of Stephen

Stephen was able to become king because the English Church, backed by Pope Innocent II, decided to support him. More specifically, the efforts made on Stephen's behalf by his brother Henry, bishop of Winchester (1129–71), facilitated his accession in 1135. Henry was very wealthy, holding the abbey of Glastonbury along with the bishopric of Winchester; but he was also the son of the count of Blois and the grandson of William the Conqueror. He therefore felt at home in the world of high politics, and he persuaded Bishop Roger of Salisbury and Archbishop

William of Canterbury to accept Stephen as king. Thereafter, Stephen exercised less control over the Church than any of his three predecessors. To an extent this was inevitable, given the political difficulties he faced after the late 1130s and the restricted geographical area he ruled effectively by the end of the reign. There was certainly a reduction in direct royal influence over appointments to bishoprics and abbeys. Of the nineteen bishops appointed during Stephen's reign, only one was a royal clerk. In fact this trend had begun during the last decade of Henry I's reign, as the old king became more pious and found room on the episcopal bench for monks, canons and archdeacons. By 1135, less than half of the standing bishops had been royal servants. And it has been suggested by Crouch that Stephen's failure directly to control appointments should not necessarily be interpreted as a sign of his political weakness or incompetence. Rather, he was content to allow churches to choose their own bishops and abbots as long as they paid him money for the privilege of doing so and came to him for confirmation of the choice which had been made. In Crouch's words, it is 'very difficult to talk of Stephen losing influence over the church in the context of appointments, for he never aspired to much in the way of influence . . . He did not, however, let the Church elect for free, even if he let it elect freely.'[15] What is more, there are examples of appointments which show the stamp of royal influence. Stephen's illegitimate son, Gervase, became abbot of Westminster in 1138, and his nephew, William FitzHerbert, archbishop of York in 1143.

Papal influence within England certainly increased after 1135. There were more appeals to the papal court, and Stephen had to deal with more papal legates than his predecessors. Again, though, such developments in England were part of a wider phenomenon: papal power was greater than ever before and acknowledged as such across Europe. And the extent to which these changes significantly reduced royal control over the Church is open to question. The legate Alberic of Ostia (1138–9) deposed and consecrated abbots and bishops at a council he summoned to Westminster in late 1138, and, whilst he was legate, Henry of Winchester became, according to Barlow, 'the effective ruler of the English Church, holding councils, deciding cases, and influencing elections'.[16] However, Stephen was still able to restrict the numbers of English bishops who left the kingdom to attend papal councils. Only five were allowed to attend the Second Lateran Council in 1139, and only three received permission to attend Pope Eugenius III's council at Rheims in 1148. When archbishop Theobald of Canterbury returned to England after travelling to Rheims without the king's permission, he was banished.

The king did face some difficult situations, in northern England particularly, which strained his relations with the papacy. On the death of Archbishop Thurstan of York in 1140, Stephen sought to have one of his nephews appointed to this post. It was the second most important position within the English Church, but also, given Stephen's problems with the king of Scotland by the early 1140s, a position of great strategic and military significance. The candidacy of the first royal nephew, Henry de Sully, was rejected by Pope Innocent II because Henry wanted to hold the archbishopric in plurality with the abbey of Fécamp; and although the second nephew, William FitzHerbert, was successfully forced on the electors, he faced weighty opposition from St Bernard and the Cistercians of Yorkshire. In 1147, William was deposed by Pope Eugenius III and replaced by Henry Murdac, abbot of Fountains and a friend of St Bernard. Stephen refused to allow Murdac to take up his post, and when he died in 1153, William FitzHerbert was restored to the see by Pope Anastasius IV. In Durham, too, the king's control over the Church was called into question by the events of the civil war. Bishop Geoffrey died in 1140, at a time when much of the diocese was under the control of King David of Scotland. He tried to intrude his candidate, William Cumin, into the bishopric. In 1143, on papal orders and within the safe precincts of York Minster, another election was held by William's opponents, and the dean of York, William de St Barbe, was chosen. By 1144, support for Cumin had evaporated and William entered Durham to take up his duties. Then, after William's death in 1152, Stephen's nephew, Hugh de Puiset, was elected bishop.

For those seeking to assert that Stephen lost control of the Church in the second half of his reign, therefore, it should not be forgotten that in 1148 both English archbishops were excluded from the kingdom by royal order, and that by 1154 two royal nephews were archbishop of York and bishop of Durham. However, on at least two occasions Stephen's treatment of and at the hands of the Church inflicted significant damage on his authority within England. Stephen's handling of Roger, bishop of Salisbury, and of Roger's nephews, Alexander, bishop of Lincoln, and Nigel, bishop of Ely, at and after his Oxford court of 1139 has traditionally been seen as disastrously inept, and as an event which tore the experienced heart out of Henry I's carefully-constructed system of royal government. More recently, it has been emphasised that royal government itself continued to function largely uninterrupted by the events of 1139. Without pipe rolls it is impossible to know for sure, but all the bishops eventually returned to court and the chancery and Exchequer may have worked as before, albeit under new management. Nevertheless, Stephen's high-handedness damaged the image of him as a trustworthy guardian of ecclesiastical interests in the eyes of many within the English Church. Even his brother, Henry of Winchester, was alienated for a time. It may be no coincidence that Matilda chose to land in England in September 1139, only three months after the events at Oxford, and at a time when Stephen's relations with the Church were at their lowest ebb. A profound impact was also made on Stephen's capacity to rule effectively by the events of April 1152 when Archbishop Theobald refused to consecrate Stephen's son, Eustace, as his successor. Theobald relied on rather shaky papal authority to justify his stance, but the real reason for the refusal was probably the bishops' wish not to prolong the civil war any longer by legitimising Eustace's claim to the throne. It was a bold position to adopt, and Theobald was forced to go into exile after announcing his decision. It did not end the civil war (Eustace's death effectively did that), but it signalled the start of a terminal decline in Stephen's fortunes.

Conclusion

There is much more to the history of the Anglo-Norman Church than has been touched on in this chapter. Nothing has been said about the conflict between the churches of Canterbury and York over the issue of primacy within the English Church. And nothing has been said about the profound influence exerted by the new monastic orders of the twelfth century, principally the Cistercians, on England's physical and mental landscape. Such omissions have been made because the principal concern here has been the evolving relationship between the Church and royal government. The Norman kings all needed the support of the Church, but they also insisted on dominating and controlling its personnel and its decision-making processes, and on using, and sometimes abusing, it for their own political, financial and military purposes. Reform was acceptable, but only if it either helped to increase royal control or at least did nothing to diminish it. The stark reality for the king was that, in Barlow's words, 'unless he could rule his ecclesiastical as effectively as his lay subjects, his power would be much diminished'.[17] Try as they might, however, the Norman kings could not counter developments in the wider Church which slowly but inevitably whittled away their power. The intellectual climate across Europe in 1154 was quite different to that which had prevailed in 1066: the pope was acknowledged as supreme within the Church, and national Churches were laying claim to a general freedom from lay control. By the second half of the twelfth century, any attempt by an English king to turn back the clock to the simpler days of William I and Lanfranc was bound to end in acrimony and conflict.

Notes

1 *Eadmer*, p. 9.
2 *JW* iii, p. 13.
3 Bartlett, *England under the Norman and Angevin Kings*, p. 395.
4 *NC*, p. 119.

5 *NC*, pp. 148–9.
6 Carpenter, *The Struggle for Mastery*, p. 130.
7 *NC*, p. 74.
8 *WMK* i, p. 559; *EHD II*, p. 183.
9 *OV* v, p. 203.
10 *EHD II*, p. 203.
11 *EHD II*, pp. 647–8.
12 Barlow, *The English Church, 1066–1154*, p. 49; Loyn, *The English Church*, p. 116; Bartlett, *England under the Norman and Angevin Kings*, p. 389.
13 *NC*, p. 166.
14 Brett, *The English Church under Henry I*, p. 62.
15 Crouch, *The Reign of King Stephen*, pp. 300–6.
16 Barlow, *The English Church, 1066–1154*, p. 110.
17 Ibid., p. 275.

Part III

Angevin England, 1154–1217

9

The Reigns, 1154–1217

Henry II, 1154–1189

1154–1161

The early years of Henry II's rule in England were dominated by his efforts to restore royal authority after twenty years of civil war. What follows here will touch on these matters in passing, but much more will be said about them in the next chapter.

After his coronation at Westminster on 19 December 1154, Henry tried to deal with his two younger brothers, Geoffrey and William. In September 1155 at Winchester, the king and his barons discussed a projected conquest of Ireland. There was papal approval for such a plan, and Ireland may have been intended for William. However, nothing came of this scheme in the short term, and William died in 1164. As for Geoffrey, Henry had promised his father on his death-bed that he would surrender Anjou to his younger brother when he became king of England. Geoffrey now wanted to take charge of what he saw as his lawful inheritance; but Henry had other ideas. In January 1156 Henry crossed the Channel and in February performed homage to King Louis VII of France for his French lands. Thus Geoffrey was deprived of a potentially important ally and he was soon quite isolated. In July 1156 he agreed to abandon his claims in return for the county of Nantes, the lordship of Loudun and an annual pension of £1,500. He died in 1158.

Henry returned to England in April 1157 and stayed until the end of 1158. He spent this time dealing with problems in Wales and Scotland. In May 1157 Henry met the young Scottish king, Malcolm IV, at Chester and demanded homage and the return of Northumbria to the English crown. When he had come to England in 1149, Henry had promised Malcolm's grandfather, David I, that all the land north of Newcastle and the Tyne, as well as Cumbria and Carlisle, should belong to Scotland forever. This of course was when he needed the Scottish king's support; by 1157 the balance of political power had been reversed, and Malcolm did as he was instructed. Henry was less successful in Wales. He obtained the submission of the two most powerful Welsh princes, Owain Gwynedd in the north (in 1157) and Rhys ap Gruffudd in the south (in 1158). The expanded frontiers of native Wales were also pushed back by Henry and acknowledged by the Welsh, but the Welsh problem had not been conclusively dealt with.

On his return to France at the end of 1158, his new friendship with King Louis was further strengthened when a marriage was arranged between Henry's eldest son, also called Henry, and one of Louis's daughters by his second marriage, Margaret. Henry was only 3 years old and Margaret was still a baby, and Louis could reasonably have assumed that the betrothal had little immediate significance. Henry thought otherwise. Margaret's dowry was to be the strategically-vital area of the Norman Vexin, and it was to be handed over when the marriage took place. The sooner Henry could get hold of this land and its castles, especially the one at Gisors, the more the security of Normandy would be reinforced.

Meanwhile, Henry also hoped to take advantage of his good relations with Louis to further his ambitions in southern France. Eleanor of Aquitaine's family had long-standing claims to the county of Toulouse, and Henry was keen to make something of them. So in June 1159 he marched south, hoping that Louis would not come to the aid of Count Raymond of Toulouse, who was married to Louis's sister. In this Henry was disappointed, and the resistance of Raymond and Louis meant that he failed to take Toulouse. A truce was agreed in May 1160, but Henry had not lost sight of the main prize, Margaret's dowry in the Vexin. After 1159, there was a papal schism, and one of the claimants to the papal throne, Alexander III, was desperate for political support. So when in November 1160 the marriage was performed between young Henry and Princess Margaret, the king had already secured papal approval for it and the Vexin was accordingly handed over. Louis had been tricked, and although he attacked the Vexin almost straight away, he could not shake Henry's grip on it. In the short term Henry had come out on top. More importantly, perhaps, in the long term, the good relationship established between the English and French kings after 1154 had been destroyed for good.

1161–1174

The 1160s were dominated in the popular mind by Henry II's quarrel with Archbishop Thomas Becket, which climaxed with Becket's murder in Canterbury Cathedral in December 1170. It is easy to think that this dispute overshadowed all else during the 1160s, and much more will be said about it in Chapter 12. Henry, however, also had other concerns. In 1163, he was in Wales, dealing unsuccessfully with Prince Rhys of Deheubarth. Then in 1165 Henry invaded north Wales, but his campaign ended in failure as the weather and the Welsh terrain made progress impossible. In March 1166 he left for the continent. A confederation of barons from Normandy and Maine had been causing trouble on the borders of Brittany, and Count Conan appeared unwilling to deal with them. So, when he arrived there, Henry deposed the count and betrothed Conan's daughter to his 7-year-old son, Geoffrey. Geoffrey would be the new count when he was old enough; meanwhile, Henry would take care of the count himself.

At the same time, momentous events were taking place in Ireland. Henry had already secured papal approval for an English invasion of Ireland in the 1150s; but any plans he had made were postponed and the invasion, when it came, was not a royal one. In 1166, the king of Leinster, Dermot MacMurrough, was driven out of Ireland by Rory O'Connor, king of Connacht. He came to England and asked Henry II for help. The king responded by issuing a general permission for any of his subjects to go to Ireland and help if they wished. Dermot was particularly successful in finding recruits among the Anglo-Norman nobility of south Wales, most importantly Richard FitzGilbert of Clare ('Strongbow'), lord of Chepstow, to whom Dermot offered his daughter in marriage and succession to the kingdom of Leinster. In 1169–70, Strongbow and his associates crossed to Ireland and were immediately successful. Dublin and Waterford were taken and, when Dermot died in May 1171, Strongbow had a kingdom at his disposal. News of the invaders' success in Ireland had reached the king by this time, and he was alarmed by the prospect of his own subjects setting up kingdoms abroad. So in autumn 1171 he travelled to Ireland himself to assert his authority. The Anglo-Norman magnates (including Strongbow) and the native rulers of Ireland submitted to him and accepted his overlordship. In return, they were allowed to keep much of the land they had seized.

Henry spent six months in Ireland, but his biggest problems by the early 1170s were with his own children. In January 1169 Henry had announced his plans for the succession. His second son, Richard, would take over the northern part of his mother's lands and become count of Poitou. His third son, Geoffrey, would eventually become count of Brittany through his intended marriage to the heiress there. His fourth son, John, who had been born in 1167, was at this stage not allocated any lands, a fact which later earned him the epithet 'Lackland'. As for his eldest son, Henry, he would succeed to England, Normandy, Maine and Anjou. 'The Young King', as he was known, was therefore crowned in

1170 so as to mark out his position as the designated heir. His problem was that he had no real power to go along with his position and matters came to a head in 1173 when Henry arranged a marriage between the 6-year-old John and Alais, the daughter and heir of Count Humbert of Maurienne. This was part of a strategy to extend Angevin control in southern France and Humbert was paid £3,333. John, too, was granted the castles of Chinon, Loudun and Mirebeau in the heart of Anjou. Nothing came of the plan because Alais died, but the damage had been done. Young Henry was furious at the grant of the castles to John: they were strategically-vital to the control of Anjou and within the lands he had been granted in 1169. His father had not even bothered to consult him about the grant. All three of Henry's elder sons joined a revolt against him, egged on by Louis VII and their mother, Eleanor, from who Henry was now estranged. Involved in it as well were the king of Scotland, the counts of Flanders, Boulogne and Blois, the earls of Chester, Norfolk and Leicester and a powerful minority within the English baronage. This was the opportunity Henry's enemies had been waiting for, and there was military activity in all parts of the Angevin lands. Initially, Henry concentrated on dealing with the rebels in Normandy and Anjou and left his representatives in England, principally the justiciar Richard de Lucy, to deal with the rising in England. After the defeat of the rebellious earl of Leicester in October 1173 and the capture of the king of Scotland in July 1174, the rebellion was effectively over.

1174–1189

After quashing the Great Revolt of 1173–4, and until the early 1180s, Henry II was at the height of his powers. His eldest son had been cowed, and his second son, Richard, was preoccupied with his new county of Poitou. Louis VII was old and increasingly ineffectual, and when he died in 1180 he was succeeded by a 15-year-old boy, Philip II, who was as yet too young and inexperienced to present any threat. And more concrete proof of Henry's supremacy was provided by the terms he imposed on the captured king of Scotland, William 'the Lion', in the Treaty of Falaise of December 1174. William surrendered Scotland to Henry, received it back as a fief and did homage for it. English garrisons were installed in the castles of Edinburgh, Roxburgh and Berwick. An independent Scottish kingdom no longer existed.

Although Henry had dealt successfully with the Great Revolt, it was only a matter of time before problems recurred, and the next family quarrel arose in 1182–3. In 1182, after having helped Richard put down a rising by his vassals in Poitou, the Young King, still frustrated by the lack of real power in his hands, invaded Poitou himself on a rather shaky pretext. Richard's opponents, whom Henry had just helped to subdue, flocked to him. In January 1183, King Henry tried to negotiate a settlement between his sons, but he failed. Geoffrey of Brittany then joined forces with his eldest brother and they found themselves up against their father and Richard. Only the death of the Young King in June 1183 stopped the crisis getting even further out of control. After his death, Richard assumed his brother's place as heir to England, Normandy and Anjou. His father now wanted John to succeed to Aquitaine, but Richard, having established his authority there in ten hard years of fighting, would not hand over the duchy; anyway he did not want to be left without practical power as his dead brother Henry had been. In 1184, Richard fought off an invasion by John and Geoffrey of Brittany, leaving John without an inheritance. He had been made 'Lord of Ireland' by his father in 1177, but had never travelled there; now seemed the right time, but his expedition of 1185 was an embarrassing failure.

After Geoffrey of Brittany died in 1186, Richard became convinced that his father intended to make John his principal heir, and he grew increasingly frustrated at Henry's unwillingness to clarify his plans. Philip II of France, too, now old enough to assert himself against the ageing and ailing Henry, was a growing threat. As the overlord of the ruler of Brittany, Philip claimed the custody of Geoffrey's daughters after the latter's death, but Henry denied him. Richard and Philip also had something in common in the predicament of Philip's sister, Alice. Richard had been betrothed to her since 1169, but there were rumours that King Henry did not want the marriage to take place because he had seduced Alice and wanted to keep her for himself. Another common bond between Richard and Philip was their desire to go on crusade. Jerusalem had fallen to Saladin in October 1187, but Richard did not feel able to go to the defence of the Holy Land until his position at home had been clarified and properly safeguarded. Finally, in November 1188, having confronted his father once again without success, Richard performed homage to Philip II of France, and Henry spent the last months of his life in a losing conflict with his eldest surviving son and the French king. Two days before his death, an exhausted Henry met his adversaries and acceded to all their demands: amongst other things, he promised to do homage to Philip for all his French lands and recognised Richard as his heir. This pathetic end to a glorious reign was made even more bitter for Henry when he received news on the eve of his death on 6 July 1189 that the rebellion had been joined by his favourite son, John.

Richard I, 1189–1199

1189–1190

After having been acknowledged as count of Anjou and installed as duke of Normandy, Richard was crowned king of England in Westminster

Abbey on 13 September 1189. He was determined to depart on crusade as soon as possible and he needed money. Some of his efforts to raise it will be described in the next chapter. Richard also tried to leave England in safe hands. He appointed co-justiciars, one a layman, William de Mandeville, earl of Essex and the other a bishop, Hugh de Puiset, bishop of Durham. William Longchamp, who had served Richard well in Aquitaine, was made chancellor and bishop of Ely.

Richard also had to make provision for his family. He dealt with his illegitimate half-brother, Geoffrey, by having him made archbishop of York. As for John, he was treated with great generosity. He was made count of Mortain in Normandy and his marriage to Isabelle of Gloucester took place. Richard also granted seven English counties, along with other important lands, to John. The king retained control over some of the most important castles in these counties, but John was allowed to take their revenues free of Exchequer supervision. Richard did make John promise to stay out of England for three years whilst he was on crusade, but their mother Eleanor persuaded Richard to give way on this demand.

1190–1191

Before Richard left England in December 1189, the earl of Essex died and Richard elevated Chancellor Longchamp to the position of co-justiciar alongside the bishop of Durham. Longchamp had become sole justiciar with Richard's consent by mid-1190. He was an able and competent administrator, but he was also arrogant, overbearing and deeply unpopular. This gave John an excuse to act, and matters came to a head at Lincoln castle. Longchamp was determined to have his men installed as castellans, but the holder of Lincoln, Gerald de Camville, refused to surrender custody. Longchamp besieged Lincoln, and John seized Tickhill and Nottingham in response. A compromise was reached in July 1191, but only the arrival in England of Richard's representative, Walter of Coutances, archbishop of Rouen, prevented the situation spiralling out of control. However, Longchamp was soon in trouble again. Richard's half-brother Geoffrey had also promised to remain outside England for three years before Richard left on crusade. However, he came to England in September 1191 to take up his position as archbishop of York, whereupon he was violently seized by Longchamp's agents and imprisoned in Dover castle. Longchamp insisted that his men were not acting on his orders, but the damage had been done, and he fled for safety to the Tower of London. At a council presided over by Walter of Coutances in October 1191, Longchamp was deprived of the office of justiciar and he left the country in disgrace. Walter then revealed that Richard had given him authority to take over as justiciar if necessary, and he remained as chief justiciar until December 1193.

1192–1194

John now began to scheme for the crown. Philip II of France had returned from crusade by the end of 1191 and was happy to help John undermine Richard's position. John was invited to Paris where, it was believed, Philip would offer to make John lord of all the Angevin lands in France if he would marry Philip's sister, Alice, now abandoned by Richard, who had married Berengaria of Navarre in Cyprus in May 1191. John was only prevented from sailing to France when his mother intervened to put a stop to these plans by threatening the confiscation of his English possessions.

Informed of John's treacherous plans and of his dangerous friendship with King Philip, Richard decided to return to northern Europe. In October 1192 he set out from the Holy Land; but on his way home he was captured by Leopold, duke of Austria, whom Richard had offended at the siege of Acre, and handed over to the German emperor, Henry VI, who demanded a ransom of £100,000. Richard's opponents, especially Philip II and John, were able to take advantage of this turn of events, and by the spring of 1193 war had broken out across the Angevin lands. At the end of January 1193, meanwhile, John had arrived in Paris and performed homage to Philip for Normandy and all of Richard's other lands including even, some alleged, England. He also promised to put aside his wife Isabelle and marry Alice, and to surrender the vitally-important Norman castle of Gisors to Philip as well as the Norman Vexin.

Philip made plans for an invasion of England. John then returned to England, announced that Richard was dead and claimed the throne. He failed to muster any serious support, and his claims about Richard were not believed. Envoys were sent to Germany to ascertain the truth and Richard's condition was soon established. John eventually agreed to a truce brokered by the new archbishop of Canterbury, Hubert Walter. More serious were the events in Normandy, where Philip had seized control of the great frontier castle of Gisors. He now laid siege to the ducal capital at Rouen. Then, in June 1193, Richard finally agreed terms for his release with Emperor Henry; on hearing this Philip sent John a message: 'Look to yourself; the devil is loose.'[1] Richard was finally freed in February 1194 and he landed at Sandwich on 13 March. John was summoned to appear before his brother at a council in Nottingham. He failed to appear, and the two did not meet until Richard returned to Normandy a few weeks later. At Lisieux John finally threw himself at his brother's feet and Richard forgave him.

1194–1199

In March 1194, Richard returned to England, but in May he left again, never to return. Whilst he spent the last five years of his life in France trying to recover the lands which had been taken from him by Philip II during his captivity, England was left in the hands of the new archbishop of Canterbury, Hubert Walter, who had been made chief justiciar in December 1193. After his plotting of the early 1190s John, too, became his brother's loyal subordinate. By the end of 1195, he had served Richard

---

DEBATE 8
Did Richard I care about England?

Neither contemporaries nor historians have doubted that Richard I was an outstanding warrior. However, his reputation as king of England is tarnished. Richard spent less than six months of his ten-year reign in England and, for most of the time he was there, he was preparing to leave. Contemporaries certainly criticised him for the lack of care he showed towards his subjects at this time: 'I would sell London if I could find a buyer', Richard is reported to have exclaimed in 1189–90, as he was frantically raising money for his crusade.[1] Then, between 1194 and 1199, whilst Richard was in France, England's resources were plundered on an unprecedented scale in order to meet the costs of his campaigns against King Philip. The idea that Richard undid the work of Henry II, neglected England and regarded it as little more than a source of funds for his foreign adventures has persisted over the centuries. The Victorian view of Richard, expressed clearly by Stubbs, was that 'He was a bad king: his great exploits . . . do not serve to cloak his entire want of sympathy, or even consideration, for his people.'[2] And for most of the twentieth century, such opinions of Richard prevailed. Recently, however, several influential historians have begun to dismantle the idea that Richard was heedless of his English responsibilities. John Gillingham in particular has claimed that Richard was no less interested in the government of England than Henry II or John. The arrangements he made for the supervision of his kingdom during his crusade were reasonable in the circumstances. What is more, Gillingham contends, going on crusade was not a vainglorious folly. It was Richard's duty to liberate the Holy Land and to help those members of his family and his Poitevin vassals who made up the ruling élite of the kingdom of Jerusalem.[3] There is no doubt either that, with Hubert Walter at the helm, supervised at a distance by the absent king, the second half of Richard's reign was a crucial period in the development of England's governmental institutions. Therefore, if Richard is viewed as ruler of the Angevin Empire rather than simply as ruler of England, his attitude towards his kingdom is more easily explained; and whilst he has not been totally rehabilitated, his priorities are now more clearly understood.

1 See Ch. 10, n. 16.
2 W. Stubbs, *Constitutional History of England*, 3 vols (Oxford, 1874–8), i, p. 512.
3 Gillingham, *Richard I*, pp. 117–22.

well enough to have had some of his lands restored to him, including the county of Mortain and the honour of Gloucester. Richard also gave him an annual allowance of £2,000. As for Richard's campaigns in Normandy, he prosecuted these with his customary vigour and military skill, and by 1199 he had gone a long way towards restoring the position he had inherited in 1189. However, as will be seen in the next chapter, Normandy was still significantly weaker and more vulnerable in 1199 than it had been ten years earlier.

Richard could not focus all his attentions on Normandy, either. The barons of his lands in southern France remained troublesome, and Philip II was happy to capitalise on this whenever he could. In April 1198, the viscount of Limoges allied with King Philip and in the following year Richard marched south to discipline him and his sidekick, the count of Angoulême. At the end of March 1199, Richard began the siege of the viscount's castle at Châlus-Chabrol. On the evening of the 26th, the king rode up to the walls to check on the progress of the siege. He was not wearing any body armour and was struck in the shoulder by a crossbow arrow fired from the ramparts. Later the iron barb, the length of a man's hand, was removed but not without serious damage to the shoulder which then turned gangrenous. The king died on 6 April 1199, probably after naming John as his successor.

John, 1199–1216

1199–1200

There was another claimant to the throne besides John: his young nephew, Arthur, the son of his dead brother, Duke Geoffrey of Brittany. It was unclear who had the better claim in law, Henry II's grandson (the son of an elder son) or the old king's younger son. It was also unclear whom the barons of the Angevin Empire, and the king of France, would support.

Regardless of the legal niceties, John quickly established his position after Richard's death. He seized the Angevin treasury at Chinon on 14 April 1199, on 25 April he was installed as duke of Normandy in Rouen and on 27 May he was crowned king of England at Westminster. Aquitaine was being held for him by his mother. Meanwhile, Arthur, already securely in control of Brittany, was accepted on 18 April by the barons of Anjou, Maine and Touraine as their new lord. Also, on hearing the welcome news of Richard's death, King Philip of France had invaded Normandy. The two kings met on the Norman frontier in August 1199 but failed to reach agreement on the succession. Then, in September, John headed into Anjou where the county's most powerful baron, William des Roches, submitted to him and abandoned his allegiance to Arthur. Deprived of this support, Arthur and his mother Constance made peace with John at Le Mans in September, leaving King Philip isolated. A peace treaty was formally concluded at Le Goulet on 22 May 1200, in which John was confirmed as the rightful heir of Richard in all the lands that his father and brother had held on the continent. John also acknowledged that he held these lands as a vassal of the king of France and agreed to pay Philip £13,333 by way of a relief. Arthur was acknowledged to hold Brittany as the vassal of John as duke of Normandy.

1200–1204

In August 1200, John married Isabella, heiress to the county of Angoulême. He did this, contemporaries said, for love; but Angoulême was also a notoriously turbulent and wealthy part of Aquitaine in which John was keen to gain a foothold. His mistake lay in not compensating Hugh de Lusignan, lord of Le Marche, and one of the most important barons in Poitou, to whom Isabella had previously been betrothed. When John compounded the offence by harassing the Lusignans in their lands and by failing to give them a hearing in his court, they appealed for justice to John's overlord, King Philip. Philip summoned John to his court, but John failed to appear and, in spring 1202, Philip pronounced sentence against him: John was a disobedient vassal and all his lands on the continent would be confiscated. The French king then accepted Arthur's homage for Poitou, Anjou, Maine and Touraine and war began.

Things went well for John at the start. He won a striking victory at the battle of Mirebeau in August 1202 when, amongst others, Arthur of Brittany was captured and imprisoned at Rouen. However, John only proceeded to alienate William des Roches, the powerful Angevin baron whose support had proved so crucial in 1199; and then Arthur disappeared, almost certainly murdered on John's orders, if not by him personally. During 1203, John's position on the continent crumbled. He had no money, few powerful allies, and the Norman nobility gave their allegiance to Philip. John left for England in December 1203 and his French lands were at Philip's mercy. The French king captured Richard's great fortress of Château Gaillard in March 1204, and in June the Norman capital, Rouen, opened its gates to him. Meanwhile, in April 1204, Eleanor of Aquitaine had died, and the barons of Poitou had sided with Philip rather than John. The Angevin Empire had collapsed, and all that remained of it was a small part of Aquitaine and the Channel Islands.

1204–1214

During these years, John was largely confined to England and he devoted most of his energies to raising sufficient funds to return to Normandy and reclaim his lost lands. However, between 1204 and 1214 John was not just gathering and hoarding his treasure. His reign was an important

DEBATE 9
Why did John lose his continental lands in 1204?

The central argument here concerns the extent to which King John was personally responsible for the catastrophe of 1204. Some historians and some contemporaries have had little doubt about this. According to Roger of Wendover, who wrote his account of events before 1234, John was feckless and lazy; in 1203 he preferred feasting and sleeping with his young bride to defending his lands against Philip II.[1] Most recently, Gillingham has pressed the case for John's inadequacies as lord and war leader; he was simply not up to the job.[2] It is certainly fair to say that John contributed directly to the way events came to a head in 1203–4. His treatment of the Lusignans after 1200 was inept and alerted barons on both sides of the Channel to his capacity for petty vindictiveness; he threw away a position of strength after his victory at Mirebeau in 1202; his involvement in the murder of Arthur of Brittany shocked and alienated many of his most important subjects; and by billeting mercenary troops on the people of Normandy as the crisis reached its climax, he persuaded many to seek out alternative lordship. However, despite these glaring failures, some historians have sympathy for John. By 1199, King Philip already had a potentially decisive grip on the Norman frontier, and the duchy was far harder to defend than it had been in 1189. Perhaps, therefore, 'Angevin rule in Normandy was, indeed, already a guttering candle when John came to the throne.'[3] To be sure, John had little of Richard I's military skill; but few men did. And had Richard lived, even he might have had difficulty stemming the tide of growing French power. Henry II had been much richer than Louis VII, but, thanks principally to Richard, England was financially exhausted by 1199. Thereafter, John could probably count at best on roughly the same annual income as Philip II, who had gradually been adding to his lands since the 1180s. So it is arguable that John lost his continental lands in 1204, not primarily because he was a bad lord, a poor soldier or an evil man (although all these things were important), but because he ran out of money at the crucial time. He was not a king who naturally commanded loyalty, and he was unable to meet the soaring costs of keeping his lands together by force.

1 *Roger of Wendover's Flowers of History*, II, i, p. 206.
2 Gillingham, *The Angevin Empire*, pp. 95–102.
3 Warren, *King John*, p. 90.

one for the British Isles as a whole. He embarked on campaigns in Scotland (1209), Ireland (1210) and north Wales (1211) and was so successful that, according to one chronicler, 'in Ireland, Scotland and Wales there was no one who did not bow to the nod of the king of England, which, as is well known, was the case with none of his predecessors.'[2] He was also involved in an ongoing quarrel with the papacy, as will be seen in Chapter 12.

By 1212, John was ready to return to France. But he had to cancel his plans when there was a rising in Wales and, more significantly, when details of a conspiracy to murder him were uncovered. There was at least some good news. In May 1213, King Philip's plans to invade England were scuppered when the earl of Salisbury, John's half-brother, destroyed the French fleet at Damme in Flanders. And John reached a settlement of his long dispute with the pope. Pope Innocent III was now John's most powerful ally. The English king also had the support of his nephew, Emperor Otto IV, and of the counts of Boulogne and Flanders as well, both of whom were anxious about continued French royal expansion. John appeared to have the initiative once again and set in motion his plans for invasion. His strategy was to try to divide Philip's forces: as John's allies took on the French king in northern France, John himself would invade from the south, using his remaining French lands in Poitou as a bridgehead. However, after he landed at La Rochelle in February 1214, John faced considerable difficulty in Aquitaine where he had to face Louis, Philip's son. And much more decisively, his allies were crushed by Philip II at the battle of Bouvines in July 1214. John's strategy was in tatters, and he returned home in October.

1215–1217

John's failure abroad bore the highest of political prices in England. Once his continental ambitions had ended in humiliation, the grievances given rise to by his governance of England over the previous ten years were quickly aired. In the famous words of J.C. Holt, 'the road from Bouvines to Runnymede was direct, short and unavoidable'.[3] Hostilities began in the spring of 1215, and the tide turned decisively in the rebels' favour when they gained control of London in May. John was forced to submit to their demands and, after lengthy negotiations, he put his seal to Magna Carta on 15 June 1215 at Runnymede, an island in the Thames near Windsor. John issued the charter in order to gain time and he almost certainly never intended to abide by its detailed provisions. He soon asked his lord, Pope Innocent III, to annul it; he was happy to oblige and so civil war began again. John prosecuted it with vigour. He took Rochester castle and then led a great expedition to the north. His opponents responded by offering the throne to Prince Louis of France. Louis landed in England in May 1216, and when John died at Newark on the night of 15–16 October 1216, a French prince was in control of nearly half the country and the future of England was in the balance.

John's death transformed the political situation. Those with grievances against him could not sustain them against his infant son, Henry, who was quickly crowned by his supporters in October 1216. In November,

they reissued Magna Carta, sealed by the leaders of the interim government, William Marshal, earl of Pembroke, and the papal legate Guala,
who was in England representing the kingdom's new feudal overlord,
Pope Honorius III. In May 1217 Louis's forces were defeated at Lincoln,
in August French reinforcements were destroyed off the coast at Sandwich, and in September the French prince abandoned his claims to the
English throne and returned to France. A further version of Magna Carta
was issued by the regency government in November 1217 along with a
separate charter regulating the administration of the royal Forest.

Notes

1 Quoted in Gillingham, *Richard I*, p. 244.
2 Quoted in Carpenter, *The Struggle for Mastery*, p. 284.
3 Holt, *The Northerners*, p. 100.

10

Ruling the Kingdom, 1154–1217

The Angevin Empire

The continental commitments of the Angevin kings dwarfed those of William I and his sons. Between 1154 and 1214, English politics and government was dominated by the fact that the English kings ruled or laid claim to territories which stretched from the north of England to the south of France. This collection of lands, usually referred to by historians as 'the Angevin Empire', came together under the rule of Henry II because, in the thirty years prior to 1154, the counts of Anjou had been successful in war, diplomacy and the marriage market; and also because they had been lucky at the right times. Consequently, the constituent parts of the Angevin dominions were distinct and separate; they had their own systems of government, laws and customs. There is no indication that Henry II, Richard I or John wished to mould them into a coherent unified 'state'. Nevertheless, their determination to keep this diverse and far-flung collection of lands together led eventually to the downfall and death of each of them.

When Henry II became king of England in 1154, he was already duke of Normandy, duke of Aquitaine and count of Anjou. It was from Henry II's position as count of Anjou, indeed, that the Angevin Empire derives its name, and south of Normandy was the ancestral heartland of the empire, Anjou itself, Maine and Touraine. Further south, Henry II was duke of Aquitaine by virtue of his marriage to Eleanor, duchess of Aquitaine, in 1152. The marriage of Henry and Eleanor was one of the great diplomatic *coups* of the twelfth century. Eleanor had only been divorced from her first husband, the French king Louis VII, in March 1152, and she should not have remarried without his permission. She acted quickly, however, knowing that Louis would be unlikely to allow her to marry Henry, who already had Normandy and Anjou under his belt. The most important parts of the Angevin dominions, however, were England and Normandy, and it was in these lands that the king/duke spent most of his time. They were richer and more directly under the control of their ruler than other parts of the Angevin Empire. Normandy, moreover, was important strategically and difficult to defend at a distance. For most of the second half of the twelfth century, there was intermittent conflict between the king of France and the duke of Normandy, and it was on the western border of the duchy, either side of the river Epte, beyond which lay the lands of the French king, that this conflict tended to be played out. If the Angevin Empire had a capital, it was probably Rouen, and when it fell to Philip II in 1204 the imperial edifice collapsed.

Other parts of the Angevin Empire were more loosely attached. Henry II had acquired *de facto* control of Brittany by the early 1170s. Henry's son Geoffrey married Constance, the daughter of Count Conan IV of Brittany. Conan was then forced out of power by Henry who took charge of the principality on his son's behalf. Geoffrey assumed personal control as count in 1181. In Ireland, too, Henry managed to obtain an acknowledgement of the English king's overlordship after Strongbow's invasion in 1169. And the relationship between the kings of England and Scotland was also redefined after Henry became king. Malcolm IV was bullied into submission in 1154, William the Lion was humiliated by his capture in the Great Revolt of 1173–4 and the terms imposed on him by the Treaty of Falaise as a result, and although the king of Scotland bought back all of his rights from Richard, John's reign saw him back-pedalling once again.

The politics of the Angevin Empire were complicated by the relationship between the Angevins and the kings of France. William I and Henry I had been vassals of the French king in their capacity as dukes of Normandy. However, in practice, before the second half of the twelfth century the French monarchy had been weak and its theoretical power had counted for relatively little. Henry II himself was much richer than Louis VII and, probably until the 1180s, than Philip II, too; consequently he remained more powerful than his French rivals for most of his reign. But things were beginning to change. Philip II expanded his authority within France after 1180 by adding to his territories. Moreover, by the early 1200s it is arguable that the Capetians were better off financially than the Angevins. The latest estimates suggest that Philip received about £52,000 a year from his lands, and that John received much the same from his in England and on the continent. However, Philip could collect his more quickly than John (he did not have to transport barrels full of silver pennies across the Channel), and he could direct them more effectively at a single point, the frontier of eastern Normandy. John by contrast had an extended Norman border and the rest of his continental lands to defend. When he returned to England late in 1203, it was not because he was running scared; he was running out of cash. At the same time, Philip had managed to articulate much more clearly and precisely the nature of his feudal relationship with his Angevin vassal. Henry II performed homage in person to the French king several times; but by 1200, when John agreed to the terms of the Treaty of Le Goulet, Philip II had the resources to make his notional power meaningful and real. He could set about regulating the relations between the Angevins and their vassals in France, hearing complaints about their bad lordship and default of justice, and summoning them to appear in his court to respond to such complaints. Philip's new approach bore its richest fruit in 1202 when John's French lands were confiscated because he had failed to come to Philip's court when summoned to do so. The constant presence in the background to affairs of the king of France also provided the Angevins' subjects with an alternative focus of loyalty when required. Richard's performance of homage to the French king in November 1188 began the final miserable phase of Henry II's reign, and John lost Normandy in 1204 in part because his subjects there preferred to have Philip as their lord. Between 1180 and 1200, therefore, there was a revolution in the balance of power between the rulers of England and France.

The restoration of royal authority

Such developments were still far off in 1154. When Henry II became king, royal power had been diminished by the events of Stephen's reign. As has been seen in Chapter 6, the extent to which royal government ceased entirely to function between 1135 and 1154 is open to question. Nevertheless on Stephen's death Henry II controlled much less land within England than his Norman predecessors had done, he was much poorer than them and his grip on the Church was looser than theirs had been. Henry's determination to recover what had been lost and to restore the power of the English king were the dominant themes of the early years of his reign. In Henry's view, Stephen's reign had never happened; 'when, then, peace had been restored after the shipwrecked state of the kingdom', said the author of the *Dialogue of the Exchequer*, 'the king strove to renew the times of his grandfather [Henry I]'.[1]

Henry wasted no time in making his intentions clear. In 1155, he ordered the surrender of all the royal lands in England which had been given away or otherwise lost during Stephen's reign. This involved a systematic nationwide inquiry into landholding across the kingdom. He also dismissed two-thirds of the sheriffs he had inherited from Stephen; half were replaced again in 1162. And he set about destroying those private castles which had been erected during Stephen's reign without royal permission. In 1157, for example, he took into his own hands the castles of Stephen's son, Count William of Boulogne and Hugh Bigod. At around the same time, the Exchequer resumed its central role in royal government. It had probably not closed down completely under Stephen, but now it was reinvigorated under the experienced stewardship of Nigel, bishop of Ely, nephew of Bishop Roger of Salisbury and the other bishop arrested by Stephen in 1139. The early pipe rolls of Henry II's reign are short and the detail they contain is scanty. It probably took as long as a decade after 1154 before the Exchequer was functioning as effectively as it had in the 1130s; nevertheless, a start had been made. Henry also took steps to re-establish the royal monopoly over the coinage. As has been seen, this had been lost by Stephen, and so in 1158 a new coinage of uniform weight and design, bearing the king's image, was issued for the whole kingdom. No change was then made to the system until 1180 – 'a deliberate mark of stability' designed to instil renewed respect for the king's traditional rights, and a successful attempt to foster international trade.[2]

Of course, Henry could not supervise all of this business himself. His foreign commitments meant that he was absent from England for all but seventeen months of his first eight years as king. Loyal and capable deputies were therefore required to govern England in his absence, just as they had been by the Norman kings. In this early part of the reign, Queen Eleanor was an active regent, but she was often away from England too, and day-to-day responsibility for the smooth running of the administration rested with two other men. One of them, Earl Robert of Leicester, was held in such high esteem by Henry II, according to the author of the *Dialogue*, 'that he not only obtained the office of president of the Exchequer, but was made justiciar of the realm'.[3] Alongside him was Richard de Lucy, not a great aristocrat like Earl Robert, but a career administrator. Both of these men had served Stephen well, but this was not a bar to preferment under Henry II. And although the office was still at a formative stage in the 1150s and 1160s, they were the first men who can properly be called 'chief justiciars'. The Exchequer, over which they both presided, was the centre of their power, and they had roles in the administration of justice, too. Until his death in 1168, Earl Robert was probably the senior partner; but after that Richard de Lucy acted as sole justiciar until he retired in 1178.

Not everything went smoothly, of course, and Henry did face opposition during his early years as king. In the north, William of Aumale, who had been appointed earl of York by Stephen, refused to give up Scarborough castle; and on the Welsh border two of the most important barons, Earl Roger of Hereford and Hugh Mortimer, offered initial resistance to the new king's orders. However, by the summer of 1155 they had all submitted and by 1157 other great men, like the earls of Surrey and

Norfolk, had also surrendered their castles. By this time, too, as described in the previous chapter, Henry had imposed his authority on his own brother and the new king of Scotland, and his overlordship had been acknowledged by the native Welsh princes. Such successes meant that, by 1158, the amount of territory subject to the English king's direct control had been restored to its pre-1135 levels. So now, sure that England was safe in the hands of his English deputies, Henry spent most of the next five years in France. But when he returned in 1163, he was more determined than ever to tighten his grip on England. As will be seen in the next two chapters, it was during this phase of the reign that Henry turned his attention to the reform of England's legal system and to the clarification of his rights over the English Church.

King and nobility

The English lay aristocracy during the Angevin period continued to be made up of earls, barons and knights. Henry II, determined not to be dominated by his powerful subjects, created no new earldoms and allowed probably half of those created by Stephen to lapse; figures vary, but there may have been as few as twelve English earls by 1200. The powers of the remaining earls were reduced, too, so that the trend begun under Henry I towards them becoming more honorific titles without real power was resumed. No new earldoms came into existence during Richard's reign either; indeed, the only new one created between 1154 and 1227 was the earldom of Winchester in 1207. Having said this, the remaining earls continued to have great power in their own lands and they were also expected to share in the government and defence of the kingdom. They and their fellow greater tenants-in-chief continued to advise the king as they had always done, they held key government posts, acted as judges and witnessed royal documents. More specifically, as has been seen, Earl Robert of Leicester was Henry II's first justiciar (although he never used this title himself), and in 1189 Richard appointed William de Mandeville, earl of Essex and one of Henry II's leading counsellors, co-justiciar alongside the bishop of Durham. The role played by William Marshal, earl of Pembroke, in the final phase of John's reign and in defending England after his death was crucial to the future of the kingdom.

Below the earls in the social hierarchy were a group of up to about 200 'barons'. There was no set definition of baronial status, and it was not an official title. However, during this period the term was used increasingly to describe the king's greater tenants-in-chief. The richest barons were by no means inferior to earls: they could both have castles, and their incomes were often equivalent. In Henry II's reign a few great lords had annual incomes of over £500, and the average baronial income was about £200. 'Knight' is another term which is difficult clearly to define. It has military, legal and social connotations. The term might refer to someone who had been knighted – that is gone through a ceremony at which he was girded with a sword by a superior. Young noblemen were usually knighted in their late teens; thus they were declared old enough for warfare. A knight might have land or not; landless knights were most likely to have been found in the household of a great lord, serving him in return for food and lodging, and hoping for land of their own in due course. Every great lord had knights in his household, who fought, hunted and dined with him. The knights of the king's household made up the core of the royal army in wartime. Others ranked as knights because they already held land. Such knights might set about building up their estates in the hope of passing them on to their children. In this way a local knightly class arose over time, and these men came to form the backbone of local administration. They attended the shire court, acted as tax collectors and coroners and, as the Angevin legal reforms began to have their effect, their role expanded even more. The Grand Assize (of which more in the next chapter) required a jury made up entirely of local knights. Royal government, especially in the localities, could not function without them. Increasingly, therefore, it became necessary to know who was a knight. At the start of the thirteenth century, the latest estimates suggest that there were between 4,500 and 5,000 in England.

So the king needed the support of his nobility if he was to govern effectively and win his wars. He also needed to control his most powerful men. The Angevins did this in part through the use of castles. As has been seen, the destruction of illegal or 'adulterine' castles was central to Henry II's attempts to restore royal authority after 1154. Thereafter, he and his sons sought carefully to supervise the construction of private castles. In 1176, the king even went so far as to take every castle in England into royal custody for a time. The Angevins also spent vast sums on building and maintaining castles of their own in England and abroad, at least £46,000 between 1155 and 1215, an annual average of over £760. Whereas in 1154 one castle in five was royal, in 1214 it was one in two. Moreover, it was not just a case of building royal castles and destroying private ones. In 1165, for example, Henry II allowed Hugh Bigod to take back the two castles in Suffolk, Framlingham and Bungay, which had been confiscated in 1157. Then over the next eight years the king built his own castle at nearby Orford at a cost of over £1,400. Bigod was powerful and untrustworthy, and Orford was designed constantly to remind the leader of local society who had ultimate power in the kingdom. It is possible that Henry's methods pushed Bigod too far: he was a leading rebel in the Great Revolt of 1173–4.

Henry also set about controlling his nobility by more exactly defining their obligations to the king. In 1166 he ordered his tenants-in-chief to tell him how many knights they had given land to. He already knew how many knights his tenants-in-chief owed him; but, as the king also knew, many of them had given land to a greater number of knights than they actually owed. So the king demanded a detailed written list (a *carta*, hence the name given to the survey, the *Cartae Baronum*) of their own tenants from each of his tenants-in-chief.[4] One of Henry's motives in having the survey carried out was political. He wanted to know the names of those to whom the tenants-in-chief had given land, so that he could obtain oaths of loyalty from these 'under-tenants'. Another motive was financial. Henry wanted to get a firm idea of how many knights actually occupied the lands of his tenants-in-chief so that he could raise scutage on that number rather than on the official *servitium debitum*. In addition, up-to-date information about the lands of his tenants-in-chief would allow the king to assess proper levels of payment for feudal incidents – reliefs, wardships and so on. And knowledge of the number of under-tenants would also allow him to raise money from them if the estates ever came into his possession after the death or dispossession of a tenant-in-chief. Of course the king might go too far and provoke his barons into opposition. In 1170, as part of the Inquest of Sheriffs described below, the king ordered inquiries to be carried out into how much money his lay and ecclesiastical nobles had received from their lands since he had last been in England four years before.[5] This was an unprecedented intrusion into the affairs of England's great men, and it may have played a part in persuading some of them to join the Great Revolt of 1173–4.

The survey of 1166 revealed the extent of the resources at the king's disposal in his capacity as the kingdom's greatest feudal lord. Such matters remained of central importance in the relationship between the king and his nobility after 1154. The king could demand reliefs from aspiring heirs, or sell wardships and the marriage of heiresses and widows. He could auction off non-feudal offices and privileges, too: sheriffdoms, hunting rights and much more. Such was the stuff of royal patronage, and down these avenues fortunes might lie. Richard, for example, made William Marshal a great man at a stroke when in 1189 he allowed him to marry Strongbow's daughter, the heiress to the county of Pembroke and the lordship of Striguil in Wales, and to the Irish lordship of Leinster. More damaging, particularly to royal finances, were the favours showered by Richard on his brother John in the same year to secure his loyalty whilst Richard was on crusade. John was allowed to marry the heiress to the earldom of Gloucester and county of Glamorgan, but he was given control of seven English counties.

The king needed to be prudent in dispensing patronage to his nobles, and he was supposed to be even-handed. If he was not, grievances could be created which festered through generations. An individual might offer a large sum of money to enter into his father's lands or acquire the wardship of a minor, for example. If he could pay up front, all well and good; the king would usually be grateful for the cash. If he could not pay everything at once, he might agree to pay in instalments, so much every year. A well-disposed king might allow these payments to be missed for a year or two (Henry II showed particular generosity to his earls in their financial dealings with the crown, for example), but for any number of reasons the king could at some point demand payment of the arrears or even of the debt in full. Thus indebtedness itself could be used by the king as a form of patronage and as a means of enforcing control or even of breaking someone completely. The king was supposed to act reasonably of course, but there were no fixed rules about what this might mean in particular cases. All the Angevin kings used and abused their powers of patronage. The pipe rolls of Henry II's later years reveal that large sums were regularly offered for offices, lands, reliefs, wardships and marriages. In 1185–6, for example, the widow of the earl of Warwick offered the king £466, in part so that she should only be married to someone of her choice. Under Richard and John, too, as their financial needs mounted, such offers continued to be made and the sums involved became increasingly large. In 1197–8, for example, Peter de Brus offered a relief of £333 in order to succeed to his father's lands. John in particular became increasingly desperate for both money and political security; consequently he used these offers as sticks with which to beat his barons, and that way lay resentment and opposition.

For the first half of this period, the most important nobles with whom Henry II had to deal were his sons. William I and his sons had had an uneasy relationship, but it was relatively smooth compared with the dynastic squabbling of the Angevins. It was good practice to produce several sons, in case one or more of them did not live to succeed their father. However, if they all survived into adulthood and the king was long-lived, too, then problems were almost bound to arise. As William I found with Robert Curthose, there were few things more dangerous for a king than an heir who had been brought up to rule but who had no power. The Great Revolt of 1173–4, and the others of 1182–3 and 1188–9 were all caused in large part by Henry II's failure to satisfy the ambitions and allay the insecurities of his sons. The Angevin Empire has been referred to by John Gillingham as 'a family firm', but what unity there was within and across the lands in question could not survive if the ruling family did not maintain its own solidarity.[6] Such quarrels also gave an opportunity to those outside the royal family who felt they had been denied 'good lordship' by the king. William de Ferrers opposed the king in 1172–3 because he had been denied his mother's inheritance and the title earl of Derby; Earl Hugh Bigod of Norfolk did the same because he had been forced to pay £666 to recover his two castles at Bungay and

Framlingham. The king had the power to deny these men what they wanted, but there were risks in so doing.

Royal government

The Angevin kings were frequently absent from England. During his thirty-five-year reign, Henry II spent 154 months in England, Wales and Ireland, 176 in Normandy and only 84 in his French lands outside Normandy. After his release from captivity in 1194, Richard I spent three of the next five years in Normandy and only two months in England. And John spent much of his time in Normandy between 1199 and 1203 defending it against the attacks of Philip II. He was only in England so much after 1204 because he had nowhere else to go. Even when abroad, the king remained in permanent, albeit sometimes remote contact with his English administration. Henry II maintained a close watch on the conduct of his deputies; and when in 1191 Walter of Coutances, archbishop of Rouen, landed in England to take charge of the government after the quarrel between Longchamp and John, he was carrying Richard's orders with him. More usually, individuals looking for the king's help in a lawsuit or with an inheritance would seek him out, and royal orders would be given and carried back from abroad. During Henry II's first years as king, his chancellor Thomas Becket oversaw the issuing of increasing numbers of royal writs and charters. The king's travelling household, therefore, remained fundamental to the way he exercised power. As well as writing his documents and issuing his orders, it met his daily needs and kept his valuables. It also contained the knights who formed his bodyguard and the core of the royal army in wartime.

The king's government in England needed to cope with his prolonged absences, and the central figure in this context was the chief justiciar. The responsibilities of the post were reasonably well defined by the time Richard de Lucy resigned from it in 1178. The justiciar was in overall charge of the law courts, and he also had general discretionary powers to act on behalf of the king as circumstances dictated. His principal duty was to ensure that the king's will was done, and he derived his power to do this from his role as head of the Exchequer. The Exchequer was running in top gear once more by the 1170s and it dominated royal government. Sessions were held twice a year, sheriffs were held to account and pipe rolls were compiled in the ways already described in Chapter 6. Lucy was succeeded by Ranulf Glanvill who, as well as having served as a royal sheriff and fought with distinction against the rebels in 1173–4, was also one of England's most important judges. The only relative failures as justiciar appear to have been those appointed by Richard at the start of his reign. The novelty of having co-justiciars, William de Mandeville, earl of Essex, and Hugh de Puiset, bishop of Durham, did not long survive the earl's death, and Bishop Hugh was appointed not for his skill but because he had paid handsomely for the office. And although William Longchamp, bishop of Ely, had become sole justiciar by 1191, he did not survive a power struggle with John. When John himself became king in 1199, and especially after 1204, the relationship between king and justiciar changed again. His continental lands having been lost, John was much more of an active presence in England than any of his predecessors except Stephen, and 'the role of Geoffrey FitzPeter as justiciar [since 1198] diminished from being viceregent to chief executive officer frequently in attendance upon the king'.[7] The man appointed to succeed Geoffrey on his death in 1213, Peter des Roches, bishop of Winchester, was an intimate of the king, and unpopular with his master's opponents. Such changes have been seen by some as part of a wider attempt by John to reassert direct royal control over the running of government. In Warren's words, 'he was absorbing the justiciarship'.[8] However, the last of the great justiciars, Hubert de Burgh, was not a man to be 'absorbed' by anyone. Appointed at Runnymede in 1215, he played a crucial role in the civil war which followed Magna Carta and in the minority of John's son, Henry III. After Hubert lost the justiciarship in 1232, the office never regained its pre-eminence.

Perhaps the most influential justiciar of all was Hubert Walter, who held the post from 1193 to 1198. Hubert had accompanied Richard I on the Third Crusade and visited him in Germany during his captivity. When he returned to England in April 1193, he was elected archbishop of Canterbury at Richard's urging and appointed justiciar in December. Hubert dealt with the revolt of Count John whilst Richard was in France in 1194, and after the king left England for the last time in May 1194, Hubert was left in sole control of the kingdom. He was an administrator of exceptional competence and ability, responsible for maintaining peace and dispensing justice, but also driven to experiment in government by the need to raise the vast sums required first to pay the king's ransom and then to enable the king to fight his wars against Philip II. His administration was 'a finely tuned machine' geared to the needs of war finance.[9] As described below, every traditional expedient (the exploitation of feudal incidents, for example) was used to raise money, along with many new ones: the carucage of 1198 was a new type of tax; and a new government office, the Exchequer of the Jews, was established to oversee Jewish moneylending in the kingdom. Between 1194 and 1198, an annual average of approximately £25,000 was accounted for at the Exchequer, not a lot more than under Henry II, but, coming on top of the payment of Richard's ransom, it seemed otherwise. According to one early thirteenth-century chronicler, 'No age can remember, no history can record any preceding king, even those who reigned for a long time, who exacted and received so much money from his kingdom as that king exacted and amassed in the five years after he returned from captivity.'[10]

Hubert was not just concerned with raising money. In the field of royal justice, which he supervised, there was an increasing specialisation in personnel. No more than twenty men served Hubert regularly as royal justices; all were men of legal expertise. In addition, under him the court of Common Bench at Westminster emerged as the chief royal forum for the hearing of civil cases. However, it is perhaps in relation to record-keeping that Hubert is most famous. The central courts began to keep rolls recording their decisions at this time, and new types of legal record were devised, in particular concerning land. Until 1195, parties to a land transfer might choose to have it witnessed by royal judges, so as to give it greater legitimacy. Two copies of the agreement would then be written on a single piece of parchment (a 'chirograph'), and each party would keep one after a jagged line had been cut between them. However, one document from 1195 expressly reveals how, at Hubert Walter's instigation, the practice of keeping a third copy for the royal archives was begun. These third copies are known as 'feet of fines' because they were written at the bottom (the 'foot') of the chirograph (or 'fine'). 'For the first time, a form of record had been deliberately inaugurated as a continuing series for archival purposes.'[11] In the chancery, too, there were profound developments. Henry II's chancery had produced more documents than its predecessors (an average of 120 surviving documents a year, compared with forty or so under Henry I), but no effort had been made to keep copies of the thousands which must have been issued in total. Almost certainly whilst Hubert was justiciar, a central record of all the letters issued in the king's name began to be kept for the first time. Royal letters fell into one of three categories by the 1190s: charters, letters close and letters patent. Charters were the most solemn, addressed generally and containing the names of many witnesses; letters close, sealed shut and addressed to individuals, conveyed routine royal orders to sheriffs and other royal officers; letters patent were sealed open and designed to be made public – royal pronouncements on a range of issues. Now, an abbreviated copy of each letter was entered on a parchment roll, and a new roll was begun each year. The first surviving charter, close and patent rolls date from 1199, 1200 and 1201 respectively, but it is probable that none of them was the first of its kind. And even if they were, Hubert would still have been responsible for their introduction, as he was royal chancellor between 1199 and 1205. Because these rolls survive in almost unbroken sequence from the early thirteenth century onwards, 'the reign of John is the first period in English history when political history can be described on a daily basis'.[12] This is a welcome development for the historian, of course; but the extent to which the sudden availability of records may make John's government appear more intensive and oppressive than his predecessors' should always be borne in mind.

Local government

Much more than their Norman predecessors, the Angevin kings controlled the English localities through the operation of the legal system. The next chapter will deal in detail with developments in this area, but one is worth mentioning here. In 1194, as part of the general eyre of that year, the royal administration under the supervision of Hubert Walter ordered that in each shire three knights and a clerk should be elected as 'keepers of the pleas of the crown'.[13] They were henceforward responsible for collecting and keeping evidence in those criminal cases which could only be heard by the king's travelling judges. These men were the fore-runners of the coroners who still investigate suspicious deaths today. However, throughout this period, although new positions were created in local government, other long-standing ones remained important. In particular, the sheriff continued to be fundamental to the enforcement of royal authority in the shires. The first point of contact between central and local government, he collected the king's money, administered justice, kept the peace, maintained castles and did anything else the king ordered him to do. Whilst still the king's deputy, therefore, the sheriff wielded enormous power within his county and could acquire enormous wealth. As will be seen below, the Angevin kings experimented in various ways to try to get more money from their sheriffs. They were also determined to exercise firm control over them in other ways. Dismissing sheriffs was clearly one way in which the king could do this. As has been seen, Henry II removed large numbers of his sheriffs in 1155 and 1162; John did the same in 1204. However, the more regular way of supervising their affairs was by making them come to the royal Exchequer twice a year to submit their accounts. These Exchequer sessions were not just money-raising occasions, therefore, but remained essential elements in the framework of royal government. The *Dialogue of the Exchequer* reveals in detail how onerous an ordeal an appearance before the Exchequer could be. Henry II was not content with such methods of investigation. In 1170 he ordered an inquiry to be undertaken (the so-called 'Inquest of Sheriffs') into malpractice in local government. The key question was how much the sheriffs and other local officers had taken from their counties 'to the burden of the land and the men'.[14] In other words, Henry's plan was to get rid of those sheriffs who were abusing their position and exploiting those subject to their authority. As a result of the inquiry, twenty-two of the twenty-nine sheriffs were dismissed. Henry was not being completely selfless here, of course; the dismissal of corrupt royal officials was a device regularly used by kings who needed political support. In 1213, for example, after John had learned of the plot to have him killed on campaign in Wales, he felt compelled to make concessions. He replaced the sheriffs of Yorkshire and Lincolnshire with local knights and wrote letters to the men of these two counties expressing how moved he had been on hearing of the extortions of the sheriffs and their officers.

Regardless of the chance of dismissal, men continued to pay for the privilege of becoming a sheriff. Richard I sold such positions both before he left on crusade and after he returned: all but five of the sitting sheriffs were replaced in 1189 and two-thirds in 1194. In 1200 William de Stuteville offered John £1,000 to be sheriff of Yorkshire. The other side of this coin was that local communities were also prepared to offer the king money if he appointed a sheriff from their own county rather than an outsider or, even more alarmingly, a foreigner. In 1204–5, for example, the men of Cornwall offered John £1,466 for a variety of privileges, including the right to have a local man as sheriff. This was therefore a matter of great importance to those at the sharp end of his activities, and John ignored such sentiments to his cost later in his reign. He relied on his local officials to carry out his financial policies, and he often chose foreigners who owed their careers solely to him to act most ruthlessly. Sheriffs like Gerard d'Athée in Herefordshire, Engelard de Cigogné in Gloucestershire and Philip Mark in Nottinghamshire were notoriously harsh administrators during John's reign.

Royal wealth

The Angevin kings needed money for the same reasons as their Norman predecessors. Everyday expenses needed to be met, and their wider military commitments soaked up huge sums of money. Henry II had much more territory to defend than previous kings, and Richard had the extra expense of winning back what he had lost whilst on crusade. As for John, the task he set himself after 1204 of recovering his lost continental lands necessitated fund-raising on an unprecedented scale. There were other expenses, too: Richard's ransom of £100,000, for example, and the relief of £13,333 which John agreed to pay Philip II in 1200. To meet these enormous demands, traditional sources of revenue (including the profits of justice and royal control of the Church, which will be discussed in the following two chapters) were tapped with increasing intensity, and new ones were developed with varying degrees of success.

The early pipe rolls of Henry II's reign suggest the extent of the damage done to royal finances whilst Stephen had been king. In 1130, some £23,000 had been paid in at the Exchequer, but the average for 1155–7 was less than half this amount. The average rose as the reign went on: £18,500 between 1165 and 1174 and over £23,000 during the 1180s; but in only three years during his reign (1177, 1185 and 1187) did Henry II's

Exchequer income match that of Henry I. What is more, the real value of these sums was declining because of the effect of inflation between the 1180s and the early thirteenth century. Over this period the prices of oxen and wheat more than doubled, and the cost of warfare for the king increased considerably, too: Henry II would have paid a mercenary knight eight pence per day; John had to pay two shillings. Prices rocketed in particular during the early years of John's reign after a series of poor harvests, and he would have appreciated the wisdom of Richard FitzNigel in the *Dialogue of the Exchequer*: 'the abundance of resources, or the lack of them, exalts or humbles the power of princes. For those who are lacking in them become a prey to their enemies, while those who are well supplied with them despoil their foes.'[15]

The royal lands

These remained the principal source of the king's ordinary revenue throughout this period, although the kings' attitudes towards them varied considerably. Henry II was extremely reluctant to grant any away, but Richard was quite different, especially at the start of his reign when he was fixed on raising funds for his crusade. In the words of one contemporary chronicler, 'he put up for sale everything he had – offices, lordships, earldoms, sheriffdoms, castles, towns, lands, the lot'. Another chronicler, writing several years after Richard's accession, reports the king as saying that 'I would sell London if I could find a buyer.'[16] But not everything was done to raise money; as has been seen, Richard granted John seven English counties in 1189 in order to secure his loyalty. None of these counties had to account at the Exchequer whilst John continued to hold them. The pipe roll evidence for this period shows the short-term success of these policies: £31,000 was accounted for at the Exchequer in 1190 compared to £21,000 in 1188. However, for the three years following Richard's departure, as his regents struggled to extract what they could from a depleted royal demesne, the average was only £11,000.

In those counties subject to royal control, sheriffs continued to pay their farms. But there was a problem here for the king. In a time of rising prices, these sums, which had become fixed by the end of Henry I's reign, came to be worth less and less in real terms. Some of the shortfall could be made up, as Richard found at the start of his reign, by auctioning off sheriffs' offices to the highest bidder. Before this, moreover, the concept of the 'increment', a fixed payment made by the sheriff in addition to his farm, had been introduced. A small number of counties had paid increments since the 1160s, but the system was significantly extended when, in 1194, Hubert Walter demanded an extra £713 from the sheriffs of sixteen counties. John continued to exact increments for much of his reign. Another experiment he tried was the appointment of 'custodian sheriffs'. In several counties from 1204, the sheriff was made to account at the Exchequer for his fixed farm and for an additional and variable sum in respect of his 'profits'. For a while, therefore, some sheriffs were paying both increments *and* profits, and royal income increased as a result. Between 1207 and 1212, John was owed an extra £1,400 every year from these sources. However, by paying more into the Exchequer the sheriff's profit was obviously going to be reduced; unless, that is, he stepped up the pressure on the people in his shire and made good his losses through harsher extortion. Increments and profits were unpopular, therefore, and gave rise to resentment.

Taxation

Henry II levied geld in 1155 and 1161; thereafter the tax was abandoned and never collected again. The reasons for this are unclear. On paper, geld was a nationwide tax payable by all freemen which required no consent before the king could demand it. In practice, by the 1150s many individuals and institutions had been exempted from payment, and raising the tax may have become too unwieldy to be worthwhile. Alternatively, its abandonment may have been a political concession by the king. New taxes on land were tried by the Angevins instead. In 1198, Richard I raised a 'carucage'. The unit of assessment was the 'carucate' of 100 acres of ploughland. John levied another carucage in 1200 but never again after that, which suggests that it was not wholly successful. No records survive to show how much was collected. More significantly in the long term, in 1166 a national tax based on income was raised for the first time. All laymen and clergy were required to swear to contribute six pence in the pound of their annual income and the value of their chattels. The sums were being raised for the defence of the Holy Land. In 1188 another crusading tax on income was raised, the so-called 'Saladin Tithe'. All laymen and clergy who had not undertaken to go on crusade were commanded by the king to 'give in alms' a tenth of their annual income and of the value of their 'moveable' (personal) property. And when Richard was in captivity his representatives demanded a quarter of all moveable wealth to pay his ransom. All of these taxes were raised for specific purposes and did not set precedents for general taxation to meet ordinary government expenditure. Further steps in this direction were taken by John. In 1203, John demanded a seventh of the value of moveable property. But most importantly, in 1207 John levied a thirteenth on the value of incomes and moveables. It was not levied for a particular campaign or to meet the needs of a specific emergency, and it was collected on the property of all classes. John took care to ensure that the tax was publicised as having been authorised by his lay and ecclesiastical magnates. It raised the remarkable sum of £60,000, and although John did not risk raising it again, it was of great significance for the future. The thirteenth of 1207 has been seen as 'the first example of the kind of national taxation which was to become normal and which replaced feudal and customary dues by public obligations'.[17] Other new expedients were introduced from time to time as well. In 1202, John instituted customs duties at the rate of one-fifteenth of the value of imported and exported cargoes. This innovation had to be abandoned after 1206 when a truce between England and France restored free trade between the countries, but it had set another important precedent for the future.

Feudal incidents

As has been seen already in this chapter, all the Angevin kings attempted to raise money by taking advantage of their position as the greatest of feudal lords. They could demand reliefs, sell wardships and marriages and so on. Increasing use was also made by them of scutage. Henry II's great survey of 1166 was in part designed to increase the amounts he received in scutage, and he levied seven scutages during his reign. Richard raised five during his. John by contrast levied eleven scutages in sixteen years (annually from 1201 to 1206), raising an average of some £2,000 from each. And not only did he use this method more than his predecessors. The highest rate at which Richard had levied scutage was twenty shillings per knight's fee. John's first scutage was at two marks per knight's fee, in 1204 it was two and a half and his last, in 1213–14, was at the rate of three marks per fee, twice what Richard had demanded. Inflationary pressures account for some of this increase, but contemporaries viewed John's exactions as harsh and oppressive. What is more, whilst scutage could be raised without consent, there was supposed to be an immediate military need for the funds. However, in 1204 and 1205 scutages were raised to meet the cost of military campaigns which never took place: John was simply abusing the system.

This was not the only feudal obligation ruthlessly exploited by John. Some of the reliefs he demanded were exorbitant: £6,666 from Nicholas de Stuteville for his brother's lands in 1205; £4,666 from John de Lacy for the lands of his father in 1213. The sixty or so sons who succeeded to their father's baronies during John's reign paid an average of about £400 each for the privilege. Wardships were exploited, too, as were the marriages of heiresses: Peter de Maulay offered £4,666 to marry a Yorkshire heiress in 1214, and in the same year Geoffrey de Mandeville offered £13,333 to marry the king's ex-wife, Isabelle of Gloucester. The widows of tenants-in-chief were also willing to pay to either remain unmarried or marry a man of their choice. In 1212 the countess of Aumale, who had already had three husbands, offered the king £3,333 so as to avoid being given a fourth. As has been seen, John did not intend that all these sums should be paid: the debts they created hung over the heads of those who owed them, and they were explosive weapons in the king's capricious hands.

The royal Forest

The Angevins reasserted their authority over the royal Forest. Henry II even expanded the amount of land within the boundaries of the Forest, and from the mid-1160s he set about exploiting it enthusiastically. Teams of forest judges headed by the chief forester, Alan de Neville, toured the country enforcing forest law and collecting money for breach of Forest offences. More than £12,000 was collected in 1175 alone. Other sums were paid by individuals to clear land within the Forest or farm parts of it as they wished; local communities also paid to have their lands taken out of the Forest. In 1190, the men of Surrey paid Richard £133 for the partial disafforestation of their county, and John sold such privileges through-out his reign. His forest eyres were particularly profitable. The fines imposed during the eyres of 1207 and 1212 amounted to over £11,000.

During the Angevin period, attempts were also made to define the substance of Forest law more exactly for the first time. Two forest assizes in 1184 and 1198 set out the activities which were permissible within the Forest and the offences which could be committed there. Responsible for the Forest across the country was the chief forester. He oversaw a network of forest officials and courts, which were presided over by justices who enforced the law on special forest eyres. There were two main types of forest offence: hunting animals reserved for the king, deer in particular, and the cutting down of trees, vegetation and undergrowth without per-mission. No bows or arrows were permitted within the Forest, and dogs could only be kept there if they had been 'lawed' by having their claws clipped.[18] Such enactments were deeply one-sided, of course, and in prac-tice the workings of the royal Forest remained largely punitive, arbitrary and deeply resented. John's administration of it in particular contributed 'to a malevolent, oppressive quality in government not experienced hith-erto on such a scale'.[19] It generated funds, but grievances as well.

Credit and the Jews

Henry II was the first English king to borrow large amounts of money. In the first phase of his reign, Henry's main creditor was the Flemish merchant William Cade. But after he died in 1166 the king began to seek finance from England's Jews. The first Jewish communities appear to have settled in England only after 1066. They were based in towns (London, Lincoln and Norwich, for example), and by the second half of the twelfth century their principal occupation was money-lending. All Christians could lend money, just as Cade had done, but they would be committing the sin of usury if they made a profit from such activity, by charging interest, for example. Like other individuals in need of ready cash, therefore, the king borrowed money from Jewish lenders, but he had an extra level of control over them. All Jews were under the king's protection and at his mercy. He could tax or 'tallage' them whenever he liked: between 1186 and 1194, at least £13,000 was raised in this way, and John's tallage of 1210 may have raised as much as £44,000. Moreover, all that the Jews had belonged in theory to the king. On the death of a Jewish lender, therefore, the king might allow the dead man's family to pay for the privilege of taking over his business; or, given that all sums owed to Jews were owed indirectly to the king, he could set about collecting them himself. The greatest money-lender of Angevin England was the Jew Aaron of Lincoln. When he died, he was owed nearly £18,500 and a special office was opened at the Exchequer to collect the sums now due to the king. From 1194, during the justiciarship of Hubert Walter, Jewish lending was supervised centrally. Two copies of all loan agreements were to be drawn up, one of which was to be deposited in a chest at one of several designated towns. A separate Exchequer of the Jews was established to supervise the new system. Such control over the Jews and their finances gave the king access to considerable funds and extra power over their debtors, whose liabilities he could choose to enforce or remit on terms. Neither Henry II nor Richard made much effort to use the Jewish debts owed to them in this way. John by contrast, in particular after 1207, stepped up the pressure on those who owed him such sums. By tightly administering a system which hitherto had been run fairy loosely, he was creating resentments and dangers for himself.

Military organisation

At the heart of the royal army during the Angevin period, as they had been since before 1066, were the trained fighters of the royal household. They formed the king's bodyguard, and they feasted, drank and hunted with him. John probably had anything up to a hundred household knights almost permanently with him and, when circumstances required, this number grew. And, on campaign, the troops of the royal household would be further supplemented by the household troops of the king's leading men. Some of these knights would serve in the royal army so as to discharge a tenant-in-chief's feudal obligations to the king. The survey of feudal landholding undertaken by Henry II in 1166 confirmed how many knights his tenants-in-chief owed him in return for their lands. Thus Robert of Stafford owed sixty knights, the earl of Essex forty and the earl of Devon fifteen, for example. The ecclesiastical tenants-in-chief (the bishops and monasteries) owed knight service, too, and this is discussed in Chapter 12. In total, the king was owed something in the region of 5,000 knights by his tenants-in-chief. It was the duty of these men to serve in the king's army or garrison his castles.

Not all of these knights were required to serve at once. Sometimes the king required the knights who did not serve to finance those who did.

Thus on Henry II's Welsh expedition of 1157 every two knights were asked to equip a third; and both Richard and John implemented similar measures at times. There were problems with the feudal levies, too. Knights serving on this basis were probably only required to stay with the king for forty days; and by the early 1200s some tenants-in-chief were beginning to question whether they were obliged to provide knights to fight outside England. Alternative sources of fighting men had to be found, therefore, and like their predecessors the Angevins were happy to use mercenary troops. Henry II used mercenaries, as did his opponents, during the Great Revolt of 1173–4, and Richard's mercenary captains, men like Mercadier and Louvrecaire, acquired fearsome reputations. Such men could be just as loyal as troops raised in other ways: Mercadier served Richard almost continually from 1183 to 1199, for example. But there were dangers in relying on them too heavily. John's use of mercenaries alienated the Norman population in 1202–3 and pushed them into the arms of Philip II; and his hired foreign captains were regarded as instruments of his tyrannical rule by 1215. Popular or not, moreover, they had to be paid for, and one way of doing this was by levying scutage. The importance of scutage has already been discussed, and the dangers the king ran by raising scutage too often have also been mentioned. John could not kick the habit and he paid a high political price.

The road to Runnymede

The Angevins breathed new life into the system of government developed by the Anglo-Saxons and the Normans. They also built on it, and under them it became more powerful and refined than ever before. Nevertheless, one thing more than any other remained crucial in determining the effectiveness of royal rule: the personality of the king. Although English government matured after 1154 so as to function very effectively when the king was absent, kingship remained an intensely personal business. The Angevins were all notorious for their fierce tempers, but there were differences between them, too. Henry II's energy was legendary. According to Gerald of Wales, 'In times of war, which frequently threatened, he gave himself scarcely a modicum of quiet to deal with those matters of business which were left over, and in times of peace he allowed himself neither tranquillity nor repose.'[20] Like William I, Henry led by example and was determined to impose himself on his kingdom by sheer force of character. Richard's personal involvement in everyday government was necessarily reduced, but he was canny, even inspired, in his choice of deputies (with the exception of those he appointed right at the start of his reign), and he was sensible enough to let them get on with what they were good at. John was different:

he was probably not the devil described by contemporaries, but he was suspicious and volatile and could be vindictive and cruel.

The personality of the king did more than just set the tone of a reign. The Angevins' *vis et voluntas* ('force and will') and their *ira et malevolentia* ('anger and ill-will') were actually vital elements in the framework of political power. Massive coercive authority remained in the king's hands for him to exercise as he saw fit. He could act arbitrarily and on a whim, violently and oppressively. Overnight or over time, he could make men and break them. To be sure, the king made promises at his coronation to 'rule justly' and 'protect the Church', but they were vague and often honoured more in the breach than the observance. Indeed, there were no clear rules to limit what the king might do, and men would pay him money simply to obtain his good will or avoid his disfavour. Henry II and Richard I acted unreasonably and vindictively at times, according to their will (*per voluntatem*) rather than according to the law (*per legem*), and on one level John only followed the example his father and brother had set. However, his failings were made more apparent to his subjects for various reasons. First, his needs were arguably greater than his pre-decessors', and he was pushed to extremes in trying to meet them. The task he set himself after 1204 of recovering his lost continental posses-sions was on a quite different scale to anything Henry II or Richard had ever attempted. Second, confined to England after 1204, John was more of a presence to his subjects than Henry or Richard had been. He knew England better than any previous king, travelling to the north, for exam-ple, in all but four years of his reign. Third, he had a huge appetite for the nuts and bolts of administration which meant that he got involved in making decisions both large and small. For all these reasons, John could be personally identified with the oppressive government he so obviously led. Moreover, he did not help himself, and his conduct regu-larly shocked contemporaries. He was rumoured to have seduced the female relatives of some of his great men; there were whispers that he had murdered his nephew Arthur; and he was held responsible for the desperate deaths of Matilda de Braose and her eldest son. Matilda's husband William had been one of John's closest associates at the start of the reign, and had done very well as a result. However, he had fallen out with the king by 1208 and fled to Ireland. In the end, the king could not get his hands on the husband so he made an example of the wife: she and her eldest son were starved to death in Windsor Castle. Such epi-sodes alienated John's subjects and meant that they were unwilling to support him when the crucial time came.

The flaws in John's character also contributed to the loss of his con-tinental lands in 1204. John's thoughtless treatment of the Lusignans after 1200 and of William des Roches in 1202–3 constituted bad lordship. To be fair, however, the disaster of 1204 was not entirely John's fault. As has been seen, he faced a more powerful and richer king of France than either Richard I or Henry II had done. What is more, Normandy was much harder to defend in 1199 than it had been ten years previously. By the time he died Richard had recovered much of what he had lost to King Philip during his captivity, but the Norman border with the French royal lands was still porous. Richard had not retaken the strategically vital castle his father had built at Gisors, for example. This allowed Philip to keep his foot in the Norman door and await his chance to kick it down.

John's determination to return to France and take back what he had lost in 1204 dominated the last decade of his reign. He needed money and set about collecting it with ruthless application and success. By 1214 John was probably richer than any previous English king. Between 1199 and 1202 an annual average of about £24,000 was received at the Exchequer. Between 1207 and 1212 the average was £49,000, and this figure does not take into account other sums, such as those received by John from the Church during the Interdict. By 1214, it has been estimated, he had accumulated a war chest of some £130,000.[21] Had John's expedition to France then been successful, and had his allies defeated King Philip at Bouvines, Magna Carta may never have happened and John's reign might have ended in triumph. But, disastrously, John's plans blew up in his face and he returned home in 1214 to face a political nation straining to exact from him the price of defeat. The enormous sums John had raised had been squeezed out of his subjects with intense ferocity. Exorbitant sums had been charged for reliefs, wardships and the marriages of heiresses. Scutage had become almost an annual tax rather than a sum raised when there was a pressing military need. The king's local agents, his sheriffs, castellans and mercenary captains, had spared little in extracting what was demanded by their royal master. John's reputation as a just king was also in tatters: inheritances had been manipulated; land had been seized without judgment; justice had been denied or put up for sale. He was also oppressive and had used the instruments of tyranny to enforce his will: mercenaries, hostages, the law of the Forest. There were innumerable individuals who sought in 1215 to get out from under the pressure of this regime. Those who owed John money, for example, made this very much 'a rebellion of the king's debtors'.[22] The novel pressure John's government had inflicted on northern England also meant that many of the leaders of the opposition he faced came from that part of the country. However, there was more to the rebels' programme than personal or even local grievances. The general thrust of the document in which their demands were eventually met, later called Magna Carta, was that the king was subject to the law and should rule according to it. In other words, 'The rising against John was the first baronial rebellion to depict itself as a just struggle for a political programme'.[23] This view is best supported by Magna Carta's two most famous clauses. Chapter 39 stated that 'No free man shall be arrested or imprisoned or disseised or outlawed or exiled or in any way victimised . . . except by the lawful judgment of his peers or the law of the land'; chapter 40 ran: 'To no one will we sell, to no one will we refuse or delay right or justice.'

Beyond these resonant statements of general principle, which appear to extol the virtues of due process, the rule of law and impartial justice, the detailed provisions of Magna Carta attempted to make its theory of kingship into a workable reality.[24] Restrictions were placed on how the king could henceforth exercise his feudal rights. Reliefs were fixed for earldoms and baronies at £100, and for knights' fees at £5. The extent to which the king could manipulate wardships, heiresses and widows was significantly restricted. Scutages and gracious aids could only be raised in future with the consent of the 'common counsel' of the kingdom – the lay and ecclesiastical nobility and tenants-in-chief. The conduct of royal officers was to be investigated and no new sheriffs would be appointed unless they 'know the law of the kingdom and mean to observe it well'. No increments were to be exacted in addition to the sheriff's farm. The oppressive workings of the royal Forest would be moderated. John's foreign captains and their troops would be removed from the kingdom and all hostages would be released. All of this and more was contained in a royal charter of great length. It is important to remember that Magna Carta took this particular form – a grant by the king 'to all free men of our kingdom'; a list of promises which the king had sealed and which he was expected to keep. Despite this, John's opponents were not naïve enough to trust his good faith, and perhaps the most remarkable part of the charter is that which set out how he would be made to keep his promises. Chapter 61, the so-called 'security clause', established a committee of twenty-five barons. They would investigate complaints about the way the king or his servants were implementing the terms of the charter. If the king failed to deal with a complaint, the committee could then discipline him 'by seizing castles, lands, possessions, and in such other ways as they can . . . until, in their opinion, amends have been made'. This was revolutionary. Not only did the charter as a whole subject the king to the law in unprecedented ways; in chapter 61 it established an authority superior to him in his own kingdom. No self-respecting king could accept this arrangement willingly or permanently.

Magna Carta therefore criticised the excesses and inconsistencies of Angevin government in general, and John's regime in particular. But it also testified to the success of Angevin rule in certain areas. As will be seen in the next chapter, the new legal remedies instituted by the Angevins had brought more people into contact with royal justice, given them an appetite for justice and educated them in how the legal system worked.

By 1215, John's conduct had simply served to make his people more aware of the need for regular and consistently-applied justice. Thus, chapter 18 of the charter stated that two royal justices were to be sent to each county four times every year to hear cases of *novel disseisin* and *mort*

DEBATE 10
What was Magna Carta?

'Magna Carta is an unrewarding document for the general reader.'[1] Nevertheless, its obscure technicalities have not prevented the Charter from gaining a mythic significance. Although hardly any of it now remains in force, it continues to be regarded as the cornerstone of the British constitution. The motives of the men behind the Charter in 1215 were, however, complex. Some have seen John's opponents as visionaries determined to protect individual liberty; others have portrayed them as selfish reactionaries, concerned solely with safeguarding their own rights and privileges. The range of the Charter's interests, not least its express application to 'all the free men' of England, demonstrates that neither of these views does justice to the unknowable combination of personal and principled reasons which led men to rebel in 1214–15. One certainty, however, is that 'in 1215 Magna Carta was a failure. It was intended as a peace and it provoked war.'[2] The rebel barons made a bold but doomed attempt to impose comprehensive restraints on an autocratic king, and to establish mechanisms to ensure that he kept his promises. For John, however, the Charter had simply provided him with a way out of a temporary difficulty; he never intended to submit to its detailed provisions. Thereafter the Charter might have been forgotten but for its revival after John's death by the supporters of his son, Henry III. Having removed its more objectionable clauses, they reissued the Charter in 1216 and 1217 (after which it began to be known as *Magna* Carta, to distinguish it from the Charter of the Forest issued in the same year), and the third reissue in 1225 became the definitive law of the land. During the next two centuries the Charter was applied in the common law courts, but it also came to represent something more than the sum of its detail; reissuing it became almost an automatic response to criticism by hard-pressed kings. Then, in the seventeenth century, after being largely ignored by the Tudors, opponents of the Stuart monarchy rediscovered the Charter's value as a weapon against absolutism. In the end, therefore, the Charter's adaptability, according to Holt, 'was its greatest and most important characteristic'; similarly, in Warren's view, 'many who knew little and cared less about the contents of the Charter have, in nearly all ages, invoked its name, and with good cause, for it meant more than it said.'[3]

1 Warren, *King John*, p. 236.
2 Holt, *Magna Carta*, p. 1.
3 Ibid., p. 2; Warren, *King John*, p. 240.

d'ancestor; and in chapter 17 John conceded that a bench of justices would sit permanently at Westminster to hear common pleas. The men behind the charter, and their tenants whose support they needed, wanted more law, not less, properly defined and justly applied. But what they wanted more than anything else, it is worth emphasising again, was to restrict the power of the king and confine it within limits. It is not surprising, therefore, that in the short term the charter failed in its purpose of reconciling John with his barons. Indeed, it only became a permanent feature in England's constitutional landscape after John's death, when it was reissued first in 1216 and 1217 by the regents for his infant son, Henry III, as a bid for support against Louis of France, and then in 1225 in return for a grant of taxation. The reissues omitted those parts of the 1215 charter (the security clause, for instance) most objectionable to the king, but they still limited his effective power in ways with which his successors would have to grapple.

Notes

1 *EHD II*, p. 575.
2 Carpenter, *The Struggle for Mastery*, p. 196; Warren, *The Governance of Norman and Angevin England*, p. 98.
3 *EHD II*, p. 563.
4 See *EHD II*, pp. 968–81 for some examples.
5 *EHD II*, p. 471.
6 Gillingham, *The Angevin Empire*, p. 119.
7 Warren, *The Governance of Norman and Angevin England*, p. 132.
8 Ibid.
9 Turner and Heiser, *The Reign of Richard Lionheart*, p. 149 and chapter 8 generally.
10 Quoted by Carpenter in *EHR*, CXIII (1998), p. 1219.
11 Clanchy, *From Memory to Written Record*, p. 69.
12 Bartlett, *England under the Norman and Angevin Kings*, p. 200.
13 *EHD III*, p. 304.
14 *EHD II*, pp. 470–2.
15 *EHD II*, p. 524.
16 Quoted respectively in Gillingham, *Richard I*, p. 117, and Carpenter, *The Struggle for Mastery*, p. 247.
17 Warren, *The Governance of Norman and Angevin England*, p. 149.
18 *EHD II*, p. 453.
19 Holt, *The Northerners*, pp. 163–4.
20 *EHD II*, pp. 415–16.
21 Carpenter, *The Struggle for Mastery*, pp. 271–2.
22 Holt, *The Northerners*, p. 34.
23 Bartlett, *England under the Norman and Angevin Kings*, p. 62.
24 *EHD III*, pp. 316–24.

11

The Kings and the Law, 1154–1217

Between the accession of Henry II to the English throne in 1154 and the death of King John in 1216, a wide range of changes was made to the way the English systems of criminal and civil justice functioned. It has been traditional to see these changes as having marked a sudden and dramatic advance in the development of the English Common Law. However, there was a good deal of continuity between the systems of justice administered at the start of the twelfth century by Henry I and at the start of the thirteenth by John. And, though much of what happened to English legal theory and practice between 1154 and 1217 was hugely significant, it is not clear that the changes formed part of a developed or coherent plan of reform. The changes were piecemeal responses to particular needs, and whilst their effects were momentous in the long term, they were not preconceived. Indeed, there were no obvious changes to the legal system for the first few years of the reign, and the period of reform can be said to have begun in earnest only with the publication of the Constitutions of Clarendon in 1164.

The background to the reforms

Henry II became king after nearly twenty years of intermittent civil war and political disruption. During that period, royal authority in general had been weakened and, as far as the operation of the law was concerned, undermined. As his power base was restricted geographically, and as his rivals competed with him for political power, Stephen had been less able than his predecessors to involve himself in legal disputes. And as direct royal influence over the operation and implementation of the law waned, people had begun to look elsewhere for redress of their grievances and solutions to their problems. Claimants to land appear to have resorted more and more to violent means to settle disputes and, on a wider scale, there is evidence of increased theft and violence at all levels of society. When Henry II became king, therefore, the need to restore peace, settle disputes and restore lost royal authority acted as a spur to renewed royal involvement in the administration of the law. More generally, the twelfth century saw growing interest in the practice and content of the law across Europe. As will be seen in Chapter 12, the study of the law of the Church, canon law, was a developing discipline, and the study of Roman law was becoming more popular, too; authorities within the Church and outside it were becoming increasingly concerned to have their powers defined and their basis explained in legal terms. Furthermore, in England between 1163 and 1170 the king was involved in a bitter dispute with Thomas Becket, the Archbishop of Canterbury. This conflict turned as much as anything else on the respective roles of secular and ecclesiastical law in society. All of this led to an increased emphasis on the categorisation and definition of royal rights and on the codification and standardisation of laws and legal procedures.

The operation of the system

The bones of the system used by William I and his sons remained intact in 1154, and continued to be central to the operation of justice thereafter. Lords' courts, hundred courts and shire courts still operated, and the king's own court still topped the system. The kings continued to hear cases in person as and when it suited them, but during Henry II's reign a new central royal court also appeared at Westminster, the Common Bench. The origins of the Bench are obscure, but by the 1170s ordinary civil litigation was being heard regularly there by the king's justices, and the Bench was to remain the principal royal court for the hearing of civil cases for the rest of the Middle Ages.

In addition, Henry II and his sons developed the legal system and their own power by increasing the amount of contact between the centre and the localities. The Norman kings had sent judges around the country to preside over cases in the shires. This practice was vastly extended by the Angevins, although it is not clear precisely when they began to do this. Certainly by the latter stages of Henry II's reign, the country had been divided into separate circuits, each made up of a number of counties. Groups of travelling royal justices were regularly sent to tour particular circuits, visit the counties within them and hear cases. Each visitation was called an 'eyre' and the judges 'justices in eyre'. By the end of the twelfth century, systematic 'general eyres' of the whole kingdom, during which all the circuits were visited simultaneously by justices in eyre, had become a familiar feature of the English legal system. Between 1176 and

1189, for example, there were no fewer than eight visitations of the general eyre.

The range of business conducted by the travelling royal justices of this period was very wide. On appearing in a county, they brought with them a list ('the articles of the eyre') detailing the business they were to conduct. The earliest surviving example of such a list dates from 1194.[1] The justices were to hear, as they always had, 'pleas of the crown new and old', and 'of malefactors and those who harbour them'. As will be seen, they also dealt with an increasingly large number of cases concerning land. They were also to inquire into royal wardships within the county and as to the position of heiresses and widows whose marriages the king controlled. Thus the eyre was concerned as much with the investigation and enforcement of royal rights as it was with the prosecution of crime and the settlement of disputes. Sessions of the eyre were therefore sessions of a nationwide *royal* court; and the justices who presided over those sessions, men appointed by the king, actually made judgments, unlike their Anglo-Norman predecessors. Such developments led to the emergence of a core group of expert royal judges, in whose hands a regular, consistent body of national law and custom began to evolve.

Whilst the eyre was stretching out the tentacles of royal justice into every corner of people's lives, juries of local men remained indispensable to the proper functioning of the Angevin legal system. In both civil and criminal matters, they were central to the system of investigation and judgment. Once again, there was nothing new about groups of local men giving evidence to the king's officials on a range of matters (this is how the Domesday survey had been conducted, for example, and the sworn inquest was ultimately an Anglo-Saxon device); but it was the Angevins who systematised the practice and standardised its operations. At the start of the eyre, for example, a jury of twelve local knights was sworn in. Their job was to prepare answers to the articles of the eyre for the justices. They also had to arrest those from their hundred who were suspected of involvement in crime, or at least provide the sheriff with the names of people whom he could arrest and bring before the justices. And after 1166, as will be seen, the so-called 'jury of presentment' came to occupy a central place in the investigation and prosecution of crime. Local juries, too, were also instrumental to the new procedures which were developed for the hearing of disputes over land.

Greater sophistication was also introduced into the system by the expanded use of documentation. Anglo-Saxon kings had used writs as formal confirmations of land transfers. As has been seen in Chapter 6, the Norman kings had done the same and had expanded the range of situations in which writs might be used. The Angevins were also quick to capitalise upon the versatility and essential simplicity of the writ. Writs continued to be used in the traditional ways, but they also acquired fresh significance in the second half of the twelfth century as the precisely-formulated instruments by means of which a whole range of new and standardised legal actions were initiated. Under the Norman kings, where a remedy was sought from the king, every royal writ was tailor-made for the specific circumstances of the case it concerned. However, it was the Angevins who oversaw 'the development of a core of writs to be reproduced in set forms for set situations'.[2] This was especially the case, as will be seen, with regard to cases concerning land. What is more, according to *Glanvill* (see next paragraph), it was a custom of the realm by the 1180s that no one need answer in their lord's court concerning their free tenement without a royal writ. In other words, anyone who claimed land held by someone else had first to obtain a writ from the king or his justiciar before the occupier of the land was obliged to defend himself.[3] This gave greater protection to tenants and greater scope for royal involvement in the judicial process at a local level; the royal presence was now felt regularly in lords' own courts. Lords seeking remedies against tenants also prompted a further increase in the number and standardisation of the forms of writs produced by the royal chancery. By such means, the royal writ became ever more important in the lives of relatively lowly landholders. The Angevin writs, as well being standardised in terms of form and content, were also 'returnable'. In other words, after carrying out the royal instructions contained in the writ, the sheriff would make a note on the back of the writ of the action he had taken. He was then obliged to produce the writ before the royal justices on the day appointed for the hearing of the case at the eyre. By making a record of what had been done, therefore, a check could be kept on the progress of the case as well as on the official conducting it.

The increasingly familiar sight of a royal writ pronouncing the king's will helped to make royal power into an everyday reality for wider sections of English society than ever before. But the ever-expanding use of standardised writs was just one way in which the Angevin kings issued orders and gathered information in written forms. As has been seen in Chapter 10, this period saw the start of the systematic keeping of government records, of which legal records were one type. Royal courts had begun to keep 'plea rolls' by the end of the century, recording details of the cases heard before them. When the royal justices held a session of the eyre in a particular county, a detailed record was kept on a parchment roll (an 'eyre roll') of the cases heard, the judgments given and, not least importantly, the money raised for the royal coffers. The government also began from the 1190s to keep its own record of agreements (so-called 'feet of fines') made in land disputes heard in the royal court. Furthermore, many of the changes in the law during this period are known about simply because the new rules were written down and kept. The Constitutions of Clarendon of 1164, the Assizes of Clarendon and

Northampton of 1166 and 1176 respectively, the Assize of Arms of 1181 and the Assize of the Forest of 1184 all set out new principles and procedures and were the forerunners of later acts of parliament. This period also saw the first real attempt to set out in coherent and logical form a record of English laws. The *Treatise on the Laws and Customs of the Kingdom of England* was written in the 1180s and is commonly referred to as *Glanvill* after Henry II's chief justiciar from about 1179, Ranulf Glanvill, who may have had some role in its composition. *Glanvill* is structured around the common forms of the new writs and explains how each of them is to be used. This emphasis on writing things down and recording information only served to standardise further the administration of justice.[4]

The reforms

Criminal law

The Angevin period saw ongoing attempts (begun under the Norman kings) to classify different types of criminal offence. According to *Glanvill*, 'royal pleas', those triable only by the king or his judges, included

> lese-majesty as tending to the death of the king, or the moving of a sedition against his person or his realm or in his army; or again the fraudulent conceal-ment of treasure trove; or again the pleas concerning a breach of the king's peace: homicide; arson; robbery; rape; falsifying [forgery]. These crimes are either punished capitally or with loss of members.[5]

Serious theft appears to have been a royal plea, too. Lesser offences, triable by sheriffs or lords in their courts, came under the general heading of 'trespasses', wrongs such as beatings, brawling and minor wounding, where breaches of the king's peace were not claimed. Thus most offences of a less serious nature would have continued to be heard in the lower courts, outside royal supervision.

Where royal jurisdiction did come into play the new procedures served to increase the power of the king's judges. Someone might be accused of breaching the king's peace, for example. If the accused man was apprehended he would have to be kept in custody until the royal justices arrived in the county on the next eyre visitation. If the verdict was not obvious, trial by battle was the most usual method by which guilt or innocence was determined (the ordeal was used if the accused was deemed incapable of fighting), and the importance of oaths in the judicial process had begun to decline. Once found guilty, the punishment for the accused in criminal pleas of the king was death by hanging or mutilation. Outlawry remained the usual result for an accused who fled. Thus, there were notable elements of continuity from the first half of the twelfth century in the way this type of offence might be tried. However, the likelihood of such cases being heard by the sheriff or a local justice in the shire court lessened dramatically as the century went on. The leading role played by the eyre and the royal justices in the hearing of such cases had brought them squarely under the authority of the king by the early 1200s.

This increase in royal authority in criminal matters was further strengthened after 1166. According to the Assize of Clarendon of that year:

[1] . . . King Henry, on the advice of all his barons, for the preservation of the peace, and for the maintenance of justice, has decreed that inquiry shall be made . . . through twelve of the more lawful men of the hundred and through four of the more lawful men of each vill upon oath that they will speak the truth, whether there be in their hundred or vill any man accused or notoriously suspect of being a robber or murderer or thief, or any who is a receiver of robbers or murderers or thieves, since the lord king has been king . . .

[2] And let anyone, who shall be found, on the oath of the aforesaid, accused or notoriously suspect of having been a robber or murderer or thief, or a receiver of them, since the lord king has been king, be taken and put to the ordeal of water, and let him swear that he has not been a robber or murderer or thief, or receiver of them, since the lord king has been king . . .[6]

Put bluntly, Henry II was trying to rid his realm of undesirable elements and, like his Norman and Anglo-Saxon predecessors, he wanted local people to bear responsibility for good order within their communities. Ordeal by water, which, unlike hot iron, gave immediate results could only help to speed up the process. According to the Assize of Northampton, which in 1176 modified that of Clarendon, those who failed the ordeal were to lose a foot and their right hand; but even success in the ordeal was not necessarily enough. According to chapter 14 of the Assize of Clarendon, those 'of ill repute and openly and disgracefully spoken of by the testimony of many', even if they got through the ordeal, were obliged to leave England under oath never to return.[7]

The more usual task for the jury of presentment was to present the royal justices in eyre with answers to the questions set out in the articles of the eyre at the start of each new visitation. Meanwhile, those who had been accused of crime between visitations were produced before the justices by the sheriff. It was then the task of the members of the presenting jury to bring forward the accusations against individuals. Until the ordeal was abolished in England in the early years of Henry III's reign, this remained the conventional way of assessing guilt or innocence in hard cases. But once ordeal was removed as an option the role of the presenting jury expanded so that they soon came close to being the judges of guilt or innocence. As a result, 'the criminal trial jury, now one of the most widely recognised characteristics of common law, was emerging'.[8]

The success of these changes is more difficult to assess. Certainly, through the eyre and the use of presenting juries, royal control over criminal cases increased. Royal revenue increased, too. The chattels of convicted felons fell to the crown and could be sold, and there was a wide range of financial penalties for failure to appear in court, the unsuccessful prosecution of a claim and other omissions by litigants. But whether the tide of crime was stemmed or not is unclear. Most offenders probably continued to flee, regardless of their own views about their guilt or innocence. And one area royal control failed to impinge upon was that of crimes committed by clerics. This was a central cause of contention in the Becket dispute, but Henry II's attempt to bring clerical crime under the supervision of royal rather than church courts was a failure.

Civil law

Under Henry II new forms of action called 'assizes' were developed to deal with questions concerning the possession of land. The eyres spent an increasingly large proportion of their time dealing with such cases. The two most important of these were the assizes of *novel disseisin* and *mort d'ancestor*.

Novel disseisin

This was the appropriate action where an individual complained that he had recently been 'disseised' or dispossessed of some land without a court judgment. This might happen, for example, where a new lord wanted to introduce new tenants into lands which were already occupied. If the plaintiff felt that he had been disseised in this way, he could go to the chancery and purchase a royal writ in this form:

> The king to the sheriff, greeting. *N.* has complained to me that *R.* has unjustly and without a judgement dispossessed him of his free tenement in such-and-such a village since my last voyage into Normandy; *therefore I command you that, if the aforesaid N. should make you security for prosecuting his claim, then you shall cause the chattels taken from the tenement to be restored to it, and you shall cause the tenement with the chattels to be in peace until the Sunday after Easter*, and in the meantime you shall cause twelve free and lawful men of the neighbourhood to view the land, and have their names enrolled. And summon them by good summoners to appear before me or my justices prepared to make the recognition. And summon *R.* (or his bailiff if he cannot be found), under safe pledge to be there at that time to hear such recognition. And have there, etc. Witness, etc.[9]

When the sheriff had received the writ the plaintiff and defendant had to provide guarantors that they would turn up in court on the day fixed, and then the jury was empanelled to view the land in question. The case then came before the court; claims and defences were made. The jurors then swore to give a truthful verdict, deliberated and returned to give their findings. If the plaintiff was successful in establishing that there had been a disseisin without judgment, the sheriff restored him to possession of the land; if he was unsuccessful for whatever reason, he would be penalised financially for having brought a false claim.

Mort d'ancestor

This was the appropriate action to bring where an heir of someone recently deceased claimed that he was being denied his inheritance by the lord of the land in question. Again, the first step was to purchase the appropriate writ from the royal chancery and give it to the sheriff:

> The king to the sheriff, greeting. If G. son of O. shall make you security for prosecuting his claim, then summon by good summoners twelve free and lawful men of the neighbourhood of such-and-such a village to attend before me or my justices on such-and-such a day, prepared to declare on oath if O. the father of the aforesaid G. was possessed of his demesne as of fee of one virgate in that village on the day of his death, if he died after my first coronation, and if G. is his nearest heir. And in the meantime let them view the land, and you shall cause their names to be enrolled. And summon by good summoners R., who holds the land, to be there then to hear such recognition. And have there the summoners and this writ. Witness, etc.[10]

Similar procedural steps to those which took place in a case of *novel disseisin* then followed until the jurors reached a verdict on the questions put to them in the writ. If the decision went in the plaintiff's favour, another writ was issued ordering that he be put into possession of his lawful inheritance.

There were many other forms of action developed to deal with other specific sets of circumstances. Two which concerned the Church were of particular importance. The assize *utrum* summoned a jury to declare whether land was held free of service by a church or by a layman; and that of *darrein presentment* was designed to determine who had the right to appoint a priest to a church. All of these actions had certain things in common, no matter what the nature of the case was. They needed a royal writ to initiate them, and they were all designed to be simple and straightforward, and to provide expedient remedies: speedy procedures to deal with immediate problems. The local jury played a central role in the system, too: it would not have worked without their local knowledge and sense of communal responsibility. And the new system was limited in other ways. These actions were only available to freemen, and the king's own tenants, his 'tenants-in-chief', could not use them against their royal lord or against each other; the king was not prepared to dilute any of his traditional powers over his own vassals. Furthermore, these actions dealt only with basic questions: was someone dispossessed without a judgment? Was someone in possession of the land on the day he died? And because they only deal with the short-term issue of possession, they are often referred to as the 'possessory assizes'. They did not deal with the more fundamental question of who actually had the *right* permanently to occupy the land in question. To settle this more profound issue, separate procedures were required, and central to these were the writ of right and the Grand Assize.

Actions of right

The Norman kings had issued writs commanding individuals to 'do right' in legal disputes. Under the Angevins, the use of the 'writ of right' was extended and standardised in conjunction with the Grand Assize. The claimant could obtain a writ from the chancery usually addressed this time not to the sheriff, but to the lord of whom he claimed to hold the land in question:

> The king to the earl of *W.*, greeting. I command you without delay to grant full right to *N.* concerning ten ploughlands in Middleton which he claims to hold from you . . . of which *R.* the son of *W.* had dispossessed him; and unless you do so, the sheriff of Nottingham will do so, lest I should hear any further complaint about this through default of justice. Witness etc.[11]

The king's message was clear: unless you carry out your duties as lord, I will do it for you. The procedure upon a writ of right could be long and complex. In essence, though, the plaintiff would make his claim and the tenant who was in occupation of the land would defend it. There were two ways of doing this. One was trial by battle. This was in essence the same as trial by battle in criminal cases, but there were some differences. In civil actions, swords would be used by the combatants, and the plaintiff would be represented by a champion, whereas the tenant could fight himself if he wished. If the tenant was defeated, the land would be surrendered to the plaintiff.

An alternative to battle was the so-called 'Grand Assize'. The use of the Grand Assize automatically took the case into a royal court. A writ was obtained by the plaintiff addressed to the sheriff which provided that four knights of the neighbourhood were to elect twelve other knights of the same neighbourhood 'who best know the truth of the matter', who were to declare on oath before a royal judge which of the parties had the better rights to the land in question.[12] Whoever was found to have the greater right gained or kept possession of the land. Local knowledge was central to this process once more, but only knights could sit on a Grand Assize jury, whereas freemen were sufficient for the jury on a possessory assize: this reflected the more profound question which the Grand Assize was supposed to investigate.

The effects of the reforms

Because the new remedies in actions over land were only available to free men, and because only knights could sit on Grand Assize juries, it became increasingly important to know who fell into particular social categories. Thus it is arguable that the Angevin reforms led to clearer lines being drawn between different groups within English society. However, as Hudson puts it, 'the reforms' most obvious impact was to bring a greater number of parties and cases into contact with royal justice'.[13] The new criminal procedures were harsh and exacting, but the new speedy remedies available in land cases proved to be very popular. Moreover, the readiness of the royal courts to deal with disputes between lesser men about small areas of land arguably led to a decline in the importance of local and lords' courts. And such a result has prompted some historians to suggest that the Angevin legal reforms were elements of a deliberately 'anti-feudal' royal policy; in other words that Henry II in particular set out to reduce the power lords exercised over their tenants through their courts and to replace their power with his own. But such an argument assumes too great a degree of conscious planning on the part of Henry and his servants.

The reforms were not comprehensive, moreover, and they did not touch all groups within society to the same extent. The unfree (peasants, villeins, serfs, call them what you will) were unaffected by them and, in the eyes of the law, women, even high-status ones, remained second-class citizens. But, most importantly, one individual more than any other emerged from the reforming process with his traditional powers and prerogatives relatively untouched: the king himself. Whilst his tenants could no longer exercise their own lordship arbitrarily without running the risk of legal procedures being instituted against them, none of the new procedures operated against the greatest lord of all, the king: after all, how could he issue writs against himself? Thus, whilst royal control over the system of justice increased during this period, the king was arguably less subject to laws and rules than ever before. The Angevin reforms therefore left one big question unanswered: how did you stop a tyrannical king? It was in part this hole at the heart of the new legal system which Magna Carta set out to fill.

Conclusion

By 1217, English law was no longer based simply on local custom and tradition but on firmly established principles and concepts (the king's peace, royal pleas, the right of all freemen to hold their land unless a royal writ was brought against them, for example), and on regular and standard mechanisms for investigation, prosecution and trial (the writ,

DEBATE 11
Was Henry II the founder of the English Common Law?

In the opinion of arguably England's greatest legal historian, 'the reign of Henry II is of supreme importance in the history of our law, and its importance is due to the action of the central power, to reforms ordained by the king.'[1] For Maitland, Henry II was the genius who personally presided over a revolution in England's system of criminal and civil justice: new laws were enacted, new legal systems were established and an ancient, incoherent structure was swept away to be replaced by one which was uniform, consistent and 'common' to the whole kingdom. Until the 1960s, most historians followed and built upon this argument; one referred to the second half of the twelfth century as the period of 'the Angevin leap forward' in legal matters.[2] More recently, however, and although one contemporary claimed that Henry II 'was clever in devising new and undiscovered legal procedures', the degree to which the king was directly involved in the changes his reign witnessed has been questioned, as has the extent to which those changes and their effects were consciously planned.[3] Moreover, there has also been an effort to show that the legal developments of Henry II's reign would have been impossible without the considerable achievements of his predecessors. Wormald in particular has argued that the key stages in the formation of the English legal system took place before 1066. The Anglo-Saxon system was not standardised across the kingdom, but the royal administration was strong enough to exert considerable authority in legal matters and the notion of 'the king's peace' was established by the time the Normans arrived. Hudson has emphasised the ways in which royal control over the legal system was extended between 1066 and 1135, and how such progress 'permitted the administrative and intellectual developments of the Angevin period which completed the formation of the common law'.[4] Nevertheless, the contribution of Henry II and his advisers was still immense. Between 1154 and 1189, through the use of kingdom-wide judicial visitations or 'eyres', royal judges who actually gave judgments, the keeping of written records and other processes, a coherent, nationwide system of justice began to emerge which applied national laws and customs consistently in all parts of England. Henry II's reign saw the creation, therefore, of 'something quite new and . . . radically different from the fragmented, localised and inefficient system he had inherited'.[5]

1 Sir Frederick Pollock and F.W. Maitland, *The History of English Law before the Time of Edward I*, 2 vols, 2nd edn (Cambridge, 1968), p. 137.
2 D.M. Stenton, *English Justice Between the Norman Conquest and the Great Charter, 1066–1215* (Philadelphia, 1964), ch. II.
3 *EHD II*, p. 419.
4 Hudson, *The Formation of the English Common Law*, p. 21.
5 Brand, 'Henry II and the Creation of the English Common Law', p. 102.

the jury, the eyre). Many elements of the system would still have been familiar to an Anglo-Saxon audience, but much had changed, too. Hudson has summed things up well: 'The achievement of the Norman and Angevin period was immense. Key elements of thirteenth-century and later common law were established: a court system with a definite focus on the royal courts, local or central; much substantive law with regard to land-holding; consistent forms of litigation in land cases; classification of offences against the person and moveable goods; the availability of the jury to decide criminal cases. A common law had been formed, both in the sense of a law common throughout the realm and a law with definite continuity into the law of later centuries.'[14] The kings had played a central role in these developments. By subjecting more and more cases to the authority of their courts they had spread their influence and filled their coffers. In the process, however, it is arguable that they had made the dilution of their traditional powers inevitable.

Notes

1 *EHD III*, pp. 303–6.
2 Hudson, *The Formation of the English Common Law*, p. 143.
3 *EHD II*, p. 504.
4 *EHD II*, pp. 495–513.
5 *EHD II*, p. 495.
6 *EHD II*, pp. 440–1.
7 *EHD II*, pp. 444, 442.
8 Hudson, *The Formation of the English Common Law*, p. 179.
9 *EHD II*, pp. 508–9. The words in italics are my translation of this part of the original Latin; there appears to be a mistranslation at this point in *EHD*.
10 *EHD II*, p. 506.
11 *EHD II*, pp. 504–5.
12 *EHD II*, pp. 500–1.
13 Hudson, *The Formation of the English Common Law*, p. 205.
14 Ibid., pp. 236–7.

12

The Kings and the Church, 1154–1217

The relationship between the Angevin kings and the English Church was dominated by two quarrels: the first between Henry II and Archbishop Thomas Becket, and the second between John and Pope Innocent III. Both disputes arose in large measure from each king's determination to govern the Church in the same ways as he thought his predecessors had done. However, they also arose because fundamental intellectual and political changes were taking place across Europe during the twelfth century, over which English kings had little if any control. As has been seen in Chapter 8, whilst the royal grip on the Church had been loosened during Stephen's reign, this was not simply a consequence of his political weakness or incompetence. By the 1150s, ecclesiastical authorities were becoming generally more assertive in their own cause, more conscious of the need to stand apart from the lay power and more successful in so doing. These trends continued apace into the Angevin period, and so no matter how valid Henry II and John thought their arguments were about traditional royal customs and prerogatives, they could not govern their Churches, and therefore their kingdoms, effectively without acknowledging the influence and power wielded by other forces, particularly the Papacy, within their territories. Having said this, the authority exerted over the Church by Henry II, Richard and John remained extensive and, times of obvious crisis apart, there was much about their relationship with it that the Norman kings would have been happy to accept. Times had changed, therefore, but governing the Church, albeit now within more constrained limits, remained fundamental to the way the Angevin kings governed England.

The Papacy and canon law

In the century or so before Henry II became king of England, the Papacy had been at the forefront of developments in the Church. The principles of the reformers who had taken control in Rome in the 1040s were generally accepted across Europe by the 1140s. The Church needed to be pure; its personnel needed to be chaste and uncorrupted. But more than this, by the middle of the twelfth century, the authority of the pope as the supreme spiritual leader of western Christendom was universally recognised, and his influence cut across territorial borders. A key factor in the growth of papal power had been his success in intervening in the affairs of national Churches. Papal legates acted in the pope's name within kingdoms; decisions made locally, relatively trivial in themselves but cumulatively a remarkable testament to the growing confidence in papal authority, were sent to Rome for appeal; the pope demanded the attendance of archbishops and bishops at his councils wherever they were convened. 'In 1100 traffic between England and the curia had been rare, by 1200 it had become the norm, largely by volition rather than compulsion.'[1] Kings, of course, English ones no less than others, struggled to restrict the exercise of these powers and, when forced to accept them, to minimise their impact. But other developments only made their task more difficult. As the power of the Papacy grew, more interest was taken in defining its basis and extent. As a result, the study of 'canon' law, the law of the Church, was revolutionised during the twelfth century. The Bible was studied perhaps more intensely than ever before, and the works of the so-called 'Church Fathers', men like St Augustine and St Jerome, were perused to find justifications for the concept of papal supremacy and for the view that members of the clergy were different to others – separate and distinct with their own rights and privileges. During the 1140s the most comprehensive and authoritative compilation yet of canon law, the *Decretum*, was produced by Gratian of Bologna, and it remained the standard textbook of canon law for most of the Middle Ages.

It was not by chance that the *Decretum* was produced at Bologna, because by the middle of the twelfth century the university there was the acknowledged international centre for the study of ecclesiastical and secular law. Indeed, there was a general expansion of education in the twelfth century, and education was the preserve of the Church. At a local level, sometimes individual priests, but more usually monasteries and cathedrals became increasingly active as providers of the scholarly nuts and bolts, namely a knowledge of Latin. Ambitious young men who had proved their aptitude for Latin, and who were interested in the study of the law, might then make their way to Bologna, but those more interested in philosophy and theology would make for Paris and, by the end of the twelfth century, the fledgling university at Oxford. In an increasingly mobile world, then, England was not cut off from these developments. There were English students studying at Paris and Bologna from about 1100, and between 1179 and 1215, one in three Paris 'masters' (graduates) whose origins are known were English. Nearly a third of the English bishops appointed between 1180 and 1223 were masters. Thus, along with the refined techniques of philosophical dispute and argument, the latest ideas about the status of the Church within society were brought to England by a new generation of men who had been educated to the highest available standards in the fields of philosophy, theology and law.

Therefore, by the time Henry II became king, the western Church was governed more coherently and more hierarchically from the centre than ever before. Ever more emphasis was being placed by the powers within the Church on the establishment of its own sphere of authority and jurisdiction, separate from and independent of that of the lay ruler. It had its own leader, its own personnel, its own laws and its own courts, and its claims to autonomy were capable of more or less clear definition according to canon law. However, this was still an ongoing process, far from completion in 1154. The Papacy was regularly politically weak and unable to act assertively; lay and ecclesiastical jurisdictions in England still overlapped considerably; and the powers the king had over the affairs of the Church were still of real practical value. Much remained ill-defined, then, in the relationship between king and Church, and it was to be in these grey areas, where the rivals for power pulled against each other in the struggle for control, that conflict erupted.

Royal expectations

Having said all this, for lengthy periods during the reigns of Henry II, Richard and John the English Church was dominated, used and exploited by them much as it had been by their Norman predecessors. They controlled appointments to bishoprics and abbacies and vacancies as much as they could, and royal servants continued to figure prominently as bishops. Of the sixty-three men appointed to bishoprics between 1154 and 1216, twenty-nine were royal clerks. Royal attitudes are encapsulated in a famous writ of Henry II which was alleged to have been sent to the monks of Winchester after the death of Bishop Henry of Blois in 1171: 'I order you to hold a free election', the king said, 'but nevertheless forbid you to elect anyone except Richard [of Ilchester] my clerk.'[2]

Members of the clergy also continued to work at all levels within the royal administration. Clerks were the mainstay of the chancery and the Exchequer; they produced the ever-increasing volume of documentation emerging from central government during this period. Higher up the ladder, royal chancellors and justiciars were often bishops. The most notable example of all was Hubert Walter, archbishop of Canterbury (1193–1205), who held both posts at different times under Richard and John. As has been seen in Chapter 10, his contribution to the development of English government was immense. Some appointments were less successful, of course: Bishop William Longchamp of Ely (1189–97) was a failure as chancellor and justiciar during the early part of Richard's reign.

The kings also continued to regard their bishops and abbots as great barons who owed them loyalty and service. The most detailed replies submitted in 1166 after Henry II's great inquiry into feudal service came from individual churches. The archbishop of York, for example, owed the king twenty knights and gave a lengthy list of all the tenants he and his predecessors had enfeoffed. He also made it clear that he was sending the king these details 'being one of those subjected in all things to your orders . . . and in this return I am declaring all these things to you as my lord'.[3] In all, the bishoprics and abbeys which sent their details to the king in 1166 owed him approximately 775 knights of the 5,000 or so owed by all the king's tenants-in-chief; about 15 per cent of the total.

Nevertheless, royal control over the Church was not as extensive as it had once been. If nearly half of the bishops appointed under the Angevin kings were royal clerks, necessarily more than half were not. Some, as in previous periods, were monks, but the rest were clerks who had established their reputation outside royal government, by serving within a bishop's household, perhaps, or as archdeacons or cathedral canons. Under Henry II more of these 'ecclesiastical clerks' became bishops than did men whose early careers had been within royal government. This may have been in part because of a growing unease within ecclesiastical circles about the continued involvement of churchmen in lay affairs. Some bishops, notably Hubert Walter at Canterbury and Peter des Roches at Winchester (1205–38), felt few qualms about devoting themselves to royal service; others, like Hugh de Puiset of Durham (1153–95), even paid for the privilege. But certainly, some scruples were sincerely felt. Thomas Becket resigned the royal chancellorship after becoming archbishop of Canterbury in 1162, and Geoffrey Ridel resigned the same office when he became bishop of Ely in 1173. By the early thirteenth century, too, there was increasing disquiet felt about the appropriateness of churchmen sitting as royal judges. Bishops had traditionally presided over the shire court, and under Henry II many acted as judges in the central or travelling royal courts. However, this required them to pass sentences which might involve the shedding of blood, and for reformers who demanded that the clergy should be untainted by worldly concerns, such participation was unacceptable. Clerical involvement in government was to continue for the rest of the Middle Ages and beyond, but by the end of John's reign it was no longer taken for granted that members of the clergy had a natural role in the administration of lay affairs.

Henry II and Thomas Becket

Therefore tensions were developing not far beneath the surface in 1154. Having said this, there was every sign at the start of Henry II's reign that his relationship with the English Church was going to be a traditional one. Like any new king, he needed ecclesiastical support and was keen not to stir up controversy. He was also busy abroad until the end of the 1150s. However, by 1162 Henry was firmly established on the throne, and there was a vacancy at Canterbury, Archbishop Theobald having died in 1161. This was Henry's chance to make his mark on the Church and to begin the process of recovering those powers and rights which had been lost to the English king during Stephen's reign. The king's nominee for the archbishopric was Thomas Becket. Royal chancellor since 1154, Becket had served the king dutifully and enthusiastically, and Henry had every reason to think that he would continue to do so after becoming archbishop. He was duly elected in May 1162; and the ease with which Henry imposed his choice on the monks of Canterbury suggested, superficially at least, that royal dominance over Church appointments was being reasserted after the relative slackness of Stephen's reign. But almost as soon as he had taken up his new post, and to the king's dismay, Becket resigned the chancellorship and, overnight it seemed, was a changed man. Gone was the high-living, extravagant chancellor who had loved finery and display; in his place now was the ascetic, zealous archbishop who wore a hair-shirt beneath his vestments. No longer the defender of the king's interests, his priority now was the defence of the Church he led.

It was not long before several minor disagreements had soured the relationship between the king and the archbishop. However, the hostility between them crystallised over one issue: what should happen to 'criminous clerks', members of the clergy who committed crimes? This was a bigger problem than it might at first sight appear. Perhaps as many as one in five of the adult male population of England at this time was a member of the clergy. Most were in 'minor orders', below the rank of priest, and would not have been ordained; many would have lived lives like ordinary laymen. Despite this, for Becket and the theorists who argued for the distinctiveness of the clerical caste, it was for the Church alone to deal with wrongdoers from within its own ranks. For Henry II, by contrast, one of his primary duties as king was to keep the peace and punish all criminals, regardless of their position in society. To make matters worse for the king, the punishments inflicted on criminals by lay and church courts were quite different. A layman found guilty of even a minor offence might suffer mutilation or even death; for the church courts, however, the most serious punishment available to them was to strip the offender of his clerical status. The dispute over criminous clerks, therefore, went to the heart of what the king was able to do within his kingdom. For Henry, the Church's claim that its personnel were solely its concern impacted profoundly on his ability effectively to govern, and it undermined his attempts to restore law and order in England after the chaos of Stephen's reign. For the Church, its right to apply its own laws and inflict its own punishments in its own courts was a touchstone of its independence from lay control.

The king raised the issue of criminous clerks with his bishops at a council held at Westminster in October 1163. He demanded that clerks found guilty in ecclesiastical courts of serious offences should be handed over to his officers for punishment. The bishops, united behind Becket, rejected this demand. Matters then came to a head at another royal council held at Clarendon near Salisbury in January 1164. Henry demanded that the assembled bishops assent to a list of what he presented as the traditional customs of the kingdom, those which in his view had regulated the relationship between the king and the Church in the reign of Henry I. The bishops, behind Becket again, though some of them reluctantly, swore in general terms to observe traditional practices, but unusually the king then insisted on writing these customs down and requiring the bishops to put their seals on copies of the document, known since as the Constitutions of Clarendon.[4] This was a step too far for most of the bishops, given the specific terms of many of the clauses they were asked to approve. A few were uncontroversial, but many were not: clause 4, for example, stated that bishops and archbishops were not permitted to leave the kingdom without royal consent; clause 8 held that no appeal could be made to the pope in an ecclesiastical case without the king's permission. Such provisions probably did represent what had happened under Henry I, but they ignored completely the extent to which views about the freedom of the Church had developed since then. No self-respecting bishop who considered himself a loyal servant of the pope could accept them without being seen to countenance a backward step away from reform. But most problematic of all was clause 3, which attempted, not very clearly, to deal with the problem of criminous clerks. The royal view appears to have been that accused clerks should first be brought to a royal court. If their clerical status was established, they could then be sent to a church court under the supervision of a royal official. If then found guilty and punished in the church court, the accused should be handed back to the royal court where the appropriate secular penalty would be imposed. This interpretation seriously impinged on the Church's right to supervise its own personnel, and it exposed clerks accused of crimes to punishment in both royal and church courts. For Becket, it was impossible to accept.

The issue of the Constitutions of Clarendon resolved nothing (they 'were the consequence of the dispute as much as its cause'[5]), and only increased the bitterness on both sides. By the autumn of 1164, the king had decided to get rid of Becket once and for all, and he summoned him to appear at his court on a charge that he had failed to deal with the complaints of one of his vassals in his own court. Becket failed to appear in response to this summons and when he finally met the king at Northampton in October 1164 he was charged with contempt. He appealed to the pope for assistance, in direct contravention, the king claimed, of clause 8 of the Constitutions of Clarendon. On the night of 13–14 October, the archbishop fled from court and escaped across the Channel. He looked to the pope for support, but Alexander III was preoccupied with his struggle against Emperor Frederick 'Barbarossa'. He could not afford to alienate another powerful ruler and so, whilst he was sympathetic towards Becket, he could not take drastic steps against Henry II. The dispute rumbled on unresolved, therefore, and Becket spent the six years between 1164 and 1170 in exile in France.

The stalemate was broken in June 1170 when Henry II decided to have his eldest son crowned in order to consolidate his plans for the succession. Since there was no archbishop of Canterbury to perform the ceremony, the king relied on the archbishop of York to carry it out. When Becket heard what had happened, he was outraged at this insult to his position. After a threat by Alexander III to punish the king, and some abortive attempts at reconciliation, Becket finally returned to England in December 1170. His target now was not the king but the bishops who had performed the coronation ceremony. He excommunicated them, whereupon several of their fellows travelled to France to complain to Henry about Becket's high-handed conduct. Shortly afterwards the king lost his temper over Becket's behaviour for the last fatal time. In a furious outburst he appeared to invite his followers to take drastic steps against the archbishop; four of his knights immediately travelled to England and hurried to Canterbury where they arrived in the late afternoon of 29 December. Having tried without success to get Becket to absolve the excommunicated bishops, they cornered him in his cathedral and hacked him to death. Miracles were soon reported at his tomb, and only just over two years after his murder, in February 1173, Thomas Becket was canonised.

If Henry II had not intended Becket's murder, he was deeply implicated in it and eventually had to perform humiliating penance to atone. In July 1174, at the height of the Great Revolt against him led by his eldest son, the king came to Canterbury as a barefoot penitent and was publicly scourged outside the cathedral. By this time, in fact, much of the heat generated by the quarrel with Becket had dissipated. In May 1172, Henry had formally submitted to the pope's legates at Avranches. In addition to providing knights to go on crusade and agreeing to go himself, Henry undertook to allow unimpeded appeals to Rome and to abolish all customs hostile to the Church which he had introduced.[6] In other words, the king had given some ground, but he had not lost very much as a result of the archbishop's death. And after 1172 good relations with the papacy were restored, as was much of the traditional emphasis on royal control of the Church. By 1180 most of the contentious parts of the Constitutions of Clarendon had been negotiated away, including the problem of criminous clerks, and the king was successfully nominating his men to vacant bishoprics and taking the profits from vacant sees. Superficially at least, it was almost as if the Becket dispute had never happened.

On one level, the controversy had been so intense only because of the personalities of the men involved. Both Henry II and Thomas Becket were obstinate and bloody-minded in their determination to defend what they considered to be their rights and privileges. Once one of these characters was removed from the stage, it could be argued, normal service was likely to be resumed as far as the relations between the king and his Church were concerned. To an extent this is fair, but the dispute arose from more than the stubbornness of former friends. It also turned on something fundamental in the developing relationship between Church and state in twelfth-century Europe: where did power ultimately lie and to whom was loyalty ultimately owed?

John and Innocent III

Many of the same forces which gave rise to the Becket dispute also lay behind the breakdown in Anglo-papal relations which took place during the reign of John. In July 1205, the archbishop of Canterbury, Hubert Walter, died. Like his predecessors, John considered that he should have a significant say in nominating the next archbishop, a tenant-in-chief of the crown and one of the king's principal counsellors, and he put forward the name of John de Gray. Gray was bishop of Norwich (1200–14) but also one of the most important officials within John's government. For their part, the monks of Canterbury were keen to assert their right to choose their own archbishop (a sign in itself of the growing independence of the Church), and they elected in secret their sub-prior, Reginald. On hearing of this, John was outraged and by the end of 1205 he had bullied the monks into holding another election, as a result of which John de Gray was unanimously elected.

News of the confusion at Canterbury reached the ears of Pope Innocent III in Rome. He was unhappy about the candidacies of Prior Reginald and Bishop John, and so he quashed both elections. He then proposed a third candidate, Cardinal Stephen Langton. Langton was English and he had made his reputation as a distinguished teacher at the university of Paris. He was an acceptable candidate for the monks as well as the pope, but not for the king, who was furious at this turn of events. Not only had his traditional rights to be involved in the nomination procedure been ignored, he claimed, but Langton himself was a quite unacceptable arch-bishop. He was unknown in England, and he had lived among John's enemies in France too long for him to be considered trustworthy. Never-theless, Langton was consecrated archbishop in Rome. John refused to allow him into England, expelled the monks of Canterbury from the kingdom and confiscated their lands. Stalemate ensued.

John's fundamental objection to Langton's appointment was not un-reasonable. None of his predecessors would have tolerated papal med-dling on this scale in the affairs of the English Church. However, times had changed and Innocent III was a formidable opponent at the head of a formidable institution. Initially, there were hopes of a compromise, but by 1208 no solution had been found and Innocent III had run out of patience. In March 1208, England was placed under an interdict by the pope, and in 1209 John was excommunicated. The first measure meant that no church services could be performed in England: no masses, no marriages, no burials, no religious provision at all except the baptism of children and the confession of the dying. The second meant that John's immortal soul was at risk if he died without being reconciled to the Church. Just as significantly in practice, it also meant that his subjects were no longer obliged to be loyal to him.

This novel situation placed the English clergy in a dilemma which brought to a head many of the developments of the past century. When the crunch came, to whom was their loyalty owed, king or pope? The bishops of London, Ely and Worcester immediately went abroad after pronouncing the sentence of interdict in 1208. They were followed in 1209 by the bishops of Bath, Lincoln, Rochester and Salisbury, who felt unable to serve an excommunicate king. Other bishops died after 1208 and no replacements could be consecrated. By 1211, only one bishop, Peter des Roches of Winchester, was left in England. Lower down the social scale, it is hard to determine what the effects of the Interdict were on priests and people, but there is no reason to doubt that its impact on the conduct of ordinary religious life was significant.

For his part, John appears to have been largely unmoved by the sen-tences pronounced against him and his kingdom. Indeed, he was able to use the period of interdict to his financial advantage. The lands of the Church were confiscated by the king in 1208 and only returned to the religious communities in question on the payment a stiff fee and the promise of a share of future income being given to the king. When churches became vacant as bishops fled abroad or died, John retained their lands in his own hands and took the profits. By 1213, seven bishoprics and over a dozen abbacies were controlled by him, and the income must have amounted to hundreds if not thousands of pounds per year. In the year 1212 alone, he received no less than £9,275 from the bishoprics in his hands, and he may have received as much as £66,000 from the Church during the Interdict as a whole. John might even have been happy to let the Interdict continue indefinitely, indeed, had it not been for political developments elsewhere. By 1212, he felt ready to return to France and recover the lands he had lost in 1204. However, before he could do so, a settlement with the pope was necessary; frustrated at the king's refusal to capitulate over Langton's appointment, Innocent III was threatening to depose John and give his support to a French invasion of England. Therefore, in May 1213, John agreed to accept Langton as archbishop and, most drastically, surrendered England and Ireland to the Papacy only to receive them back as the pope's vassal. Suddenly John, absolved from excommunication, was the favourite son of the Papacy and Innocent III was his most powerful ally. The Interdict was lifted in the following year after the amount of compensation to be paid by John had been settled. It has been said of John's decision to submit to the pope that 'in the wider political context, it proved to be a masterstroke'.[7] The way was now cleared for his invasion of France, and John had the weight of papal support to throw at his opponents within England; any defiance of him would be defiance of the pope as well.

Like the Becket dispute, however, John's quarrel with Innocent III may appear to have generated more heat than light and to have been of little long-term significance. John's domestic government was not affected significantly by the Interdict; indeed, he profited from it financially and used it as a means of enforcing even tighter control over his subjects. In addition, once it was over, John picked up where he and his predecessors had left off, and bishoprics continued to be filled with royal servants. However, the price John had to pay in order to try to recover his continental lands was submission to the Papacy. In 1080 William I had rejected Gregory VII's claims to overlordship of England; in 1214 it was the English king who actively sought and willingly subjected himself to the superior authority of a foreign power. It was certainly a clever diplomatic manoeuvre by John, and it allowed him to pursue his plans in France as a loyal son of the Church. That it was deemed necessary, however, demonstrates the extent to which papal authority had developed since the late eleventh century. The real importance of papal backing became clear only after John's continental plans had collapsed. It was Innocent III who condemned Magna Carta and who stood behind John in the civil war that followed. And the papal legates Guala and Pandulph, who came to England before and after John's death, contributed significantly to the stabilisation of England in the early years of the minority of his son, Henry III.

Notes

1 Harper-Bill, 'John and the Church of Rome', p. 297.
2 Quoted in Warren, *Henry II*, p. 312.
3 *EHD II*, p. 971.
4 *EHD II*, pp. 766–70.
5 Carpenter, *The Struggle for Mastery*, p. 208.
6 *EHD II*, pp. 825–7.
7 Harper-Bill, 'John and the Church of Rome', p. 308.

The Principal Narrative Sources and their Authors, 1042–1217

This is not a full list of all the available narrative sources for this period, only of those used most regularly in writing this book. There is an obvious imbalance here between the number of sources listed which come from the Anglo-Saxon and Anglo-Norman periods, and those which come from the Angevin period. This is not because Angevin narrative sources do not exist: far from it, they are plentiful and frequently excellent. It is more a reflection of their relative unavailability in accessible and up-to-date translations. My policy throughout has been directly to refer only to sources which readers have a reasonable chance of studying for themselves.

Full citations for all the works mentioned will be found in 'Suggestions for Further Reading'.

The Sources

The Anglo-Saxon Chronicle

An annalistic account of English history, in English, from 494 until the mid-twelfth century. Its compilation was begun, it seems, in Wessex at the end of the ninth century, and it was continued in a number of monasteries thereafter. There are eight surviving manuscripts of the *Chronicle* in all, but for the period covered by this book, three are more important, namely those written at Abingdon (text 'C'), Worcester ('D') and Peterborough ('E'). Whilst these were all probably based on a common source, they each contain important differences of fact and interpretation, and each betrays its own local concerns and sympathies. After the Norman Conquest, the *Chronicle* was continued in English at Peterborough only.

The Bayeux Tapestry

A stunning visual source which provides an account of the final months of Edward the Confessor's reign, Duke William of Normandy's preparations for invasion and the Battle of Hastings. Although the main character in the tapestry's version of these events is Harold Godwinson, he is not sympathetically portrayed; the story is of his perjury and inevitable defeat at William's hands. It is generally thought that the tapestry was designed and made in Kent in about 1070 on the orders of Bishop Odo of Bayeux, William I's half-brother. His plan may have been to display it in his cathedral; it is still kept and displayed in Bayeux.

Eadmer of Canterbury

An Englishman, born *c.*1064, Eadmer spent his career as a monk at Canterbury where he served in the household of Archbishop Anselm. As well as writing a biography of the archbishop, Eadmer compiled a history of his own times up to 1121, the *Historia Novorum* (*History of Recent Events*).

Gesta Stephani (*The Deeds of Stephen*)

An anonymous history of the reign of King Stephen, begun *c.*1147, and written either by Robert, bishop of Bath (1136–66) or by someone close to him. It is more sympathetic to Stephen than other contemporary or near-contemporary accounts of the reign.

Henry of Huntingdon

Born *c.*1088, Henry was the son of an English mother and a Norman father who was also archdeacon of Huntingdon. When he was about 12, Henry was placed in the household of the bishop of Lincoln to be educated; and in 1110, on his father's death, he succeeded to the latter's archdeaconry. Henry began his *History of the English People c.*1123–30, at the prompting of Alexander, bishop of Lincoln, and he completed it in 1154. He is a well-informed and entertaining historian who used existing sources to which he added his own details and stories; he is the source of the story of King Cnut and the waves, for example, and his description of Stephen's reign is the only complete contemporary account.

The History of William Marshal

Written in nearly 20,000 lines of Norman-French verse by 'John', who knew William Marshal personally, this is the only surviving biography from this period of a layman who was not also a king. Commissioned by his family to celebrate the life of the Marshal on his death in 1220, and finished between 1226 and 1229, it provides a fascinating insight into the aristocratic life of the period, and is one of the principal sources for Anglo-French politics for the fifty years or so either side of 1200.

John of Worcester

The chronicle written at Worcester during the first half of the twelfth century has traditionally been attributed to a monk of Worcester named Florence. However, it is now generally thought that the author of this work was another Worcester monk, John. John wrote his history between *c.*1124 and *c.*1140, using a copy of the *Anglo-Saxon Chronicle* which has since been lost. This copy appears to have differed significantly from other surviving versions of the *Chronicle*, so John's work is of great historical value.

Orderic Vitalis

Born in Shropshire in 1075 of mixed English and Norman parentage, Orderic was sent to become a monk in the Norman monastery of St Evroult when he was 10. In about 1114 he began to write a history of the Church in Normandy; but over the next thirty years his *Ecclesiastical History* turned into something much more extensive. Despite living a cloistered existence for all of his working life, Orderic was immensely well-informed about the affairs and histories of the leading Anglo-Norman families. His huge work is thus of immense value as a guide to events on both sides of the English Channel up to 1141, when he stopped writing.

Roger of Howden
Roger began his *Gesta Regis Henrici Secundi* in the early 1170s. He was a trusted
and loyal royal clerk, and a great admirer of Henry II. However, his detailed
narrative provides an extremely valuable, and largely reliable, insider's account of
high political events until his death in 1201.

Roger of Wendover
A monk at St Albans, Roger of Wendover wrote an account of John's reign in the
mid-1220s and included it in his *Flowers of History*. Roger was hostile to John, and
his influence on later students of the king's rule and character has been considerable. Many of his more colourful anecdotes, however, amount to little more than
dubious gossip.

Vita Edwardi Regis (*The Life of King Edward*)
An anonymous work, dedicated to Queen Edith, daughter of Earl Godwin and the
wife of Edward the Confessor. It was probably written in two parts either side of
the events of 1066; the first part *c.*1065–6, and the second *c.*1067. Part I provides
a partial history of Edward the Confessor's reign, but is particularly concerned
with the fluctuating fortunes of Godwin and his sons, Harold and Tostig. Not
surprisingly, given the author's dedication, this part of the *Vita* is decidedly pro-
Godwin. Part II is a more hagiographical account of the (by then) late King
Edward's saintly qualities.

William of Jumièges
A monk at Jumièges near Rouen, William wrote his *Gesta Normannorum Ducum*
(*The Deeds of the Dukes of the Normans*) *c.*1070 and dedicated it to William the
Conqueror. William's descriptions of the lives and careers of the early dukes owed
much to earlier sources, but his work also contains plenty of valuable information
about English history either side of 1066. Having said this, William's purpose in
writing should always be borne in mind when reading his version of events: his
aim was to legitimise Duke William's succession to the English throne.

William of Malmesbury
A monk of Malmesbury Abbey in Wiltshire, William was born *c.*1095 and died in
1143. He was a prolific historian and, by the standards of his day, an outstanding
one. By the 1120s he had produced separate histories of both the kings and
bishops of England up to his own day. His *Historia Novella* (*History of Recent
Events*) was dedicated to Earl Robert of Gloucester and provides a contemporary
description of the last years of the reign of Henry I, and the early years of King
Stephen.

William of Poitiers
Orderic Vitalis (who used William of Poitiers' work extensively) relates that William
was the son of a noble Norman family and that as a youth he had served Duke
William as a knight. He then opted for the religious life, becoming first the duke's
chaplain and then archdeacon of Lisieux. Probably during the first half of the
1070s, William wrote what survives of his *Gesta Guillelmi Ducis Normannorum*

et Regis Anglorum (*The History of William the Conqueror*). It is a well-informed insider's account. However, even more than William of Jumièges, whose work William of Poitiers certainly used, the latter's purpose was to exalt the career and character of William the Conqueror, and to provide justification for the conquest of England.

Suggestions for Further Reading

This is not a comprehensive bibliography. I would refer those seeking something along those lines to the bibliographical essay by D.A. Carpenter which accompanies his *The Struggle for Mastery*, and which can be found on the website of the King's College London History Department: http://www.kcl.ac.uk/history. The books mentioned below are those which I have found particularly helpful whilst writing this book, and which should help those seeking a deeper understanding of the areas I have discussed, and/or a wider appreciation of the period as a whole. Wherever possible, I have tried to cite books which are reasonably accessible and generally available.

The place of publication is London unless otherwise stated.

Primary Sources

The best collections of translated primary sources are *English Historical Documents II 1042–1189*, ed. D.C. Douglas and G.W. Greenaway, 2nd edn (1981) and *English Historical Documents III 1189–1327*, ed. H. Rothwell (1975). Also very useful for the earlier part of this period is *The Norman Conquest of England: Sources and Documents*, ed. R.A. Brown (Woodbridge, 1984). Together these provide a good selection of administrative and legal sources – writs, charters, leases, assizes and extracts from Domesday Book and the pipe rolls. They also contain extracts from many of the principal narrative sources; in particular *EHD II* includes full translations of the *Anglo-Saxon Chronicle* and *The Dialogue of the Exchequer* as well as a reproduction, albeit in black and white, of the Bayeux Tapestry.

However, these collections omit substantial extracts from some of the more important narrative sources I have referred to. For the late Anglo-Saxon and Anglo-Norman period, these include the *Vita Edwardi Regis*, which can be found in *The Life of King Edward who rests at Westminster*, ed. and trans. F. Barlow (1962); *The Chronicle of John of Worcester*, ii, ed. R.R. Darlington and P. McGurk, trans. J. Bray and P. McGurk (Oxford, 1995), and iii, ed. and trans. P. McGurk (Oxford, 1998); *The Ecclesiastical History of Orderic Vitalis*, 6 vols, ed. and trans. M. Chibnall (Oxford, 1969–90); William of Malmesbury's *Gesta Regum Anglorum: The History of the English Kings*, 2 vols, ed. and trans. R.A.B. Mynors, R.M. Thomson and M. Winterbottom (Oxford, 1998–9), his *The Deeds of the Bishops of England*, trans. D. Preest (Woodbridge, 2002), and his account of the early years of Stephen's reign, *The Historia Novella*, ed. and trans. E. King and K.R. Potter (Oxford, 1998); and *Eadmer's History of Recent Events in England*, trans. G. Bosanquet (1964). A valuable and affordable recent addition to the list of translated sources is *Henry of Huntingdon: The History of the English People: 1000–1154*, trans. D. Greenway (Oxford, 2002).

Only limited extracts are provided in *EHD III* from the narrative sources for the later Angevin period. Generally, indeed, these are much less accessible than those for the years up to 1154, and there are few modern editions. Nineteenth-century translations of *The Annals of Roger of Howden* and *Roger of Wendover's Flowers of History* have been reprinted by Llanerch Press. A notable modern version of an important text, however, is *The History of William Marshal*, ed. A.J. Holden and D. Crouch, trans. S. Gregory (Anglo-Norman Text Society, 2002); although, as the first volume of three to appear, it only covers the years up to 1194.

General Works

Two works together deal exclusively with the development of English government before, during and beyond the period covered by this book. These are H.R. Loyn, *The Governance of Anglo-Saxon England 500–1087* (1984) and W.L. Warren, *The Governance of Norman and Angevin England 1086–1272* (1986). Seminal as far as the development of written government and literacy in general are concerned is M.T. Clanchy, *From Memory to Written Record: England 1066–1307*, 2nd edn (Oxford, 1993). Other works are wider in scope, covering politics, government, law, the Church, society, the economy and culture. Two recent ones are fundamental: D.A. Carpenter, *The Struggle for Mastery: Britain 1066–1284* (2003) and R. Bartlett, *England under the Norman and Angevin Kings, 1075–1225* (Oxford, 2000). These are both dynamic works, full of insight and novelty, which wear their profound learning very lightly. Also very stimulating is M.T. Clanchy, *England and its Rulers 1066–1272*, 2nd edn (1998); and F. Barlow, *The Feudal Kingdom of England, 1042–1216*, 5th edn (1999), remains comprehensive and very helpful indeed. A new work, which covers much of the same ground as this book, is C. Daniell, *From Norman Conquest to Magna Carta* (2003).

The most accessible and comprehensive introduction to developments in the law during this period is J. Hudson, *The Formation of the English Common Law: Law and Society in England from the Norman Conquest to Magna Carta* (1996). The best and most recent overview of the economies of Britain in the Middle Ages is C. Dyer, *Making a Living in the Middle Ages: The Peoples of Britain 850–1520* (2002). For the development of towns, see S. Reynolds, *An Introduction to the History of English Medieval Towns* (Oxford, 1977) and R.H. Britnell, *The Commercialisation of English Society, 1000–1500* (Cambridge, 1993).

Chapter 1. The Reigns, 1042–1066

The standard biography of Edward the Confessor is F. Barlow, *Edward the Confessor*, 2nd edn (1997), whilst Harold's life and career are studied in Ian W. Walker, *Harold: The Last Anglo-Saxon King* (Stroud, 1997). The standard account of the battle of Hastings is R.A. Brown, 'The Battle of Hastings' in *Anglo-Norman Warfare*, ed. M. Strickland (Woodbridge, 1992). The most recent and detailed analysis of the battle, however, which questions many of the generally-held assumptions about it, is M.K. Lawson, *The Battle of Hastings, 1066* (Stroud, 2002).

Chapter 2. Ruling the Kingdom, 1042–1066

The best introduction to all aspects of the Anglo-Saxon period is *The Anglo-Saxons*, ed. J. Campbell (1991). The last chapter is particularly relevant here. P. Stafford, *Unification and Conquest: A Political and Social History of England in the Tenth and Eleventh Centuries* (1989) is thorough and a reissue is overdue. A. Williams, *Kingship and Government in Pre-Conquest England* (1999) is often impressionistic but always stimulating. Chapters 7–11 are of particular relevance here. Other useful works which deal with the end of the Anglo-Saxon period are N.J. Higham, *The Death of Anglo-Saxon England* (Stroud, 1997) and F. Barlow, *The Godwins* (2002). R. Fletcher, *Bloodfeud* (2002) does a remarkable job of disentangling the obscure web of northern politics during these years. Chapters 8 and 9 are directly relevant here, although the earlier chapters contain some fresh and fascinating discussions of aspects of Anglo-Saxon culture and society in general. *The Blackwell Encyclopaedia of Anglo-Saxon England*, ed. M. Lapidge, J. Blair, S. Keynes and D. Scragg (Oxford, 1999) is a treasure-house of useful information and perceptive explanation arranged alphabetically.

Chapter 3. The Kings and the Law, 1042–1066

Accessible introductions to the workings of the late Anglo-Saxon legal system are thin on the scholarly ground. Most of the general works covering this period contain some discussion of the subject. However, the most important recent work has been done by Patrick Wormald. More ambitious readers might seek out the relevant parts of his *The Making of English Law: King Alfred to the Twelfth Century. Volume I: Legislation and its Limits* (Oxford, 1999), or some of the essays in his *Legal Culture in the Early Medieval West: Law as Text, Image and Experience* (1999), especially in this context, perhaps, ch. 12.

Chapter 4. The Kings and the Church, 1042–1066

The best introduction to the history of the eleventh-century English Church before the conquest is F. Barlow, *The English Church, 1000–1066*, 2nd edn (1979). There are also relevant chapters in H.R. Loyn, *The English Church, 940–1154* (Harlow, 2000). For a good selection of images of Anglo-Saxon artwork of all kinds, and useful introductions to it, see *The Golden Age of Anglo-Saxon Art, 966–1066*, ed. J. Backhouse, D.H. Turner and L. Webster (1984). Michelle P. Brown, *Anglo-Saxon Manuscripts* (1991) is a very helpful and well-illustrated introduction to its subject.

Chapter 5. The Reigns, 1066–1154

A lively new work which deals accessibly and insightfully with the main events of the Anglo-Norman period, reign by reign, is D. Crouch, *The Normans: The History of a Dynasty* (New York, 2002). As for books on individual rulers, D. Bates, *William the Conqueror* (1989) is the best introduction to its subject, whilst D.C. Douglas, *William the Conqueror* (1964) is older but still very useful. F. Barlow, *William Rufus* is lively and thorough, whilst Emma Mason's 'William Rufus and the Historians' in *Medieval History* 1/1 (1991) provides a stimulating view of the historiography of the reign and includes her discussion of the circumstances surrounding the king's death. C.W. Hollister, *Henry I* (2001), published posthumously, is the product of a lifetime's intensive study of its subject and his times. There are several good books on Stephen's reign: both very useful are R.H.C. Davis, *King Stephen*, 3rd edn (1990) and K.J. Stringer, *The Reign of Stephen: Kingship, Warfare and Government in Twelfth-Century England* (1993). Best of all, however is D. Crouch, *The Reign of King Stephen, 1135–54* (2000). On Matilda, M. Chibnall, *The Empress Matilda: Queen Consort, Queen Mother and Lady of the English* (Oxford, 1991) is excellent.

Chapter 6. Ruling the Kingdom, 1066–1154

M. Chibnall, *Anglo-Norman England, 1066–1166* (Oxford, 1993) and B. Golding, *Conquest and Colonisation: The Normans in England, 1066–1100* (1994) are essential reading, as are the works of Judith Green, in particular *The Government of England under Henry I* (Cambridge, 1986), and *The Aristocracy of Norman England* (Cambridge, 1997). J.O. Prestwich, 'War and Finance in the Anglo-Norman State', in *Anglo-Norman Warfare*, ed. Strickland, is seminal. W.L. Warren's view about the 'myth' of Anglo-Norman efficiency in government is handily summarised in his *The Governance of Norman and Angevin England 1086–1272*, ch. 3. M. Bennett, *Campaigns of the Norman Conquest* (Oxford, 2001) provides a useful and extremely well-illustrated guide to the military situation in England in the first few years after 1066.

Chapter 7. The Kings and the Law, 1066–1154

Chapters 2–4 of Hudson, *The Formation of the English Common Law* provide the best short introduction to the workings of the Anglo-Norman legal system.

Chapter 8. The Kings and the Church, 1066–1154

The best introduction to the history of the post-conquest English Church is F. Barlow, *The English Church, 1066–1154* (1979). There are also relevant chapters in H.R. Loyn, *The English Church, 940–1154*. M. Brett, *The English Church under Henry I* (Oxford, 1975) is essential. Chapter 2 of J. Burton, *Monastic and Religious Orders in Britain, 1000–1300* (Cambridge, 1994) is also very useful.

Chapter 9. The Reigns, 1154–1217

The standard biography of Henry II is W.L. Warren, *Henry II* (1973). It is long and detailed, but comprehensive and still very impressive. The best biography of Richard I is J. Gillingham, *Richard I* (1999). R.V. Turner and R.R. Heiser, *The Reign of Richard Lionheart: Ruler of the Angevin Empire, 1189–1199* (Harlow, 2000) is a very helpful overview which takes in much of the most recent work on the reign. W.L. Warren, *King John* (1961) is still a most enjoyable and stimulating biography. The Yale edition of 1997 also contains a useful introduction by D.A. Carpenter on the recent historiography of the reign. Of the more recent works, R.V. Turner, *King John* (Harlow, 1994) is the most valuable.

Chapter 10. Ruling the Kingdom, 1154–1217

J. Gillingham, *The Angevin Empire*, 2nd edn (2001) is the best introduction to the wider concerns of Henry II and his sons. R. Mortimer, *Angevin England, 1154–1258* (Oxford, 1994) is a good overview of its subject. On the restoration of royal power by Henry II, the main work is E. Amt, *The Accession of Henry II in England: Royal Government Restored, 1149–1159* (1993). J.E.A. Jolliffe's *Angevin Kingship*, 2nd edn (1963) is old and out of print; it is worth seeking out, however, as it reveals the harshness and irregular force at the heart of Angevin rule like no other work. For the achievements of Hubert Walter, see Clanchy, *From Memory to Written Record*, pp. 68–73. The works of J.C. Holt are fundamental for a proper understanding of John's reign and Angevin government generally. Both indispensable are *The Northerners: A Study in the Reign of King John* (Oxford, 1961), especially chs IX–XII, and *Magna Carta*, 2nd edn (Cambridge, 1992). These books are not straightforward and presume a good knowledge of the subject on the reader's part. They amply repay careful study, however. A good, short introduction to Magna Carta can be found in D.A. Carpenter, *The Minority of Henry III* (1990), pp. 5–12. Chapter 8 of Hudson, *The Formation of the English Common Law*, is very good on John's administration of justice and on Magna Carta, too. *King John: New Interpretations*, ed. S.D. Church (Woodbridge, 1999) contains many valuable papers. Of particular note is D. Power, 'King John and the Norman Aristocracy', an essential discussion which casts valuable light on the reasons behind the loss of Normandy in 1204. D. Crouch, *William Marshal: Court, Career and Chivalry in the Angevin Empire, 1147–1219* (Harlow, 1990) is an excellent biography which looks at the history of the Angevin Empire from the perspective of one of its most important and remarkable personalities.

Chapter 11. The Kings and the Law, 1154–1217

Chapters 5–7 of Hudson, *The Formation of the English Common Law* provide the best introduction to the changes in the legal system during this period. P. Brand's essay, '"Multis Vigilis Excogitatam et Inventam": Henry II and the Creation of the English Common Law', reprinted as ch. 4 of his *The Making of the Common Law* (1992) is also an admirably clear and succinct analysis of the importance of the reign of Henry II in English legal history.

Chapter 12. The Kings and the Church, 1154–1217

There is no full modern treatment of the English Church under the Angevin kings. However, all of the general works on the period deal with the areas I have covered. The most recent biography of Thomas Becket is F. Barlow, *Thomas Becket* (1986). And the most recent study of John's relations with the papacy is C. Harper-Bill, 'John and the Church of Rome', in *King John: New Interpretations*, ed. Church. This essay also includes a good, brief analysis of the strengths and weaknesses of the English Church at the turn of the thirteenth century.

Index

The following abbreviations have been used:

EC: Edward the Confessor
HarII: Harold II
WI: William I
WII: William II
HI: Henry I
S: Stephen
HII: Henry II
RI: Richard I
J: John
HIII: Henry III

Persons are indexed under their surnames unless convention dictates otherwise. Where names are the same, the clergy precedes the laity; the order is then according to rank. Page numbers in italics indicate references to 'The Principal Narrative Sources and their Authors'.

Places in England are identified by abbreviated reference to their historic county.